D0500385

A HANDBOOK FOR

Sharing the Blessings of Your Marriage, Family, and Home

MINISTERS' WIVES

A HANDBOOK FOR

Sharing the Blessings of Your Marriage, Family, and Home

MINISTERS' WIVES

DOROTHY KELLEY PATTERSON

FOREWORD BY TIM AND BEVERLY LAHAYE

BROADMAN
& HOLMAN
PUBLISHERS

NASHVILLE, TENNESSEE

0–8054–2063–0

Published by Broadman & Holman Publishers,
Nashville, Tennessee

Dewey Decimal Classification: 253
Subject Heading: MINISTERS' WIVES

Scripture quotations are from
The New King James Version,
copyright © 1979, 1980, 1982,
Thomas Nelson, Inc., Publishers.

1 2 3 4 5 6 7 8 9 07 06 05 04 03 02

Dedication

To First Ladies who have been special to me—

To my mother, who is the First Lady of my daddy's heart and ever the encourager in my life;

To Honey, my mother-in-love, who modeled devotion to Christ as she served as Patée's First Lady in the First Baptist Church of Beaumont, TX, in which I was reared;

To Sarah Eddleman, who gave me my first opportunity to learn and preside over hospitality in the home of a president during my years as a student at New Orleans Seminary;

To Rhonda Kelley, my sister-in-love and the First Lady of New Orleans Baptist Theological Seminary, where my brother Chuck is President, who is my kindred spirit for exchanging ideas and for encouragement in the work we love;

To my sisters Eileen, who is her pastor husband Steve's First Lady, and
    Charlene, who has also served as her husband Russ's First Lady
    when he was a pastor, and to Kathy who has a lot of work to do to
    keep up with all these First Ladies;

To my daughter Carmen, whose pastor husband selected her to be his
    First Lady; she inspires and helps Mark as he serves the First Baptist
    Church, Little Rock, AR; she faithfully nurtures Abigail and
    Rebekah; she presides over her household;

To Rachel, who has become the First Lady in the heart of my son
    Armour;

To Paige, the pastor—and now president—who made me his First Lady; he
    has generously provided for me, faithfully protected me, passionately
    loved me, and consistently intertwined our lives in ministry; he forgives
    my weaknesses and praises my strengths, and more than any other he
    finds and enriches my giftedness.

Contents

Foreword

After thirty-seven years of service as pastor and wife in three different churches, we can readily identify with Dorothy Patterson's often humorous and very practical evaluation of "the pastor's wife, who must also serve as mother and dedicated servant of Christ and a dozen other jobs she never envisioned when she said, 'I do.'" They say it takes one to know one, and Dorothy certainly qualifies. She was the wife of Dr. Paige Patterson when he was the associate pastor of the great First Baptist Church under Dr. W. A. Criswell. She knows the ecstasy of God's hand on her life and ministry, but she also knows the sadness when others would criticize and wish they could lay hands on her and her husband.

Yet she has an uncanny ability to take criticism and objection as a part of the job and always maintains a Spirit-filled joy, even in the midst of the most difficult pressures of the ministry. She has been her husband's greatest cheerleader, encourager, and best friend for over three decades. During that time she was a vital part of raising their two dedicated children and now can rejoice at their availability to God in their adulthood.

We remember praying with Dorothy amid the tensions of denominational difference when she and her husband were the brunt of much criticism. Never did she lose faith that God was in control, even when things seemed out of control. Her long reliance on the Lord and His ability to see them through to the perfect will of God was a powerful encouragement when Paige needed her most, and she served as an example of what God can do when a person is faithful.

Now they serve as president and president's wife of one of the finest seminaries of the Southern Baptist Convention—Southeastern Baptist Theological Seminary. There she has endeared herself to the students by her incredible sense of humor and her deep insights into God's Word. One visit to their chapel services, and you will find she is a favorite among the students and their wives.

Any pastor's wife or prospective wife will benefit from this book, based as it is on the Word of God and filled with practical helps in the multi-faceted role every pastor's wife must fill. This book could not have been written by anyone who had not been a pastor's wife. Anyone who reads it will find it a blessing!

Tim LaHaye	Beverly LaHaye
Author, Educator, Minister	Author, Educator
	Chairman of Concerned Women of America

Acknowledgments

To write and publish a book always brings together a team. There is inspiration and vision, research and recording, editing and refining, not to mention encouragement and support services.

First, I am blessed to have a husband who especially inspired this effort because he included me in his pastoral ministry and then challenged me to pass on lessons learned first in the setting of the Bible college we served in Texas, then on the seminary campus here in North Carolina, and ultimately through the writing of this volume for ministers' wives to the women who now serve alongside their husbands in ministry or who are preparing to do so. My children and extended family are always involved in my writing projects by supplying wonderful illustrations, offering words of encouragement, and by personal input along the way.

Second, I am helped by a wonderful staff at Southeastern Baptist Theological Seminary here in Wake Forest. Computer problems are solved by our IT staff under the direction of Tim Shidal. Our reference librarian Terese Jerose helps to uncover even the most insignificant details of documentation. But more than any others, our Magnolia Hill staff members—Chris Thompson, Bobbi Moosbrugger, Kirk Carlisle, and Jim Elliott—go beyond the call of duty in pouring out themselves in our hospitality ministries so that I can devote periods of time to writing and research for such a project as this.

Finally, I appreciate my literary agent Bruce Barbour and the editorial staff at Broadman & Holman Publishers, who remind me to stay on schedule and meet the deadlines to which we have committed.

Dorothy Patterson
Magnolia Hill

Introduction

Too often there exists a distorted and even ridiculous image of the preacher's wife. Some view her as a brainless airhead, prey for the juiciest gossip and a sitter for the nursery. She is homely and dowdy in appearance, with out-of-date and ill-fitting clothing, a deathly countenance, no makeup, and no ornamentation. She has a spongelike ability to absorb all criticism, graciously and without complaint, accepting martyrdom for her lifeless but pious body. She is one of the walking wounded, discouraged, lonely, stripped of all self-worth, bereft of any friends, neglected by her husband, and unappreciated by her children. With no identity of her own, she remains in the shadow of her husband and is measured according to his success or failure. An Anglican bishop's wife once quipped, "Clergy ought to be celibate . . . because no decent, right-minded man ought to have the effrontery to ask any woman to take on such a lousy job!"[1]

On the other hand, others expect the preacher's wife to be Super Server and Wonder Worker. A woman idolized by all, emulated by many, and kept on a pedestal by her family and friends, she presides over House Beautiful—enhanced by clean picture windows, drawn-back draperies, and open doors for all to observe perfection among the living. Many extol this saint's virtues; her reputation spreads far and wide.

With all fantasy aside, the minister's wife deserves a serious look. She is usually a lively doer who takes great joy in funneling her unbounded creativity and energy into her family and congregation, thereby putting her own personal stamp on the kingdom of Christ. This woman needs to be extraordinary to fulfill the expectations of her family, not to mention the congregation her husband serves.

The church looks to her for a shining example of biblical womanhood. The world wants to see in her the refreshing breeze of sincere, Christlike servanthood ready to meet community needs. Her children are looking for a steady rock to which they can cling during the storms of life. But her preacher-husband just wants the made-to-order bride and helper who God promised would labor at his side in life and ministry.

An informal survey conducted among pastors and their wives revealed that 63 percent of the women, compared with 44 percent of the men, believed that the pastorate is a two-person job; 78 percent of the men and 75 percent of the women agreed that the wife's active participation in church activities is necessary for the pastor to be perceived as successful. Further, 60 percent of the women and 73 percent of the men acknowledged that wives attend some activities just because they are expected to do so. However, the survey's saddest revelation is that 54.4 percent of the wives believed that their husband's first priority is the church, and 36 percent of the pastors agreed. In this framework a survey placing clergy divorces as the third highest among professional people is not too surprising.[2]

What does it mean to be a minister's First Lady? Unfortunately, the modern age has moved from "getting two for the price of one" to "settling for one for the price of two." The U.S. government actually has a law prohibiting members of the presidential family from being on the payroll, as a result of former President Kennedy's appointment of his brother to a cabinet-level position. Hillary Rodham Clinton, as America's First Lady, had no government salary, but she received much money for support staff, travel, and entertainment. A cloud remains over her husband's administration regarding how she used taxpayers' money and unbelievable perks coming out of the White House to launch an unprecedented campaign for the Senate.

A pastor's First Lady has no written job description, yet she walks into a role with amazing expectations and sometimes overwhelming responsibilities. She is her husband's wife and thus, according to the biblical mandate, *his helper*. She has a function and role given by God—regardless of any occupation she might choose. This handbook's focus is the religious arena in which the minister's wife is not called by the church to a particular position. Although there is no law prohibiting her paid service on the church staff, the church does not assign a salary to a minister's wife for her work as First Lady.

The role of First Lady is still a demanding one. Most people still consider the preacher's wife to be an extension of her husband and the functional equivalent to the pastor. Yet this volume will present the minister's wife as a woman with duties and responsibilities that supersede whatever she does in the church without limiting her prerogative to carve out her own unique role in kingdom ministry. Unity with diversity is the hallmark of the teamwork and partnership needed by the minister and his First Lady as they labor in the kingdom vineyard. They may have different gifts and conflicting ideas, but with grace and lovingkindness they will work together to maintain a strong family and vibrant congregation.

CHAPTER 1

Position Demands Passion

As a minister's wife, to attempt to mold your life into meeting the expectations of your parishioners will send you to disaster and disillusionment
on the fast track. You aren't meant to busy yourself dancing for the pipers,
nor are you called to perform on a ministry platform under the scrutiny of
eyes and glare of lights. Rather, your task is genuine and sincere commitment to the responsibilities God has given you. The rest of the script will
unfold according to God's plan for you.

You are not defined by your husband's work or even your own labor, as
important as it may be; your identity and worth are not judged by personal
skills or giftedness but by your intimate relationship to Christ. The passion
in your heart will manifest itself in your position in the kingdom.

Beauty from the Inside Out

The essentials for living the Christian life and making a difference in the
kingdom are not determined by your physical appearance, your intellec-
tual acumen, your personal charisma, or even your personal giftedness.

> "My worth to God in the public sector is no more than the substance of my walk with him in private."
>
> —DOROTHY PATTERSON

Working from the inside out, your greatest resources are found in the heart's spiritual sensitivities, which have been developed through a consistent walk with the Lord (Prov. 31:30; 1 Pet. 3:3–4).

The Holy Spirit must occupy the throne in your heart. As your Guide, He will enhance your character with His fruit (Gal. 5:22–23). He will give and develop your gifts (1 Cor. 12:8–11). You may know the contents of the Bible; you may be familiar with church polity and organizations. However, to model the Christian life and equip the saints, you must be intimately acquainted with the Spirit of God. He alone can prepare you for your task. Mary of Bethany chose to sit at the feet of the Savior. She focused on Him without being distracted by her family or other responsibilities.

Hearing the Word of God, gleaning the inspiration found in corporate worship, and seeking the edification that comes from great men of God are all important. Many preachers' wives are Bible teachers in their own right and spend much time studying the Bible to prepare for teaching responsibilities.

How can you bring the presence of God into your life? Jesus more than anyone practiced the presence of God. By studying His life, by adopting His priorities, by living as He lived, and by doing what He did, you can become like Him. Robert Murray M'Cheyne, dead by age thirty, said, "It is not talent God blesses but likeness to Jesus."

The Requirement of Solitude

What did Jesus do? He sought solitude and silence—uninterrupted time to communicate with the Father. In the modern penal system, solitary confinement is used to break the strongest will. Spiritually, you need solitude in order to overcome external pressures and develop and nourish a relationship with God. The absence of interruptions and removal of human influences create a vacuum into which God fits. Silence moves beyond quiet or solitude because it closes out all distractions—music, words, or noises. Whether the desert, your closet, or any isolated spot—to be silent and still and wait on the Lord is a prelude to hearing His voice (Ps. 46:10).

Moses found his strength and preparation for ministry in the wilderness. Jesus, too, spent a time of solitude and deprivation in the wilderness—the cauldron in which He developed strength. He prayed and meditated. He quoted Scripture. He adopted a simple and sacrificial lifestyle; He expended His energies in service to others.

No woman will adopt such a lifestyle just by *meeting* Jesus; she must *live* with Him in order to become like Him. You must learn how to invest your time and energies in a lifestyle that puts you not only in touch with but also in harmony with the Lord. By tapping His resources, you can carry out an otherwise impossible ministry assignment.

When endowed with spiritual disciplines, you can do what needs to be done when it needs to be done. You use your will in proper choices and activities. You practice the presence of God until you respond automatically and without thinking in your choices.

These disciplines seem to be givens—things taken for granted for the wife of a preacher. Yet many preachers and their wives meet the Lord only in order to prepare for teaching or other ministries. Their Bibles may be dog-eared from use, but their hearts have not been crammed with Scripture. Suffering from spiritual starvation, they are spiritually weak, not because God will not endow them with strength but because they have deprived themselves of the necessary nourishment. As a result they are left mutilated, their growth stunted, their testimonies weakened, their ministries deformed.

For spiritual disciplines you must purposefully embrace specific tasks using your heart, mind, and body as well as your passion, will, and spirit. Your personality and the way you order your life must be molded by a power beyond yourself as you yield and bow to the Lord's control of your life. You incorporate this discipline through times of solitude (prayer, meditation on Scripture, fasting) and celebration.

The Reward of Sustenance

Your soul and heart must be laid bare before the Lord as you read and meditate on Scripture for your own personal nourishment. I prefer to use my time reading the biblical text, but some enjoy using a devotional book as a companion. Read the Word every day. I read a chapter from Proverbs daily because it is practical for my life as a wife, mother, and grandmother. In addition, I am now reading through Psalms each month, finding comfort and encouragement.

Taking your petitions, confession, intercession, thanksgiving, and praise out of Scripture is the best way to pray according to God's will. My prayers are not confined to the written Word of God, but I weave His words throughout my prayers. Especially is this true with my daily portions from Proverbs and Psalms. I pray aloud as I personalize them; I write my initials or those of one for whom I am praying as I claim the promises and cling to the comfort they bring.

My mother-in-love read through and marked a Bible for each of her children and grandchildren. In the Bible prepared for me, she has written notes that are especially meaningful to a wife and mother. There are devotional thoughts, insights gleaned from the text, and even some notes of love from her to me. As I read my Bible, I put initials of family members or friends next to verses as a way of identifying my special prayer for that person. You can do the same for your loved ones—read through and find a way to personalize a copy of Scripture for the one you love and give it as a gift on some special occasion.

Seeking the sustenance you need for spiritual power is a quest of its own. Reading a few verses here and there is not sufficient. You must have a heart commitment to study Scripture systematically, to meditate on what you read, to contemplate its meaning for your own life, and to memorize helpful verses for recalling at later times. Meditation does not allow your mind to drift aimlessly without focus.

Meditation is putting your mind and heart on a single verse or thought, mulling its words over in your mind (Ps. 1:1–2; 63:5–6; 143:5; 119:48, 78, 148; Josh. 1:8). You cannot be hurried, and you can meditate only when your mind is free from outside distractions. Disciplined thought brings insights and lays the foundation for practical application. Read the verse through again and again—perhaps aloud to hear the words and cement them in your mind.

Memorizing the verse or passage focuses your mind on its words and message. Calling to mind the verses throughout the day in conversation, teaching, or counseling will help to implant its message in your heart.

Personalizing the verses you read brings comfort to your meditation. Insert your name as you contemplate each verse. Use different translations and paraphrases to see new insights and renew old truths. Doing your devotional reading in a copy of Scripture you have not used before allows you to mark verses with fresh vision.

A Verse Especially for Me

"Fear not, for I have redeemed Dorothy;
I have called Dorothy by her name;
She is Mine.
When Dorothy passes *through* the waters, I will be with her;
And *through* the rivers, they shall not overflow Dorothy.
When Dorothy walks *through* the fire, she shall not be
 burned;
Nor shall the flame scorch her."

Adapted from Isa. 43:1–2

—Dorothy Patterson

> ### *Practicing the Presence of God*
>
> - Reading and studying Scripture systematically
> - Meditating on specific verses
> - Memorizing key verses
> - Personalizing verses with your own name
> - Seeking inspiration in corporate worship
> - Finding edification in great women of God

The payback from meditating on God's Word is worth the time and energy invested. You make your ministry deep through personal quiet time, and the Lord will make it wide through unlimited opportunities for service. You meet the Lord in ways you've never known Him before (Jer. 9:23–24; Col. 1:9–10). Your mind and heart will be encased with a protective shield (Phil. 4:6–7). Your mind will be renewed with His thoughts (Ps. 119:38; Prov. 23:7), and you will have a clear channel for divine direction in your life (Prov. 3:5–6). Meditation transfers what you have read in God's Word into spiritual strength and wisdom and a lifestyle lived for the glory of God just as digestion of food appropriates what you have eaten to the physical needs of your body.

Another source of comfort and edification is the hymnal. The Book of Psalms is the hymnal of Israel and contains some of my favorite devotional readings. Many of the great hymns of Christianity are full of theological truth and provide an excellent source for meditating on Scripture.

The Responsibility of Submission

Reading the Bible is not the only way to "hear" the Word of the Lord. Prayer is also an indispensable tool God uses to speak to your heart. The metaphor "garden of prayer" is appropriate to define prayer. You set the boundaries for your garden—a place to blend personal imagination, memories, dreams. It must be a sanctuary from the cares of life; it must be private and accessible to you alone or only to guests you invite; it is a place for renewal and revival.

Selecting the best time varies with the individual, but your most important meeting of the day is with the Lord. Unfortunately, most preachers' wives are "time impaired" because of their overbooked lives. You live by the calendar; you can schedule and organize God right out of your life. In ministry you can set out with great intentions to spend a lengthy time with the Lord and then be swallowed up with one interruption after another until the maximum becomes the minimum.

What could be more fortifying than beginning and concluding your day with God! Before you venture out to the challenges of the day, you seek His help; and when you have completed the day, you return to thank Him and ask for renewing strength through the night. God clearly expects His children to spend time with Him (Matt. 6:33). In fact, He created the man and the woman for fellowship; He planned for them to have intimate communication with Him (Ps. 25:14; 27:4).

A church historian once commented that Martin Luther was quick to say that when faced with a tremendous amount of work to do in an unusually short time, he would more than ever need to spend several hours in prayer before he began such an arduous schedule. Luther knew the real source of power and realized that he was too busy and his work was too important not to connect with God in preparation for the task.

Getting up in time to meet the Lord is not as easy as it may sound. You start by going to bed on time the night before. The easiest way to achieve time with the Lord is to make the time for your going to bed and arising in the morning habitual. Your quiet time will not be meaningful if you are not at your best physically as well as mentally and spiritually. If you are so tired as to be half asleep, you will be unable to concentrate.

You need to have the same time and the same place reserved for Him. I've always had a cozy corner in my home—not only a place to relax in body and mind but also a place to meet God. This place is comfortable and familiar; I am not only drawn there, but I want to linger. What a delightful place for intimate conversation with the Lord or a tea party with a special friend. I can have piped-in praise or worship music, but often I have silence, which may be the most important "sound" for communing with the Lord.

How much time does it take to commune with the Lord? Quality does not supplant quantity in the sense of giving yourself time to hear from God through His Word, speaking to Him with your prayers and praise, and then meditating long enough for Him to work in your heart. Certainly fifteen minutes is minimal. The time does not have to be exactly the same every day, for there will be times when you find yourself extending the time without even realizing it.

My prayers, and the prayers my husband and I share together, are wafted from many different settings. I love my comfortable blue chair. I can go there at the end of a challenging day and find a blessed retreat with the Lord. The prayer garden—an enclosed oasis to which our bedroom opens—has a bubbling fountain, fragrant floral beds, and a giant Texas-shaped stone, reminding me of my home-state roots. Two large Indonesian chairs carved out of massive teak trunks offer a place to recline with a small table for a cup of tea and my Bible. The deck overlooks a wooded area and is marked by the sounds and movements of a variety of birds. The sunset is visible through the trees; the wind chimes add music; the hanging baskets frame the painting of nature. There are comfortable chairs and the solitude necessary for a time with the Lord.

Although I would prefer an isolated beach or a wooded path with sights and smells that heighten my senses, I can always find relaxing solitude in a long walk in any setting—hotel corridors or parking lots, through the seminary campus, on the treadmill in my bedroom, while I am at home or on a trip. Most important is the solitude and quiet that allows me to talk with the Lord as I would in conversation with an intimate friend. Walking and talking with the Lord just seem to go together!

Prayer walking is one of my favorite settings for quiet time. I read Scripture before or after I walk; but while I am walking alone, I pray aloud. For me it is an intimate visit with the Lord, and I have the added benefit of physical exercise, which without the prayer time is drudgery!

You can also have a portable prayer setting. My sister-in-love Rhonda gave my mother a basket filled with wonderful helps to enhance prayer time. I began giving prayer baskets to brides or new mothers or friends celebrating a birthday or holiday.

My personal prayer basket has my Bible; a pen; highlighters; a journal with family photographs and space for recording prayer requests and answers; selected birthday photographs from my Southeastern Baptist Theological Seminary prayer box; facial tissues and a special handkerchief (my "tear bottle" always seems to be overflowing); cards for notes of encouragement to students, missionaries, friends, or family members for whom I have prayed; a favorite Scripture card done in calligraphy by my daughter Carmen; Magnolia Hill bookmarks with instructions for how to brew a proper cup of tea. You could include a tea cup and saucer with tea bags, a devotional book, a scented candle, or some carefully chosen tapes or CDs.[1]

Debbie Baker designed a prayer box, an organized system to pray weekly for church members and prospects. She prepared an index card with the church member's photograph, name, address, and telephone number on the front. On the back she added information about the person (directions to his home, prayer requests and answers, cards sent, visits or calls made). She alphabetized and divided the cards into groups for each day of the week. For prospects, she used a different color of card. This idea could be used for family, friends, Sunday school class, Bible study group. For a larger group of names, you could recycle biweekly, monthly, or, as I do, annually. This routine can be in your personal quiet time, or it may be used in prayer time with your husband or family. Debbie shared the benefits she received from this prayer program: an organized way to pray for the church family and prospects, a reminder of prayer requests and answers, a record of ministries to members and contacts of prospects, a source of information including telephone numbers and addresses.

How do you connect with the Lord? First, you seek Him with your whole heart (body senses, intellect, and emotions). Time with Him must be a priority. You must be willing to let Him govern your life and faith. You can *see* the beauty of creation; you can *hear* classical music presentations or even the melodious singing of the birds; you can *smell* the aromatic flora and fauna as well as spices and herbs; you can *touch* a family member or friend with feelings of affection and delight. Not only do your senses connect you with the Lord, but also your emotions add feelings of joy and personal experience, enabling you to praise the Lord and celebrate His goodness. Alongside your emotions is your intellect, which helps you find answers to your questions. Although you can never explain God, you can learn more about Him as you read and meditate on His Word.

Prayer offers personal guidance to get you through daily activities. It puts a protective shield around your husband and children. Prayer is not merely a means for getting God to do what you want Him to do; rather, its purpose is to lead you to God's will on earth. Prayer should make you single-minded with God.

The subject of your prayers includes known events coming as well as unknown challenges. Occasionally I like to write out my prayer in a journal or on stationery as if I were writing a letter to the Lord. These intimate epistles then chronicle my walk with Him and serve as encouragement in the future. I also find it therapeutic to list my petitions in a prayer journal. I note God's response from His Word, using Scripture to find comfort and strength; and I record answers. In looking back, I wish I had put my prayers and petitions into a

> "Read and study your Bible in the highways of life—an opportunity for witness; pray in your closet—a source of power."
>
> —DOROTHY PATTERSON

set-apart journal to follow the trail of God's answers and promises over a lifetime. When I do read past journals, prayers and answers are always there, reminding me that God is sufficient for my every need!

A student designed a spiral-bound prayer Rolodex, writing prayer requests on the index cards. She stands it as an easel on the kitchen table. For the mealtime blessing she flips to the next card to lift its request to the Lord. She notes answered prayer on the card. When a card noting answered prayer appears again in the cycle, the family thanks God for answering that prayer!

> ### Dottie's Dictum for Prayer Power
> - Write a letter to the Lord.
> - List your petitions in a journal.
> - Record your answers to prayer.
> - Walk while you pray to keep the adrenalin flowing.

The Great Escape

Only by spending time with the Lord can you look like Him (Ps. 17:15), think like Him, talk like Him, and act like Him (Prov. 16:3; Ps. 91:1; 19:7–11; 16:8–9). Taking time away from normal routines and people who have been woven into your life is a necessity just as are eating and sleeping. Solitude is an antidote for stress and fatigue that allows you to withdraw long enough to regroup and regain momentum and composure. By isolating yourself from interruptions and distractions, you find new thoughts, unique wisdom, and workable solutions.

Solitude must be balanced with intimacy. It is different from aloneness, which might suggest

> "Don't seek a ministry, but expect the fruit of a disciplined life."
> —JOHN WESLEY

loneliness. Solitude suggests time for replenishment from within. You can invigorate your spirit with enthusiasm, renew your body with energy, and restore productivity to your life.

Once the personal spiritual disciplines are in place, then the minister's wife is prepared to assume responsibility as a willing and eager helper to her husband and to emulate the Christlike lifestyle before her children. Children, too, must be taught to make solitude a part of life, for only then can they pursue personal Bible study and prayer. They, too, need to be separated from daily burdens and responsibilities of life in order to meditate and build personal spiritual strength.

None of these disciplines should be done because you are the minister's wife but rather because you are the Lord's child. Everything done should be motivated by your love for Christ. Your service to husband, children, family, and church must be done "as unto the Lord."

In addition to the daily time with the Lord, consider a special personal retreat—a time for examining your own heart, reviewing what has gone before and contemplating what is to come. Such a time might be scheduled on your birthday, as you begin the new year, as you move from season to season, or as you complete one major project and prepare for another. It may be a quiet place in your own home or a secluded spot somewhere else. You should visibly seek God's wisdom, His guidance, His blessing. You will come out strengthened spiritually and prepared to meet whatever problems, temptations, or trials may come to you (Isa. 40:29–31).

> I sought him whom my soul did love,
> With tears I sought him earnestly;
> He bow'd his ear from Above,
> In vain I did not seek or cry.
> In my distress I sought the Lord,
> When nought on earth could comfort give;
> And when my soul these things abhor'd,
> Then, Lord, thou said'st unto me, Live.
> —Anne Bradstreet, First Lady of Massachusetts Bay[2]

Joy in the Journal

Any view suggesting that God is against fun, play, relaxation, amusement, and pleasure is distorted. In fact, Satan would like nothing better than to make the Christian life look unattractive and negative, when in truth Christ offers a life of joy and blessing, vitality and enthusiasm, even in the midst of adversities! Instead of negatives, it projects positives. The emphasis is not on what you can't do but on what you should do in order to have the maximum joy and blessing. Long for God (Ps. 63:1); come to God (Ps. 65:2); cry out to God (Ps. 84:2); bless His name (Ps. 145:21).

Journaling is the way to record your spiritual journey. Through the years I have kept many different journals. I have had the general journal in which I recorded daily events, family milestones, Paige's preaching texts, and decisions made in his ministry; travel journals in which I described the daily itinerary, evaluated the hotels and restaurants, listed favorite shopping places and the purchases made, noted guides and other people with whom a future contact might be made; journals that are dedicated to spiritual struggles; journals planned for my children and granddaughters and even for nieces and nephews if I live long enough! Putting my gratitude to God into words, recording blessings and answered prayers for praise now and in the future is great therapy for responding to future doubts and frustrations, questions and anxieties. Only God and my journal really know the depths of my despair, the heat of my anger, and the pit of depression into which I can fall.

Journals can become a personal "life file." Every minister's wife needs a record of the road traveled—whether done as a series of letters carefully written in sequence or paragraphs detailing and keeping track of the highlights and personal events of life recorded in an orderly and organized fashion. Keeping diaries, filing personal letters, and saving mementos can all dovetail into journaling.

Every minister's wife needs some reservoir for dispensing strength for the journey. If you aren't into journals, you may want to try a Blessing Box or Provision Present or Joy Jar. When God does something wonderful for you—meeting a mundane need, unfurling a genuine miracle, or sending a serendipity into your life—you can record that on a small scroll of paper or a business card and drop it into a box, gift-wrapped present, or jar. Then at Thanksgiving, New Year's Day, on your birthday, or anytime you need encouragement, you can dip into that reservoir of documented outpourings of God's love to remind yourself of the divine loving-kindness and tender care of the Heavenly Father.

Ordering Your Private Life for Public Ministry

Most activities open to a pastor's wife are worthy, and many women married to pastors are doers. How can a pastor's wife determine the most effective and efficient way to use the time available to her? As you choose what to do and when to do it, hallow your priorities by Scripture. The Bible speaks to this vital question with some general principles.

Personal quiet time—sustaining your personal relationship to Christ— is unequivocally the first priority. This time is not for the work of the church or for attending its regular services. Rather, this daily prayer and Bible study lets God speak in the most intimate communication (Matt. 6:33). Nothing produces any more heat in prayer than the light of the Word of God. This discipline is that from which all else must flow; it is the

An Anonymous Prayer

Lord, I have been so good today. I haven't raised my voice to anyone. I haven't called anyone rude names. I haven't yelled and screamed, ranted and raved at anyone. I haven't even broken anything or hurt anybody. But Lord, I'm getting out of bed in about five minutes, and I will probably need Your help then. Amen.

governor of all that is to come; this intimate fellowship with the Heavenly Father cannot be omitted without the gravest consequences.

The second priority became mine when I chose to marry. I am a divinely appointed helper to my husband (Gen. 2:18–24; Eph. 5:21–33; 1 Pet. 3:1–7). For a preacher's wife the task of caring for her husband's mundane needs is only the beginning. She and her husband are also partners in ministry, and that seems to blossom into another full-time job!

The third priority is another result of my decision to marry and bear children. Rearing children goes beyond providing custodial care for those whom God entrusts to you. Their spiritual nurture, educational training, and preparation for citizenship in the world are all under your supervision.

The fourth priority is the extended family. Scripture gives ample evidence that God views the family as spanning the generations. He planned for family members to minister to one another at various stages of life (Deut. 6:1–9; Ps. 68:6; 78:4–7). Inevitably there will be emergencies— sickness, death, or tragedy—which touch the entire family circle, awakening a compassion and determination to pull together and rely on one another in bearing the burden (Gal. 6:2) and carrying the load.

The fifth priority is one I share with my husband, who is president of a seminary. Its ministries as well as the students on the campus are an opportunity for kingdom investment. This assignment does not minimize the work of the local church, nor does it preclude support of community causes and civic service.

Perhaps my experience will help other ministers' wives in making these choices. However, you dare not seek to do the work beyond until Christ has done the work within. Ultimately it is not how intelligent you are, what physical beauty you have, or even how many gifts and talents are in your grasp; rather, the seed for all you will ever accomplish in your home or in the church or community lies within your own heart and spirit— what Peter calls the "gentle and quiet spirit" (1 Pet. 3:4) and what the wise Solomon describes as a "fear of the LORD" (Prov. 31:30). These qualities of a woman's inner life can be developed only under the tutelage of the Holy

Spirit, who is the Guide unto truth (John 16:13), the Teacher for all things (John 14:26), the Intercessor to the Father (Rom. 8:26), the Agent for renewal (Titus 3:5), the Comforter in sorrow (John 15:16), and the Bestower of spiritual gifts (1 Cor. 12:8–11).

In summarizing the attributes of a minister's wife, you must begin with the genuine experience in which heart and life are committed totally to the Lord Jesus. Close behind this personal relationship with Christ is the determination to set up priorities according to divine directives. Whatever the minister's wife plans to do in the Lord's vineyard must be secondary to her complete support of the ministry of her preacher-husband. Believing in what her husband is doing is absolutely indispensable, and supporting him in his ministry takes hard work. Women do not question paying the cost for necessities, and they seldom question spending whatever is available for luxuries; but some seem to think that spiritual things are not worthy of the cost, despite the clear biblical admonition (2 Tim. 2:15).

Time Management

Praying about your daily schedule every morning will keep you sensitive to the Lord's direction for your life. Praying with your husband about how to order the day ahead will help you both. Another effective way to manage time is to work smart. A personal survey of how you spend your time is a prelude to using your time wisely.

The concern is not how much time you have but how you use that time. Everyone has the same number of minutes in a day, but some people seem to accomplish a lot more tasks in a lot less time. The key is to break life into manageable segments of time. You must have long-range goals and a lifetime vision; but to conquer the big things, you must start with short-term goals and step-by-step plans. List all the responsibilities and projects before you for the day. Generally, using your freshest energies on the most important and getting the worst done early paves the way for more productivity on the minor things.

Prioritizing your to-do list is essential. You may use letters or numbers or symbols or even colors. Most important are things you must do to avoid serious consequences; next are tasks that would cause only mild repercussions; then would come things without real consequences, and finally anything you can delegate or pass along to someone else.

In your prioritizing, consider your own unique abilities and special skills. Your efficiency, not to mention your pleasure, is greatly enhanced if you pursue what you do best.

Even motivated and efficient people sometimes waste time by procrastination or putting off the things they need to do but don't enjoy doing. Perhaps the formidable task needs to be divided into parts to be tackled one at a time. Or maybe you need to set aside a block of uninterrupted time to complete the task. Stopping and starting greatly increases the time required and stifles the effectiveness of the time you spend. I have addressed this problem in my life by trying to block certain days for writing—no appointments, no classes, no telephone calls (except from family), nothing to interrupt!

Sometimes it helps to identify the time of day when you are sharpest and most efficient in order to assign to that time your most challenging projects. My most productive time is from 10 A.M. to 6 P.M. Before 10 A.M., I work through my beginning-the-day rituals. In the evening I do less-demanding tasks—going through the mail, reading the newspaper, organizing my schedule. You do not have to reach every goal to accomplish something important.

You must keep flexibility by regularly evaluating how you use your time. Time for message preparation and other essential duties should be blocked well in advance. These time allotments should not be disrupted by unnecessary interruptions. The preacher's calls can be screened by a secretary in the office and his wife at home. Making and receiving telephone calls should be assigned a time rather than letting them chop up your entire day. Sometimes a call should be forwarded to another person who can better answer a question or handle a situation. Long telephone cords must have been made for women like me. What a challenge to see how many things you can do at once!

Developing shortcuts will enable you to use time otherwise wasted. Women have genes that enable them to do at least two things at once. In addition, you should not only use the time-savers you already have but look for others to make you more efficient.

Paige and I have a calendar with engagements set for two to three years in advance—board meetings, church commitments, seminary events, family gatherings. We update that calendar quarterly and carefully block time for family fellowship, spiritual renewal, and writing assignments. A detailed weekly schedule is churned out for staff and family.

Your home should also have a message center. We have used mailbags hanging on bedroom doors, monogrammed magnets on the refrigerator, chalkboards, and bulletin boards. Now my husband and I each have a monogrammed leather pouch to pass messages and information back and forth.

Making lists is one of my spiritual gifts! I can affirm the words of President Teddy Roosevelt: "I will always believe in going hard at everything I do." Even during planned holiday celebrations, I create a list for each family member so that the labor is more evenly distributed and nothing falls through the cracks. At Magnolia Hill we have lists for home maintenance, lists for hospitality events, even a list for changing the clocks twice a year.

There are two glaring weaknesses in my time management: scheduling for emergencies and taking a day off regularly. I heartily recommend both, and I continue to strive to incorporate these principles since I know they would ultimately be time-savers. Obviously, interruptions or emergencies may make your carefully laid plans worthless, but nevertheless the planning itself is invaluable—at least as a starting place.

Here is a summary of tips for getting the most from the least amount of time:

1. Simplify your life by getting rid of clutter—not just things but time wasters (too much television, too many catalogs, too often idleness). Having too much may be a deterrent against using what you have.

2. Organize what you do and plan how to do it. Record how you are organized. The calendar should be your nerve center. I color-code my calendar—pink is my color; blue is my husband's; yellow is for seminary dates. When the children were at home, they also had colors. When we were scheduled to do something together, we had a rainbow! All birthdays are on the calendar; flight schedules are entered for easy reference. Make your lists of tasks to be done (daily, weekly, less frequently); mark them according to priority or category and person responsible. Beware of the tyranny of the urgent! Learn to distinguish between what must be done immediately, what is important but can be done whenever possible, and what falls into the category of dreams and will be done if possible.

3. Be efficient in the way you work. Handle papers only once. For example, when you open mail, have Post-it notes of different sizes, pen, paper clips, stapler, rubber bands; direct the piece to filing, to someone else, or to dictation (you could have note cards and dictaphone nearby in order to answer mail that needs a response). Handle the paper now or give it a place on your to-do list. Family shopping and errands should also be done at regular intervals and with a list. You can combine tasks: listen to a teaching tape while folding clothes; prepare food as you set the table and clean up as you move through the process. Do gift buying in the midst of other shopping throughout the year and maintain a gift closet for expected and unexpected gifts. I never have to hit the mall during the holiday season or rush out for a belated gift!

4. Delegate to helpers, whether family, friends, staff, or even labor-saving devices. Don't be afraid to ask for help. When you hesitate or even refuse to ask for help, perhaps because you think such

vulnerability would tarnish your own reputation, you are denying the joy of service to someone else. Involve the family in the work to be done. For example, everyone can place dirty clothes in a designated hamper, sorting them in the process.

5. Prepare for what is to come. I like to make my list and view my calendar in advance. Decide what is really important. Remember that you are allowed to say no. Don't be so deceived by preoccupation with what others may think or by your own importance that you do not consider requests in light of what you have the talent or time to do and even more important what God wants you to do. In this process you must connect with God. Ultimately He is the only One whose opinion matters. Take into consideration the level of stress accompanying every task, and consider each in the overall schema of life.

One of my helpers paid me a compliment I appreciated: "Mrs. Patterson, working for you has taught me to use minutes!" By planning ahead, you can always be prepared to use unexpected minutes. A canvas bag of catalogs, magazines, newspapers, notepad, Post-its, and pen is always ready to go—to the beauty shop, to the doctor's office, for a long car ride across town. My entertainment bag can fill the moments of waiting as I read, tear or clip, write notes, or make lists. When I sit down in front of the television to watch the evening news or a selected program, I have a stack to fill commercial breaks—mail to open and handle, notes to write, functions to plan.

Women who take their nurturing responsibilities seriously tend to load themselves with more than they should. Overcommitment becomes a way of life. Henry David Thoreau spoke of a "broad margin" as the model for time management. Everyone needs to leave some open spaces in the day if for no other reason than to give thanks to God for the blessings He bestows so faithfully. When a day is overscheduled and time for spontaneity is underestimated, you lose the present completely; you have no time to savor the past; and you place in jeopardy the future. The less you pack into a day, the better you can enjoy its events and the people who cross your path!

Time Management—the Short List for Preachers' Wives

- Establish your priorities, beginning with an inviolate commitment to spend time with the Lord.
- Make your marriage the most important human assignment you have. Determine to help your husband in all his duties. Do acts of love, including maintaining sexual intimacy. Take seriously your responsibility to be your husband's best friend and most cherished companion.
- Nurture your children. Model biblical marriage before them. Instruct them in biblical truth. Guide them in going God's way via consistent discipline.
- Make your home a secure haven—a dwelling of delight. Use your creativity and energy to provide a place for the family to retire for comfort and renewal, and provide your guests gracious hospitality.
- Treat your body like the temple of God, since it is! Get proper rest; eat nutritious meals; exercise with purpose.
- Dress attractively. Establish your own style; make choices of clothes and accessories that are flattering to you. After all, you not only reflect on yourself and your family but on the King of Kings, whose daughter you are.
- Simplify your life. Take charge of your schedule. Keep a calendar. Make lists. Create your own efficiency; use every means to get the most done in the least time. Organize yourself but with enough flexibility to pick some flowers along the way. Be willing to say no graciously and without guilt.

- Improve yourself after determining your gifts and skills. Read, attend refresher courses, observe women doing what you like to do, set goals, and plan a strategy to reach those goals. Stretch yourself; serve others; set your compass on the Lord.
- Accept disappointments, trials, suffering, and pain as your opportunity to drink of His cup. "This, too, will pass." Rest before you get tired; renew your energy and spirit before you succumb to burnout or depression. Take time for fun and fellowship. Laugh and play. Separate your public life of ministry from your private moments for rest and renewal.

What Will Keep You Going?

As I am preparing this manuscript, I am in a wilderness or desert season of my life. Both my hands are in splints because of degenerative arthritis, my parents have experienced awesome challenges in the aging process, a member of my extended family has gone to prison, my only son chose and married a wife whom I had never met. A loving husband, sensitive friends, caring sisters and brother, and a comforting mother are part of my life, but

Knowing the Joy of His Presence

- Make a commitment to the main thing—sitting at His feet every day.
- Plan your time with Him—when, where, what—but be flexible and creative enough to adjust without giving up meeting Him.
- Expect Satan to use every means at his disposal to distract and divert you from this intimate fellowship.
- Remember God's faithfulness through the generations and especially His blessings to you.
- Learn to wait for Him.

they have not been enough! Only the God of all comfort has healing balm, and I find myself sitting at His feet and clinging to Him as never before. Over the months the burden gets lighter.

Satan has many ways to sabotage your prayer life. You can become so self-absorbed that you are whining about your own problems rather than interceding for anyone else. Perhaps an even greater challenge is the tendency to pray sporadically when you are in trouble or have some urgent petition to put before the Lord rather than to maintain a consistent time to be alone with Him. Do you pray only when you feel the need? Such emotional bondage to feelings will often cause you to neglect the one avenue you could take to restore your warm and intimate fellowship with the Heavenly Father. Your faith makes your prayer rewarding and effective.

Before I entered high school, I was meticulous in preparing a schedule for each day of the week. I wrote it out in my own hand and carefully calculated the time to be allotted to each task, beginning with my daily devotional time. I had a chart plotting the reading of the entire Bible in a year, which I kept with my daily schedule.

Although I did adjust the daily routine from time to time, I followed this discipline with some success—until I married a preacher! Right away I became chronically ill with what was later diagnosed as asthma and allergies; my academic scholarship was withdrawn because my father, who no longer supported me, "made too much money." Just as the asthma and allergies began to respond to treatment, I became pregnant and several months later lost the baby.

The schedule began to falter, and it seemed that most of my prayers failed. I really didn't feel like praying. Besides, each class in the Christian university I attended began with prayer, and I spent entire class periods studying the Bible! I also had to prepare Sunday school lessons and Bible studies for the women of the church. Meantime, it seemed more expedient to perform my duties at home, in the classroom, and in the church. I was in a busy Baptist church, not a quiet monastic convent; people were calling or coming by, and there was no solitude living next door to the church. I knew that I ought to pray, but I just didn't feel like it.

Here I am almost four decades later. Has the frustration ended? No. As I struggle in a desert season, as I don't seem to have God's ear, as He seems so far from me, as my petitions seem to be going to call waiting or perhaps being recorded on some divine answering machine, now more than ever I must seek His presence; but it is not because I feel like reciting what could be interpreted as futile petitions. Rather, it is because I know that I cannot get through the dreary days without Him. So my will sends me into His presence with purpose again and again. I cry more than ever before Him because my emotions have joined my will in this spiritual pilgrimage. I know He has been listening; and He has been there all the time, or I could not have borne the burden. I also can say with the psalmist, "Yet I will praise Him" (Ps. 42:11).

The wife of a preacher thinks nothing of draining her cup daily as she pours out service to her family and others, but she often forgets that her cup must be filled again and again in order to be ready to pour out the next time. Oh, that you might be haunted by what God has done and hungry for what God can do!

CHAPTER 2

A Particular Pilgrimage

Genuine character is not what personal skills you have or how well you have been trained to do a job but rather who you are within. The passage specifically directed to the wives of church leaders is found within the context of the qualifications for deacons in 1 Timothy 3, "Even so must their wives be reverent, not slanderers, temperate, faithful in all things" (v. 11). These character qualities should mark the life of every godly woman, but the minister's wife—even more than the wife of a deacon— is in a unique position to model godly character qualities for the women of her congregation.

The word translated *reverent* (Greek, *semnas*) carries the sense of honor, not only personal honor but a moral ascendancy that calls for honor in others. *Slanderers* (Greek *diabolous*, literally "casting through") is undoubtedly a warning against gossip and backbiting. *Temperate* (Greek *nēphaleous*), an antonym for *intoxification*, suggests one who is completely unaffected by wine, without any mental fuzziness, perhaps referring to the self-control necessary for kingdom work. *Faithful* (Greek *pistas*), from the same root as *believe* and its derivatives found throughout the New Testament, conveys the heart of a faith commitment to God.[1]

Christian character—marked by love, joy, peace, kindness, goodness, faithfulness, gentleness, self-control—is important. These things are beyond your reach except for diligence in personal prayer and Bible study. A commitment to your calling and contentment in being your husband's helper are also important. I was encouraged by poll respondents in a *USA TODAY* snapshot indicating that clergymen, together with nurses, were perceived as having the highest ethics.[2]

Calling the Equipped or Equipping the Called

When a woman marries a minister, she not only chooses a life partner, she also accepts a life's work. God's leading you to a life's partner equals His calling you to a life's work. Having a career of being the minister's First Lady lasts "till death do us part." She can use her position as a channel for her talents and abilities and even her dreams. Is it a ludicrous or ambiguous or even superfluous question to ask if a pastor's wife should be "called," especially if she has experience and tenure in laboring in the vineyard of the Lord?

Every Christian experiences a call before beginning a personal spiritual pilgrimage (Ps. 40:8). How do you know a ministry is right for your husband and you? What makes a ministry the right one is that God calls you to it. Finding God's will for your life begins with a committed relationship. God is not an autocratic master looking for a spineless puppet, but rather He becomes a strong hand ready to fill a flexible glove. Mary, the mother of Jesus, had this committed relationship to the Heavenly Father.

Pursuing God's will also demands an intelligent response and determined decision on your part. When Mary's call to service came, she responded, "Let it be unto your handmaiden as you have said." God's call on your life will never contradict His written Word. Have you ever felt that God's call to you was in contradistinction to His call to your husband? Maybe you are in ministry a long way from home, and suddenly a church in your hometown is without a pastor, and the committee contacts your husband. God has spoken to you to start packing, but your husband hears the Lord saying, "I'm not through with you here." Who is right? The written Word of God makes clear that the husband has been assigned the task of leadership in the home. The Holy Spirit will not give you a message that would encourage you to reject your husband's leadership.

The decision-making process is never easy. You cannot hope to make wise choices unless both you and your husband are in communication with the Lord and with one another. The Book of Proverbs is also clear that you need some godly counselors (Prov. 11:14). Counselors may be family, others in ministry, intimate friends, or even a stranger whom the Lord sends into your life.

In your humanity you will make mistakes. Fortunately, God is experienced in handling the mistakes of His children. God's will survives despite human error. Wrong choices have consequences; but with the right commitment to God's plan, you can redeem the time and move forward. He is able to use your biggest mess and most foolish choice to teach you lessons and ultimately to accomplish His purposes. He is greater than you or your mistakes! Ninety percent of knowing God's will is having His mind and being willing to do or accept His will, however illogical or impractical it may seem.

The Call to Salvation

Scripture is clear concerning the call to salvation: "Ho, every one that thirsts, come to the waters,

> "God plays no game of hide and seek—the more intimately you draw to the heart of God, the more clearly you know the will of God. While He blindfolds you from the blueprint, He reveals His will day by day and unrolls the scroll line by line."
>
> —JUNE HUNT

and he that hath no money; come, buy, and eat" (Isa. 55:1 KJV). "Come to Me, all you who labor and are heavy laden, and I will give you rest" (Matt. 11:28). "If anyone desires to come after Me, let him deny himself, and take up his cross, and follow Me" (Matt. 16:24).

Certainly no woman could think of bearing up under the burdens of the parsonage without the assurance of a personal relationship with Jesus Christ. If the matter of your personal relationship to Jesus Christ has not been settled, you must seek Him with your whole heart.

The Call to Marriage

Most women who become pastors' wives never hear a divine call to ministry; rather, they marry men who have had such a call. This fact underscores as never before the importance of seeking God's will in choosing a life partner. Human love may wane under the strains and pressures of a pastor's life and work; but when God has been at the heart of every decision, He will supply the strength and wisdom needed for any woman to function ably and faithfully in this role.

A ministry wife's realization of this calling is often a slow unfolding of God's will through the working of the Holy Spirit in her heart. One thing is certain: God never has separate plans for a husband and wife because He has made the two one in His plan for marriage (Gen. 2:24). Some wives are paralyzed with fear about how they can perform in this challenging role. They are told that they will make or break their husbands' ministries by how they order their lives and what they do in the church. Still most of them enter the high-profile First Lady position with little if any preparation. They feel ill equipped and doomed to failure before they even begin.

The wives of ministers generally live with a stereotype of what they are expected to be and do. Nothing is so discouraging as feeling you are not adequate for the task you have been given. Having married their husbands before they became pastors, some ministry wives were thrown into the arena of public service and expected to function as if they were trained for the position.

Ministers' wives are expected to be more spiritual than other women or men (except perhaps the pastor) in the church. They are supposed to have superior knowledge of the Bible, and they are expected to be present for all services, and, of course, women's meetings, of the church. Their homes are to be cleaner and better organized than others, and they are expected to provide instant hospitality for any and every occasion.

Anyone who faces the unknown without preparation or training would feel intimidated. You will never please everyone and cannot live your life controlled by what others expect and demand. However, you do have Someone to make the path straight and provide light along the way.

Mary Granville's aristocratic family was less than enthusiastic about her marriage to Dr. Patrick Delany, an Irish clergyman of humble origin and modest means. However, they later testified that this marriage unlocked "strong creative elements" in Mary. Indeed, after her marriage Mrs. Delany pursued an exciting artistic venture of penning beautiful flower drawings. Her flower collages—still admired today throughout the world—gave her a unique entrée to the British royal court.

Mrs. Delany was greatly loved by her husband's congregation. She announced that Tuesdays would be "public days," which meant that she and her husband were at home to anyone who wished to call. She also arranged their Sunday lunch at a public house to which she invited the townsmen and their wives by turns to join them for dinner. She also made arrangements for a room at the house where her husband could rest before returning to church in the evening.

Mrs. Delany did not give up her interest in fashion when she married a pastor. Rather, it alerted her to the restrictions on the export of Irish cloth, which hurt the local traders. She took it upon herself to persuade the ladies to wear dresses of Irish cloth. Using the contacts that came with her First Lady position in the community and the experience she had enjoyed in attending the finest court functions in England, Mrs. Delany was just the person to set this example. The women trusted her good taste and followed her, and the tradesmen were grateful beyond expression.[3]

God's plan for marriage does not depend on perfect people, right circumstances, or even correct choices; rather, marriage according to God's design is guaranteed to flourish if there is perfect commitment (Gen. 2:23–25). If a young woman is led into loving commitment to a preacher, God will enable her to take on the added challenges of being married to a pastor. All burdens are accepted and borne as unto the Lord. In this light the duty of the marriage becomes the beauty of the union. The difficulty of being a pastor's wife is swallowed up in the opportunity of being a part of the work of the Lord. The uncertainties of overwhelming sorrows in mundane ministry are merely a part of the awesome task and are balanced and even overshadowed by the glories of unbounded joy in sweet service.

When God links you with your husband, be assured that He has made you to be the woman your husband needs. Your ministry to your husband and children will by far be the greatest ministry you can offer to your church. When you are doing your job at home, your husband will be able to come refreshed each day to serve the people in your congregation.

Emma Moody was described as making a ministry out of being a wife and mother. She took it upon herself to do everything within her power to relieve Dwight Moody of all the mundane tasks that would keep him from doing his work for God. She considered her husband's effectiveness in the work of the kingdom very important, and to that end she sought to minimize his weaknesses and maximize his strengths. She shielded him from interruptions, handled his correspondence, served as his troubleshooter, presided over their household, and nurtured their children.[4]

Erase the lists of qualifications you have heard touted for the perfect pastor's wife. You are one of a kind; you are the woman only you can be; you will meet needs of your husband only you can meet. When you try to fit a mold or grid someone else has fashioned, you are neglecting the gifts of the woman God created especially for your husband in the process. You are still developing and changing and even improving and learning, but the Lord is the Master Potter who gives shape and symmetry to your persona.

As the pastor's wife, you are not an average parishioner. You are the wife of the pastor. You should be a complement to the pastor. Anything you say or do is scrutinized by church members and often tells the congregation more about the pastor than what he reveals about himself. The pastor, too, is first and foremost a husband.

To see your faithfulness as a minister's wife to support the programs of the church is in itself a vital part of your husband's ministry. Whether your gifts make your contribution a public one, your sweet spirit and gracious smile can be a rewarding testimony of your commitment to the Lord and to your husband. Nevertheless, nothing you do in the church can equal the importance of your ministry within your home and to your own family.

The Call to a Vocation

There are women, and I am one, who receive the call of God personally. This call is to serve Christ vocationally in assuming a task in the kingdom. It is a call to equip others to serve Christ.

My call to vocational Christian service came in childhood before the Lord revealed to me His plan for my marriage to a preacher. The call to marriage completed and brought into focus God's plan for my life. In my case the call to marriage was a complementing call, linking my life to one with the same commitment and purpose.

The average young woman chooses a husband, and her only commitment is to him. Her highest joy and first duty is that of being a good wife to her chosen mate. Certainly, the pastor's wife can offer no less to her husband. If she did nothing more than to make her husband happy and meet his needs for nurturing shelter, tender love, and loyal companionship, through the effect of her faithfulness as wife and lover and friend, she would have done more for the church than all other services she could possibly render.

Nevertheless, how much better for you who marry a preacher to realize that you are choosing not only a life's partner but also a life's career. You seek no retreat or escape from the divine assignment to labor alongside your husband as his helper in the home and church. You are faced with a most versatile and challenging career since your position as the pastor's wife is a ready and effective channel for your talents and abilities.

The Lord does not leave you without the ability to do what He has called you to do and what you have committed yourself to do. The Lord places in the heart of a woman committed to Him a spark of heavenly fire. That fire may be only a smoldering coal through the season of prosperity and peace, but it will blaze as a raging flame during the dark hour of adversity.

One of the most common temptations for ministry wives lies in the area of spiritual giftedness. Jesus was tempted by Satan to use His gifts for personal gain. How much easier prey are you to Satan's appeal to use your gifts to your best advantage. You could make a contribution to the kingdom. Some preachers who have been superb in homiletical ability and theologically accurate in message content are brilliant orators but spiritually useless because their walk did not match their talk.

The pastor's wife is caught in a quandary of deciding what she can and cannot do within the church. Should she participate in the music program? Should she teach in Sunday school? Should she be an officer in the Woman's Missionary Union or direct the women's ministries? She must walk a tight line. On one side are those who think that her leadership in any area of church ministry is an attempt to run the church. On the other side are those who view her staying in the background as being aloof and disinterested in church life.

God's call to total commitment does not depend on your circumstances. Everyone will be shaped by family and even community, but your response to the plan and purpose of God and His call to live out that plan in service to Him ultimately depends only on your personal relationship with Him and how you respond to His direction. Most ministers and their families experience a period of deprivation during which many of the family's legitimate needs are not met sometime along the way.

Paige and I learned in times of poverty that God does care, and He is there! Understanding God's sufficiency (Phil. 4:13), you must seize the promised divine help (1 Cor. 10:13; Rom. 8:37–39) by plugging into His power (2 Tim. 1:7) and accepting His willingness to assist you (Isa. 41:10).

Training in the Trenches

Many women married to preachers are untutored in theology; some have little education. Jill Briscoe once said, "They [the disciples] didn't need a master of divinity; they had been with the Master of Divinity!" Certainly God does specialize in ordinary women who become extraordinary under His tutelage, for then He gets the glory. God never gives you an assignment that He doesn't equip you to do. However, you should not take this reasoning as an excuse to refuse opportunities to study formally in the classroom or informally through the many tools available for self-study.

For almost three decades I have been offering theological education to women. I am immensely grateful for graduate and post-graduate theological degrees that have enabled me to open the Word of God to women more effectively. You should take advantage of every opportunity to "be diligent to present yourself approved to God, a worker who does not need to be ashamed" (2 Tim. 2:15).

Women need to prepare themselves to serve their families and the Lord. A man does not have a corner on the Word of God just because he is a preacher with an ordination certificate hanging on his wall, a kingdom bag in his hand, and a one-way line to heaven upon which he expounds his particular theological jargon for God to endorse. Rather, the opportunity for a thorough understanding of God's Word and sufficient knowledge to read it in its original languages is available to anyone who would seek it and invest the time and effort to acquire the tools for research and study.

My husband and I have had the common goal of working together as a team for the Lord. Accordingly, he allowed and encouraged me to prepare with him so that our ministries could be both successful and cooperative with the help of the Holy Spirit. The Holy Spirit operates in your life as a hand in a glove. When the glove is empty—without a hand to fill it, the glove responds to only one command, "Lie there." However, when that glove receives and welcomes the hand, suddenly it can respond to many commands, "Wave, pick up, stand up, fasten a button, open a door." It is the hand that moves the glove and empowers the glove and controls the glove.

A preacher's wife should study and grow (2 Tim. 2:15). There are ways of marking that growth. First, a woman who is growing spiritually is going to hunger for God's Word. She will desire fellowship with other believers. She will have a plan for personal growth—intensive Bible study, direct and specific prayer. A woman who is growing spiritually will have a sensitivity to sin and a growing hatred toward sin (James 1:14–15). She will develop self-control; she will rejoice in serving the Lord; she will have a desire to witness and share her faith (1 Pet. 3:15).

How much or how little education you should have is what God makes available to you! However, I would caution you not to imply that you possess more expertise than you have. Use the training and gifts God has given to you, knowing He will stretch you and your ministry beyond anything you ever imagined. If your husband is in seminary, you will find wonderful programs—at least in Southern Baptist seminaries—at little cost and with great flexibility for varying schedules.

If you are already on the church field, you can enter a self-training program of directed reading, workshops, conferences, talking to women who have been there and done that. You may even be close enough to enroll in a Bible college or theological extension center. Whereas biblical and theological studies and even public speaking are very important, don't underestimate the importance of learning how to decorate and manage a home, develop and live within a budget, practice hospitality and care for guests, show common courtesies, as well as how to nurture your children and inspire your husband.

One of the smartest things I ever did was to develop my own filing system for ideas and helpful hints on managing my household and doing ministry. I have a wonderful set of traditional files on a myriad of subjects. My file inventory notebook lists these files alphabetically and stays on my desk so that I can quickly look to see if I have a file on any given subject without having to do a drawer-by-drawer search. I can also look to see how my files are styled when I add a new item in order to avoid duplicate folders with several different headings on the same subject.

In addition to these files, I have an information book with categories like *household maintenance* (hints on cleaning, caring for our houseplants, suggestions for home efficiency), *hospitality events* (functions, guest lists, menus with recipes attached, table centerpieces and settings, notations for special dietary needs, plus ideas for enhancing hospitality), *Christmas list* (to update throughout the year), *calendar, guest houses* (names of guests, dates of visit, and ideas for improving accommodations), *general information* (membership of boards, members of congress, special resource personnel), Southern Baptist Convention (agencies and institutions), SEBTS (information pertaining to the seminary where my husband and I serve). My third notebook contains the recipes and menus used most often here at Magnolia Hill. It is divided according to food category plus a special holiday section.

Still I am learning and stretching myself to do better, and I've been working at this job for four decades! Although I am not employed, I am a working woman. I spend hours and days studying and preparing to be the best First Lady I can be, and I work at that task with all my energy and creativity and a big investment of my time.

Giving up a second paycheck demands a sacrifice even to this day. Obviously, more money means more things. As a professional woman with graduate and post-graduate degrees, I could command a worthy salary. However, I am pleased with my choices and with how I have decided to invest myself.

Independent study has been rewarding to me. If I had counted on only what I was taught in the formal classroom, I would have been limited and unprepared for the responsibilities of my life. Yes, I had a wonderful formal education, but I have also taken an exhilarating informal education at my own initiative. I have sat at the feet of the Lord as did Mary of Bethany by reading through the Bible again and again just for my personal edification. I have learned from my theologian/preacher husband as Mrs. Isaiah of the Old Testament may have done. I have continued in personal study through the years, poring over a variety of volumes in our library—evangelical commentaries as well as volumes in church history, biography, and spiritual formation. I keep up with current newspapers, periodicals, and journals. I have studied my own denomination, including its most recent confession of faith. My reading is not limited to current publications. I have dipped deeply into the classics—volumes published long ago but still much honored and used. I attend workshops and professional conferences, and I continually take advantage of learning from those who cross my path.

Called or Conscripted?

God reveals His will in two primary ways. His most important communication with me is through His written Word, which the psalmist describes as "a lamp" to your feet and "a light" for your path (Ps. 119:105). Never try to use your personal experience or any person's experience to exegete or interpret Scripture. Rather, you must use Scripture to dictate your experience. Your answer can come anytime or anywhere on any subject from God's Word. The absolute principles God provides are the foundation for life; they help you make decisions. Therefore, the Word of God must be engraved on your heart.

Not only does God give you unchanging principles, but He also arranges changing circumstances in the unfolding of His will, at which time your response is the critical issue. For example, if your pastor husband is fired and loses his position, your understanding of the ultimate control of God and His providence enables you to allow yourself to be borne along through the tragedy of uncertainty and anxiety. It is more important to know who holds the future than it is to know what the future holds. There is a time for you to quit studying the problems in your life and start studying the promises in God's Word.

Esther, an orphan Jewess from a minority race, found herself in the harem of a cruel pagan king—Ahasuerus of Persia. She could have whined in despair or rejected her faith and heritage, but instead she responded to each tragedy or crisis by making right choices. She continued to obey her surrogate parent as much as was in her power to do; she made no demands and kept a gentle and quiet spirit, which endeared her to members of the court.

When Esther became the queen of Persia, she still remembered her family and faith. When God called her into action, she started with "I can't." But quickly she was ready to risk all in obedience to Him. She determined, "God can, and I want Him to use me."

Because God's name is not mentioned in the Book of Esther, the book seems to be a collection of coincidences in a story with a happy ending. But these coincidences were actually "God incidences," God's way of remaining anonymous so that His Hand and power are evident without a word on His part. His acts of providence build a bridge to Himself. Esther was seemingly powerless, but she did what she could; she responded appropriately to the choices before her, trusting divine providence. No tragedy excused her from obedience to Scripture.

You may not enter a pagan harem or marry an unbelieving tyrant or have an edict of death over your head as did Esther. Instead you will have your own set of challenges—a husband who is a spiritual leader for the congregation but indifferent to your spiritual needs, parishioners who are willing to take your time and creativity without any gratitude and then stab you in the back, and a parsonage that was perfect for the last pastor but completely inadequate for your family. Again, the key is not how quickly you can change all of the aforementioned problems but how completely you can trust and obey in your response to life's unexpected setbacks, which were allowed—but not necessarily directed—by God.

Surrendering to God's will is a journey. You must learn not to be afraid, not to give in to anxiety and worry, not even to run away. God deals firmly with His children. When you step out from under His umbrella of protection and run from His assignment, remember the prophet Jonah. Ann Landers once commented on careless drivers: "It's not only a car that can be recalled by its maker!"

When you run from God or carelessly bring shame to the kingdom of Christ, God can turn His back, but He may deal with you in whatever way is best for the kingdom of Christ. Learn to wait on the Lord and to praise Him as you go His way. Think for a moment what any caterpillar might be thinking as it looks up at the butterfly winging about: "You'd never get me up in the air like that!" And certainly no butterfly would want to inch along in the dirt like a caterpillar. That's because caterpillars and butterflies have different mind-sets. It takes a complete metamorphosis to change the caterpillar into a butterfly. Spiritually, the Lord must do the same to you if you are going to be the First Lady He wants you to be.

God gives a map of your life's journey. You know the direction to head, and you soon become aware of stops along the way as well as of places to avoid. You do have choices, but making right choices does not presuppose the absence of inconveniences and even disasters along the way any more than following a map from place to place can exclude all interruptions from construction or heavy traffic. God's plan may include side trips you don't want to take. But getting the map is only the first step. You must then pack your bags and focus your mind and heart on the road ahead.

Finding and doing the will of God is an overwhelming task with choices to which you must respond with a commitment to obey the truths and unchanging principles of Scripture. You must also be willing to respond to the circumstances of life with whatever adjustments must be made without becoming bitter and rebellious. In addition, your response should be with joy!

Jonah knew exactly what God wanted him to do—go to Nineveh and preach the gospel. However, Jonah did not want to go to Nineveh, and he certainly did not want to do evangelism in that pagan city. Therefore, he made alternate plans—selected his own map and headed his own way. As a result, he ended up in a whale of a mess! Fortunately, God lovingly pursued Jonah and brought him back to the right road. On the other hand, many women continue to cling to their own maps, refusing to do what God directs (James 4:17).

Fixing the problems in life can be overwhelming. Unrealistic expectations will defeat you faster than anything else. You will be more disappointed, more frustrated, and more overwhelmed. What do you do? Start with one thing you want to change and then pursue that one change with passion day after day. I remember when I wanted to get serious about a quiet time with the Lord. I never seemed to read the number of chapters in my Bible reading plan. I decided to read through Proverbs, trying to do a chapter per day but not being discouraged if I only read a few verses. The key for me was to be faithful, even if I didn't reach my final goal. To this day I am reading through Proverbs each month, and it is as natural as brushing my teeth—it is habit! A great gulf is fixed between earthly enjoyment and spiritual joy. Circumstances bring earthly enjoyment, but genuine joy comes when you bring God pleasure.

Your calling need not be something mysterious and earthshaking; it may be as simple as the "still small voice" Elijah heard after the wind, earthquake, and fire (1 Kings 19:10–18). God's calling may simply be God's leading—daily, step-by-step, a slow unfolding of God's will for your life through promptings of the Holy Spirit and circumstances. God will reveal His will to you wherever you are because He wants you to know His plan for your life (Acts 22:14).

God's will may not please you. God's plan may seem unpleasant and even impossible; it may include sorrow and suffering (Ps. 119:71). Your thoughts are not His thoughts, and His ways are not your ways (Isa. 55:8).

> "God always reveals
> His will to the person
> willing to do His will."
>
> —June Hunt

By immersing yourself in His Word, you will find His principles for a lifestyle He honors, and you will become acquainted with women and men of faith who have gone before, leaving their footprints on the pages of Scripture. He will initiate drawing you to Himself, but you must determine to line up under His Word (Ps. 119:133). When you follow your own desires, you are not seeking God with your whole heart, and you are not trusting Him. Your feelings are not reliable. God expects you to make your decisions by His standards and to act on His direction.

On the other hand, God speaks to the husband as the leader of the home, and the Lord expects a wife to bring her will and desires into line with what is presented to her from the Lord through her husband. If the husband makes mistakes, he answers to God; the wife's responsibility is to follow her husband's leadership (Eph. 5:22–24). To whom and for what is not nearly so important as the commitment to the task.

How Do You Know God's Will?

Your first and most reliable criterion for knowing the will of God is His Word. If He speaks to the question or challenge in His written Word with clear principles, then you have a clear answer—perhaps not one you want to hear but nevertheless one that is reliable and right every time. For this reason you must memorize Scripture and saturate yourself with its truths in order to trigger in your mind and heart a word from God on any given subject!

On the other hand, if Scripture does not address your decision, the Holy Spirit is available to lead and guide you. He will in no way lead you to make a decision that contradicts Scripture! Also, the Spirit will give you peace when the right decision is made (Phil. 4:6–7). Any decision you make should not impede your spiritual growth but should edify and build you up so that you are more like Christ (2 Cor. 3:18).

There are other guidelines for the decision-making process. Ask yourself how your choices would affect other people and what impact your choices would have on your testimony for Christ (Rom. 14:21). Never deceive yourself in believing your choices have no impact on anyone but you—or even only you and your immediate family! Your example has far-reaching influence (1 Tim. 4:12). Consider also how any decision you make will affect the Lord. Anyone who bears the name of Christ represents Him in a unique way. Everything a Christian does reflects on the Lord Jesus Christ (1 Cor. 10:31).

Dreams and visions do have a place as you meditate before the Lord and seek His direction (Prov. 29:18). Sometimes the greatest achievements and grandest work come as a result of a dream or vision. An oak tree starts as a small acorn; a bird is hatched from an egg; a baby begins as an embryo in the mother's womb. James Allen said, "Dreams are the seedlings of realities."

Some of you, as I, have been forced to make compensation for impairment in vision. My "glasses" are merely magnifiers. When I reached the point of seeing what were once legible words as fuzzy and illegible phrases, I had to find a way to make those words clear and precise again. Your spiritual vision, too, may grow fuzzy so that your weakness forces you to take a second look through God's magnifiers. Scripture and time spent in His presence will magnify and make clear the way before you.

What's in a Name?

What do people call you? Although such is relative and dependent on many factors, if you resent being Mrs. Surname, you have a problem far greater than identification. When you choose to marry, you are choosing to link your life to one man with whom you become one. Your lives are to be so intertwined that no one thinks of one without thinking of the other. His name links you to him with the same logic as your name before marriage identified you with your father—the head of household for your birth family.

On the other hand, something about your personal given name marks you with more precision. To be identified with your forename is fine. However, there are several cautions. Being a First Lady is a position of respect and responsibility. Sometimes too much familiarity breeds its own set of problems, especially in a culture in which respect for authority and age is waning, as is seen both in the school classroom and in neighborhood play. For people to address you and your husband with your title and surname is a way of recognizing your position of leadership within the church family. For adults to honor this custom is the best tool for teaching children and young people to do the same.

For believers, your identity is in Christ so that it is not as much who you are as whose you are. A woman of godly character does not make decisions based on her feelings and experience but rather upon what is right and true. Her standard is the Word of God. When the Lord, through Aaron, prescribed a lifestyle for the priests of Israel, He distinguished between holy and unholy, between clean and unclean; and He did so in order that these priests would teach the children of Israel His statutes (Lev. 10:8–11). Surely the Lord expects those who are set apart to represent Him in spiritual leadership to order their lives and habits so that the church and the world know they belong to the Lord.

How many times have you heard a woman say, "I could never be a preacher's wife; it would be too hard"? There have been days when I have felt the same way, but I am happy to report that they have been few and far between. Nor have they stuck in my memory as have the good times! The rewards have far outweighed and overshadowed the discouragements.

No one can please everyone, and church members do seem to have their expectations—many of them unrealistic—for the preacher's wife! One of my hairdressers was continually frustrated with how to fix my hair. Since I have always left the styling to experts, I was no help. I wanted to sit in her chair and work on my projects. But she had other clients from our church. Some wanted her to put my hair up because it added maturity (I was in my mid-twenties); others advised her to stop putting my hair up because it made me look too old. I suggested that she satisfy herself, thereby pleasing me, and forget the expectations of others.

Don't Blame the Mirror

Any husband needs a wife of whom he can be proud, and preachers are no exception. The husband who was sitting in the gates with the elders of the land had a wife who dressed in fine fabric and vivid colors (Prov. 31:22–23). Whatever your age or however humble and plain your exterior, you can appear attractive and stylish and even mysterious with time and imagination. Your imperfections should become challenges and not excuses.

The right hairstyle, appropriate makeup, and flattering clothing can be the perfect canvas for a smile and happy spirit. Your confidence grows as you learn to look your best. You can stand tall and project that confidence to others. In the early days of pastoral experience, limited budget and the needs of young children sapped resources and time. In our university town there were no spas or upscale salons! However, when I accompanied my husband to Dallas or New York or Los Angeles, I dipped into my personal savings to book myself in a top salon for a makeover. I always had pen and paper and plenty of questions. I was not just there for a fix; I wanted to learn everything I could!

The same is true for clothing. You should learn successful buying. A garment that doesn't flatter you is no bargain at any price. Looking through magazines and catalogs is helpful, but nothing is as effective as trying garments. Consider the color, the fit, the ease of movement. The real problem is not usually budget but the tendency to follow each year's fad in color and style with short-lived garments. If you are purchasing one garment per year instead of trying to replace an entire wardrobe annually, you will find that you can be more selective.

Every First Lady is a public figure for her constituency. The important thing for any person in the public eye is to try to be attractive and modest as you meet the public. Invest in a full-length mirror, and never leave your dressing room or bedroom without a careful look from head to toe.

Take time seasonally to look through your wardrobe, try on each garment, experiment with accessories, taking a good look in the mirror. If the garment does not fit properly or is uncomfortable, discard it. If it is damaged in some way or needs to be altered, then have the adjustments made promptly or discard it. If it is not appropriate for your lifestyle—too complicated to put on and off, impossible to launder or clean, or if you don't have accessories needed to wear the garment, then discard it. Durable fabrics hold their shape. Rotate clothing, especially undergarments. What is closest to your body ought to be comfortable, pretty, and durable. Perhaps by paying a little more you will have the garment around longer. Be satisfied with fewer garments and make them enhance your appearance.

The coordination of clothing with matching shoes, purse, and other accessories, including jewelry and scarves, makes for a more polished outfit. Generally plain and classic designs with simple lines and little ornamentation are the best foundation because you can then change your accessories seasonally. As a rule, with accessories less is best. Your accessories can provide an economical way to adapt an outfit to current trends. I make some choices based on personal preferences and style. However, I hope there never comes a day when I am not attentive to others, considering what they say without being too proud to make changes that seem prudent.

First Ladies are in the public eye in a unique way, and you must continually evaluate your appearance. You don't have to abandon being yourself. I have definite ideas on what fashion style is best for me. I love hats! A hat plopped on my head transforms me immediately. My hats are really close to my heart even though I wear them on my head. They are part of my persona. I began wearing hats while we lived in Arkansas because I found a seamstress who had been a milliner. She was talented and made hats to match my outfits.

Although I do not feel comfortable in pants when I am teaching on the seminary campus or delivering a message to women in the churches, other women wear pants almost exclusively in whatever the setting. I cannot imagine being on the platform without hosiery, especially in a short skirt; but again I have seen women older than I doing just that. Some have the notion that wearing any dress is being "dressed up." However, many dresses and skirts are in casual and comfortable styles.

The bottom line for me is that I do not want to be a stumbling block for someone else. Obviously there is more than one appropriate length for skirts and dresses as well as many modest styles that are appropriate and to be chosen according to individual taste and body frame. However, tight jeans, miniskirts, low necklines, and extensive body piercing are inappropriate for First Ladies.

Your goal is to pull together a wardrobe that is appropriate to your lifestyle, well-fitting and comfortable to your body, efficient in maintenance, and attractive enough to enhance your appearance. I would rather err on the more traditional appearance than appear to be so avant-garde that I would hurt my testimony. One test has served me well: If summoned by the queen to Buckingham Palace, would you wear this outfit? Certainly the King of Kings deserves special time and attention from you as you represent Him.

Garments you keep should be repaired, cleaned, and organized. I have my closet arranged by type of garment and color. Whether bane or blessing, it is a fact of life: Your hair, makeup, and clothing work together to frame your testimony. A pleasing presence is enhanced by an attractive appearance, happy disposition, poised demeanor, friendly nature, and gracious manner.

True beauty is not figures and fashion but the Holy Spirit's indwelling in your heart. Of course, the pastor's wife must follow the rules of modesty, cleanliness, and good taste. Study yourself and observe what styles draw compliments from your husband and others. With careful planning and wise buying of a wardrobe, you will make your family and parishioners proud of your appearance.

Watch for tips about laundering and ironing techniques. In my household notebook I keep information on removing common stains. I learned to fold my husband's shirts professionally by sending one shirt to the laundry professionals and then carefully unfolding it and making notes on how it was folded. My demonstration on how to fold shirts and suits and how to pack a suitcase is a favorite in my class for ministers' wives. I gleaned this information from magazines, books, and personal observation.

Upkeep on the Temple

The rules of good health go hand in hand with appearance. A body kept fit and in good health are important basics for the minister's wife. A figure that looks well in clothes may add years to your life and keep you healthy as well.

The more you relax and enjoy life by engaging in physical activity, the more you lower your stress. Some psychologists have even cited health benefits from joy and laughter. It is also important for adults to play. Play can actually clear your mind, increase your creativity, dissipate your anger, and defuse volatile interpersonal problems.

A success coach suggested these life changes: Go to bed thirty minutes earlier. Spend a few minutes thinking about your day before you get out of bed. Eat a leisurely breakfast. Read from a good book. Keep fresh flowers in your bedroom, and wake up to beauty and fragrance.[5]

Agatha Christie once said, "Women observe subconsciously a thousand little details, without knowing they are doing so. Their subconscious mind adds these little things together—and they call the result intuition." Use your God-given nature. Some consider imagination more important than information because it is imagination that opens new possibilities. You certainly have no time for throwing your imagination into gear if every minute of your life is scheduled. You have to build in time to dream and meditate and allow your creativity to do its work. Perhaps you need the soothing of a hot bath, the therapy of an evening walk, or the fellowship of a coffee time with a friend. You take care of your body because it is the Lord's temple and the vehicle with which you move through life in effective service for Him.

Don't Sink the Boat

Few women seem to be concerned with good manners or proper eti-

> ### Dottie's Dictum
> - Sustain your spiritual life.
> - Eat a healthy diet.
> - Exercise regularly.
> - Get plenty of rest.
> - Drink lots of water.
> - Practice good dental hygiene.
> - Take time to play.

quette. This decline has accompanied their exodus from the home and their forfeiture of family mealtime. Not only do family members suffer from rudeness and lack of respect for others in the home, but this sad demise of common courtesy has made its way to restaurants, theaters and cultural events, shopping centers, and even to increased rage on roadways.

To equip the First Lady in the parsonage with some training in how to become a model of feminine finesse and thereby set the tone for a winsome lifestyle is a great way to bring back gracious living, elegant simplicity, and common civility. To do so you must portray a gracious lifestyle in your speech, your dress, your walk, and the touch you bring to all of life. You become a master of the details of life. As one of my students suggested: You can "wrap everything with ribbon!" In other words, you add a unique and extraordinary personal signature to everything you do. With this discipline in life, you will draw others to your presence and influence, and you will have a wonderful venue in which to share the "living letter" of testimony Christ has placed in your heart (2 Cor. 4:2).

One of the most helpful things a minister's wife can do for her husband and family is to oversee a quiet and well-ordered household, managing

time so that the family can have regular mealtimes and punctual depar-
tures for church and other outings. To do otherwise is a distraction to your
husband, sapping his energies unnecessarily.

Never take your children to a dinner or other private function unless
they have been specifically invited. They probably would not enjoy the
adult event, and often it interferes with their bedtime routine. If you are
unable to secure a sitter, then you simply graciously decline the invitation.

On the other hand, what do you do when your invited guests appear
with uninvited children in tow? I have faced this challenge more often
since we have been at the seminary. With a large student body, in order to
accommodate the students and their spouses at the Christmas reception,
I have a simultaneous event for the children in the gymnasium. In addition, I have several days blocked for student families to bring their children to see the Magnolia Hill Christmas decorations and pick up a holiday
cookie. I am always amazed every year that some parents choose to ignore
the invitation guidelines. Not only are they rude to arrive at an adult
event with children, but they are also unfair to those who have followed
instructions. I try to find a way to make the unfortunate situation one in
which the parents learn a lesson, while I continue gracious hospitality.
Such disregard of common etiquette is not reserved for large receptions but
may also happen for a luncheon or dinner.

My solution begins with your invitation. Be as specific as you can in a
gracious way to define the boundaries. Always try to use positive language:

> Because of the size of the Christmas reception, we
> have supervised care and refreshments for all children in
> the gymnasium. Magnolia Hill will be open for the chil-
> dren to view Christmas decorations other days. Please
> help us divide the guest list in order to accommodate
> everyone.

When children show up unexpectedly for a meal, if a high chair is sufficient, I can usually add that to the dining room table. For toddlers and older children, I quickly set the morning room table and ask a staff member to host them. My response to parents:

> I hope these arrangements will be satisfactory for your
> little ones. I wish we had known they were coming so we
> could have prepared a bit more!

The chapter on hospitality has more information on common courtesies and rules of etiquette important to First Ladies. A First Lady should be a role model. You should be meticulous in being the best guest as well as the best hostess!

> "In the midst of these complicated labours . . . [Edwards] found at home one who was in every sense a help mate for him, one who made their common dwelling the abode of order and neatness, of peace and comfort, of harmony and love, to all its inmates, and of kindness and hospitality to the friend, the visitant, and the stranger."
>
> — Samuel Hopkins about Sarah, the wife of Jonathan Edwards

CHAPTER 3

A Made-to-Order Bride

The woman was created from and for the man (1 Cor. 11:8–9; see also Gen. 2:18). A wife is to help, assist, and undergird her own husband in whatever assignment God gives to him. Because this "helper" (*'ezer kenegdo*, Hebrew, literally "a help like or corresponding to him") was an inspired ideal before her creation, the words used to describe her had to express God's own purpose (Gen. 2:18).

Creative Design

Although in the modern day the term *helper* suggests a menial position, careful examination of the word's biblical usage does not indicate a servile role. In fact, the word is often associated with divine assistance (Ps. 30:10; 54:4). No man needs a "suitable helper" more than the preacher. The preacher's wife may well be described as the "universal spare part." She is often called upon to reverse gears and shift directions according to need, and many of these capable women are bursting with energies and commitment adequate to weather almost any crisis. The responsibility is demanding and rewarding.

> "As God by creation made two of one, so again by marriage He made one of two."
>
> —THOMAS ADAMS

God created the man with a need for the woman—mentally, he desires a counterpart; emotionally, he needs a companion; spiritually, he seeks a co-laborer; physically, he craves a lover. For the minister's wife there is no more important task and no more sacred duty than to devote energy and creativity to being your husband's exclusive lover. No one else can meet this need for your husband. You must never shrink from the duty of meeting his needs or fail to reciprocate with your loving response to his affections. For this intimacy to reach its greatest satisfaction demands a spiritual dimension.

While both see sexual intimacy as important, wives also have deep needs for emotional intimacy. The minister, as any husband, must remember that his wife is designed by the Creator to be a responder. He would do well to shower upon her tender love and affection not associated with sexual intimacy but simply because she is precious to him.

Outward acts of affection will only strengthen inner feelings of loving devotion. No greeting or departure, no awakening or retiring ought to be experienced without tender kisses and hugs. Both need communication at the deepest level and companionship as well as affirming compliments and loving encouragement. Both need to make themselves attractive and winsome for the other. Both need the enrichment of an exclusive courtship that is fun, romantic, intimate, and even a bit adventuresome. Just as a plant denied water and sunlight will eventually die, affection without loving touches and tender words will wither and fade. In other words, the sharing of affection must be a habit never to be broken!

Many people can do the work of the church, but only this chosen vessel can be the preacher's wife and mother to his children. Her influence on the minister, to whom has been committed the spiritual leadership of a group of families united to the Lord in worship and service, is an awesome task in itself.

The Lord does provide equipping for the task along the way. You can learn how to converse with strangers, how to ask questions, how to make your way to a subject of mutual interest, how to have a meaningful exchange. You can learn to appreciate the fact that you are often exposed to scintillating speakers and best-selling authors who can stretch your mind and open new horizons of interest to you. The Lord Himself will grow you up, chase away your insecurities, equip you with knowledge and expertise you didn't think possible, and prepare you for whatever exigencies you may face. He brings people into your life to encourage you along the way.

Marriage requires unconditional love of husband and wife, one for the other. You cannot have this kind of love without being willing to accept each other and without a commitment to make your marriage work. Make it a point to do things together—engage in play or relaxation, read to one

---

Dottie's Dictum for Wives

- Take care of your personal appearance.
- Keep your home orderly and inviting; greet your husband warmly when he returns home.
- Show affection consistently and openly.
- Listen and share kind and loving words.
- Avoid being dull by stimulating yourself intellectually.
- Stay involved in your husband's ministry.
- Observe family mealtime, especially breakfast and dinner.
- Plan couple time—weekend date and annual retreat away from children.

another, attend the theater, have coffee or tea, talk together, or go for walks. Develop outside activities that provide pleasure and relaxation. Encourage your husband to have hobbies and carve out time to enjoy them.

Creating a good and lasting marriage is not easy; it takes hard work and sacrifices by husband and wife. A minister's wife and children must be his priority right behind the time he spends sustaining his personal relationship to the Lord. His role modeling what a godly husband and father ought to be is part of his equipping ministry.

The minister's family should be a pattern to which the congregation can look for fashioning their own homes. A minister's wife must understand that part of that priority family commitment is the minister's responsibility to provide support for the family. As with all husbands and fathers, "the sweat of his brow" goes with the territory. Time and energy are necessary to fulfill his responsibilities in the workplace from which he receives his livelihood, and the family must be understanding of the need for him to do his work in order to support them.

Nothing binds a minister to his people like an open hearth with a welcome mat. Entertainment of "angels unawares"—members of the congregation, co-laborers in the kingdom's work, church leaders and potential leaders, unsaved men and women from the community—comes in due course. The First Lady of the parsonage has a unique opportunity to use her potential and creativity as well as her talents and energies in a joint ministry with her husband that is destined to be more fruitful and meaningful than separate ministries from either of them individually (Ps. 34:3; Eccles. 4:9–12).

Paul commended Priscilla and Aquila as "my helpers in Christ Jesus." This dynamic duo composed the most outstanding ministering couple on the pages of Scripture. Together they proclaimed the gospel of Christ and shared the

> "First, he must choose his love, and then he must love his choice."
>
> —HENRY SMITH

word throughout the apostolic world. Priscilla was very much a part of her husband's ministry and must have been a discerning student of Scripture in her own right. She impressed the learned Apollos and had a part in his edification (Acts 18:2–3, 18, 26).

Every minister needs a soulmate as Priscilla was to Aquila. She can help her husband determine life goals and work with him to reach those goals. She should approach this task with enthusiasm, believing in her husband, confident of his success, and loving their journey together. Even if you have nothing to prompt enthusiasm, manufacture it; and soon it will become a natural response. Learn to ask your husband discerning questions and never betray a confidence he has shared with you. Be attentive to what he says, giving him your full attention. Listen not only for what he says but also to the unspoken needs he has. Little things not only count; they can enhance even the most stagnant marriage. A ministry marriage should not only work but be vital and exemplary.

When your husband hits the winds of difficulty and trials, you need to encourage him along. A time may come when you need to be the one whose faith is strong. You and your husband are one; whatever may come, you are in it together for better or worse! The mountain is great for a gorgeous panoramic view and invigorating since it is closer to heaven; but there's not much growing atop the mountain; the fruit trees and vegetable gardens are in the valley. You will experience special joy and satisfaction when you reach the peak of the mountain, but your work and your personal growth generally will be found in the valleys of life.

You will never push your husband to success, but you can inspire him to realize his dreams by praising his successes and expressing gratitude for the qualities he has that will help him succeed. By your appropriate words, you help him visualize himself as the pastor he wants to be. Sincere praise and appreciation will drive him to give his best efforts to the task before him. A wife's obvious confidence in her husband goes a long way toward making him look good to others.

Polishing the Pulpiteer

How can a preacher's wife help him become a stronger pulpiteer? Sometimes a little extra help from you can give your husband the momentum he needs to become a more effective preacher. Paige began preaching in area churches while we were dating. I have been able to enjoy his pulpit ministry for more than four decades, and there have been many changes!

One of my personal ministries until now is the constructive evaluation of his sermons. I love to hear him preach, and I am always blessed even when I am hearing the same sermon repeatedly. Always I begin with the positive affirmations. I never rush; rather, I let Paige move along the discussion. While he is preaching, I relax and listen. I take notes on what he is saying—an outline, insightful quotes, additional references, unique illustrations. I am his most eager listener. I will be the first to laugh at his jokes or cry during his poignant illustrations. I am continually praying throughout the sermon for the Holy Spirit to do His work in my own heart as well as in the hearts of those listening.

When the sermon is over, I am the first to say "Well done," usually with some brief specific affirmation. After we have left the church and shared the joys of the service and its harvest, opportunity comes for constructive criticism or suggestions. No one else can do as much as I to help my husband continue to improve as a preacher. Paige continues to express appreciation for attentive listening that results in helping him be better. I have also trained myself to read widely and avidly for illustrations or quotations or other information my husband might find helpful in his sermon preparation.

Paige is blessed to have an excellent background in grammar and style, and his delivery is polished. However, the great void in grammar and verbal skills in modern education has left many preachers with a tremendous handicap in this area. A loving and devoted wife can equip herself—even if it means additional study or a night class at the local community college—to help her husband.

Preachers would do well to include their wives in their ministry. A godly wife can provide spiritual comfort, practical wisdom and counsel, and even entertaining conversation. A wife can be a wonderful sounding board for problems and challenges in the congregation. Long after everyone else is gone, she can be available to pray with him.

After almost four decades, I still feel privileged to be married to a preacher. I still sit through the same sermons and sometimes as many as four services a day in order to hear him break the bread of life. I consider it my God-given task to help him be his best and to love him along the way. Undoubtedly, I am his cheerleader and greatest fan. Often a wife can stretch her husband and add to his success by believing in him and by communicating that admiration to others. A humble man will never blow his own horn, but his wife can in subtle and tasteful ways make his accomplishments known. She can minimize his weaknesses and magnify his strengths.

Some wives are resentful because the preacher seems to get all the praise, the compliments, the thank-yous, the recognition; but I have a different view on these outward manifestations. Because of what I believe about Christian marriage—the oneness of a couple committed to one another—when my husband is applauded, when he is admired, when he is thanked publicly, when he is recognized for some achievement, I always feel that the recognition and praise is for me as well. When Paige receives applause or is honored with a standing ovation, I do not participate except to sit quietly with heartfelt gratitude. We are so much one that subconsciously I feel a part of everything he does and all he receives! Of course, I want to honor him, but I am humbled with the praise he receives because in my heart it is for me as well!

When you and your preacher-husband don't agree, and that will happen even when your hearts are knit as one, you must deal with the ensuing conflict in a Christlike way. You should never ridicule your husband or dwell on his faults. You must learn to listen to each other so that you really understand what is being said. You must also learn the art of compromising what you do without giving up what you believe. In matters of conscience in which you have a word from God, you will obey the Lord rather than any man; but in the inevitable choices of life, you will learn to give and take, to cooperate with each other, and ultimately to defer to your husband as the divinely appointed head of your household, for better or worse.

Praying for Your Husband

Although every wife ought to be committed to pray for her husband, certainly the wife of a preacher should be aware that she has no more important task. Marriage is indeed an investment that is designed to pay dividends, but you must pay interest. Each husband is unique, and no human being knows his needs better than a devoted wife, although someone did say that it really doesn't matter whom you marry today because he'll be someone else tomorrow! Actually both husbands and wives are constantly undergoing changes.

Many prayer guides are available, but you can develop your own as easily as using someone else's. What should be included in such a prayer ministry? Your husband's personal commitment to Christ and his own quiet time are good starting points.

From my observation of preachers as students or in church staff positions, denominational posts, and missionary assignments, they become vulnerable as soon as they abandon their quiet times of intimate personal fellowship with the Lord. Some mighty giants have fallen because they moved away from personal time alone with the Lord.

Pray that your husband will seek the Lord with His whole heart even in the midst of a busy schedule; ask the Lord to strengthen him with wisdom as well as discernment for using that wisdom. Pray that the Lord will guard your husband's thought life, give him chaste speech, keep him blameless and pure. Ask the Lord to shield your husband from blind ambition—seeking more public acclaim, better salary and benefits, ample media exposure, a more prestigious pulpit, better recognition from his peers. Ask the Lord to make his walk match his talk.

Then pray that your husband will take his family responsibilities seriously. Pray that he will exercise servant leadership, that he will shower you with tender affection, that he will take seriously his responsibility to provide for the family and to protect the family. Pray that your husband will not be content to serve only as the pastor of his congregation but that he will also be faithful as the shepherd of your family, leading in family worship and superintending spiritual growth for you and your children. Pray that he will spend time molding the lives of your children and that he will give them attention and training. Pray that he sees clearly the need for his presence in the home at mealtime and for times of relaxation with the family.

Pray for your husband's health. He needs to relax and create balance in his life physically, emotionally, mentally, and spiritually. His program of diet and exercise is important to maintain health and vigor for the work he must do. He needs to be able to leave his work and ministry for a time and immerse himself in family and friends. He needs a day of rest away from the demands of the church and congregation, and he needs to get enough sleep to renew his energies day by day. He needs to have regular medical checkups.

Finally, pray for your husband's ministry. He needs the anointing of the Holy Spirit on his preaching and teaching; he needs help in unlocking the truths of Scripture; he needs boldness for sharing the gospel; he needs sensitivity to the needs of the people he serves; he needs wisdom for biblical guidance to those who seek answers. A church grows by nutrition as well as addition—discipleship or equipping the saints as well as evangelism or winning the lost. He also needs encouragement when he is down; he needs comfort when he is hurting; he needs new vision when nothing is working.

Find a tangible way to express your appreciation for your husband. Set aside an attractively decorated box or a simple jar or even a journal to fill with Scripture verses of encouragement, coupons that offer personal services (polishing shoes, refreshments for the office staff, typing sermon notes), small packets of a favorite snack, or plans and a gift certificate for a date night.

Guarding the Gate

One of the greatest threats to the stability of families today is tailor-made for the home of the minister—a vulnerable wife who depends solely upon her husband to meet her physical, emotional, and spiritual needs and a husband who appears to be sold out to God but functions as a workaholic servant to the congregation twenty-four hours a day, seven days a week.

The preacher's job seems to define his ministry for the Lord and thus his purpose in life. But he may consider this job his alone. He doesn't want to talk about it—whether because he doesn't think his wife is a worthy listener or because he wants to protect her. He is shutting her out of his life.

The minister exudes piety in his public life and delivers a word from God with passion and eloquence from the pulpit. He seems able to meet the spiritual needs of every church member and even people who wander in from the street. However, he spends his time at home vegetating in front of the television or napping on the sofa. If he shows up for meals, he expects the food to be served promptly with a routine blessing of the food. He offers no spiritual leadership in the family, no family worship, no intimate conversation, no effort to meet personal needs of family members.

The minister's wife finds even greater frustration in feeling that she holds second place in her husband's life, behind the church. An esteemed senior pastor in his final years of ministry said to his congregation, "I am married to the church; I should have been a monk." His wife sat on her pew insecure, angry, and bitter, continuing her inestimable harm to the cause of Christ.

The minister's wife suffers the most not only from her personal rejection, but she is also painfully aware of the consequences of an absent father for her children. She may well try to reach out to her husband for intimate fellowship or in the challenge of spiritual struggles. Often she is patiently and creatively seeking to entice him to accept family responsibilities—especially spiritual leadership.

Even couples without children need to come together for prayer and reading Scripture. This time can be structured with use of a devotional volume, a prayer journal, or a Bible reading program; or it can simply be a segment of time set apart for spontaneous couple worship. The quiet time for spiritual focus for a preacher and his wife provides spiritual replenishment for both and becomes a benediction for the day's labor. Spiritual oneness is critically important to a vital marriage.

Hopefully your husband, as the pastor of your family as well as of the church, will initiate this spiritual leadership in your home. Most people manage to make time for the things they consider important. You can place a Bible near the table or other family gathering place and offer gentle reminders such as, "Is this a good time for us to read a bit of Scripture and pray together, or is there a better time for you?" However, a wife is not the Holy Spirit, Jr., in her husband's life. His inconsistencies are not her responsibility except to pray for him.

The minister's wife, starving for spiritual leadership, begins her pilgrimage with simple requests but probably works up to nagging complaints, pitiful crying and whining, and perhaps even bitter verbal assaults. Not only has her husband failed to accept any family responsibilities, but he also seems to have so insulated himself that he does not even notice or care that his family is hurting. In fact, he is so unaware of their needs that he becomes frustrated with what he perceives as their unrealistic expectations of him, and he withdraws further, becoming even more inaccessible to his family. He immerses himself in his work at the church where he perceives that he has respect and at least a measure of success.

Meanwhile, the minister's wife becomes increasingly frustrated and angry. She is engulfed in bitterness. The gulf between them grows and becomes increasingly apparent to their children and even their parishioners. And the minister's wife may even walk away from her home and family. In so doing, she would devastate her husband and children; she would deliver irreparable harm to the kingdom of Christ; she would probably live to regret her disobedience to Christ. The minister, too, would be overwhelmed with guilt and regrets, and often his ministry is ruined.

Such a tragedy began with the rejection of God-given responsibilities in light of what appeared to be a "higher calling." That was exasperated by a selfish response and the attempt to find human solutions. Finally, the disobedience became a family affair, and tragedy ensued.

God offers His own way of dealing with such tragedy. It may take longer, and it certainly does not short-circuit the pain and suffering that accompany any disobedience. However, to go God's way keeps you under the umbrella of His protection. A wife learns to wait on the Lord, realizing that she may yet praise Him for her husband and marriage (see Ps. 42:7). While she is waiting and praying and responding to injustice and insensitivity with extravagant love in Christlike ways, the Lord is working on her husband.

Preacher-husbands also can choose to stop in the midst of disobedience and recognize the priority of family responsibilities and determine to protect family mealtime and to exercise spiritual leadership with some form of family worship in the home—reading God's Word to the family and praying together as a family and spending time discussing spiritual matters.

Some suggest that a minister's wife will make or break him. Such an idea suggests that if a minister fails, his wife is responsible. Any minister totally dependent on his wife for success or failure is too weak for ministry. A wife by divine design is to help her husband. She should be a plus—an added blessing and an enhancement to all he attempts. She should make him better than he is in the sense that she inspires and helps him to do his work.

The Spin of Sin

More and more ministers, and their wives, are being caught in the web of unfaithfulness. A high percentage of broken clergy marriages are the result of a minister's improper handling of his pastoral relationships with women. As has been popularly stated, sin will take you further than you want to go; sin will keep you longer than you want to stay; sin will cost you more than you want to pay.

Everyone does a double take. How could a godly pastor or exemplary First Lady fall into an extramarital affair or adultery? Most of the time adultery was not the plan, but in the midst of those stresses and weaknesses common to the human family, even a servant of the Lord is vulnerable to moral compromise. Beware of placing blame on the spouse who has been faithful, saying the adultery occurred because needs of the guilty party went unmet. Far too many steps along the way are missing in that conclusion. Seeking personal gratification outside the boundaries of God's law is never justifiable. If one person is deceptive and chooses infidelity and unfaithfulness, the other who has remained faithful and chaste is not equally guilty.

Adultery is never the fault of someone else; it is a personal choice with tragic consequences. Sin may seem exciting with the offer of instant happiness. The momentary pleasure sears the conscience and removes restraints.

In some ways preachers are more vulnerable because they are put on a pedestal by most of their parishioners and even those within the community. This position makes them a target for designing women (see Prov. 5–7). But they also put themselves in the line of fire as they do their duties.

In the Line of Fire

What are some guidelines a wife might pass along to her pastor-husband when he is asked to counsel a woman?

- Your best option is always to have a woman counsel another woman. You can call on your wife or a woman staff member or a godly Sunday school teacher. Offer some simple training in biblical guidance for a core group of women who can then do such counseling effectively.
- If you must do the counseling session yourself, conduct all counseling sessions in the office during regular hours. Ask your secretary (or your wife, if you do not have a secretary) to make the appointment so that

the appointment, as other appointments, is made in a professional way. If you do not have a glass panel in your door, leave the door open. Someone should be in the outer office in either case. Again, the best wisdom is to ask someone else to join the counseling session. That person can be completely silent, simply praying throughout the meeting for you and the person you are counseling.

- Any counseling relationship can get out of hand and become time-consuming for the counselor and develop codependency in the counselee. The pastor should agree from the beginning to set only a reasonable number of sessions (two or three) and refuse to continue seeing a person who is unwilling to do what is suggested (Scripture memory, reading a helpful volume, etc.).

- Make referrals carefully. If you do not know a professional counselor who genuinely seeks to follow biblical principles in his counseling, let the individual make his or her own choice. Remember that a person who rejects biblical guidance may not really be interested in solving the problem but rather may be seeking to justify her or his own way.

What can a pastor's wife do when a woman in the church has a crush on her husband? First, she must gently alert her husband to the situation. Men are not so observant of such matters. She should make it a matter of prayer. She can adapt her schedule to accompany her husband whenever possible and thereby make it difficult for any woman to invade his private space. If none of this works, she may talk confidentially to a highly trusted friend in ministry rather than to anyone within the church. I know of situations in which a wife has found it necessary to contact another staff member or a mature and godly deacon if she has proof that her husband is inappropriately involved with another woman. Such situations are rare and extremely hurtful to the congregation, the kingdom of Christ, and to her own family; but blatant adultery cannot be tolerated.

The same care must be taken in relating to female staff members. Many pastors spend more hours a day with a secretary than they do with their own spouses. Again, strict rules must be observed. When the two of them are together alone, the door must be wide open. They do not work alone together in a deserted building; they never drive anywhere alone. Also, the pastor's love and affection for his wife should be abundantly clear to his staff and parishioners and to anyone who is observing.

How does the minister's wife interact with her husband's secretary? You must realize that the two of you should be allies in helping your husband do his job. He will be doubly effective if you can work together in his best interest. Beware of jealousy. Many days your husband's secretary has more of his time than you do. They do work together. However, if he follows appropriate guidelines and if she is the right kind of person, the time they spend together poses no threat to your marriage.

Treat your husband's secretary with respect as a trusted colleague. Don't snub her. Be gracious and considerate whether on the telephone or in person. Don't expect her to do personal tasks for you, but express appreciation for special things she does for you or your husband, which in the course of events may well happen.

All the innovative ways of dealing with female counselees and staff members will not ultimately protect your husband, however, if he is not enveloped in integrity and character.

Your husband can examine his own heart on this matter with questions like these:

- Do you have a consistent walk with the Lord? Do you have a personal time for reading Scripture and praying every day—not preparation for sermons or Bible studies but just time for you and God to meet?

- Do you nurture your relationship with your wife—calling during the day just to say "I love you"—and especially do you call your spouse when you are out of the city? Are you working to make your marriage better and to meet each other's needs? Are your needs being met in your marriage? If not, have you communicated this to your wife?

  You can take the initiative in seeing to it that the two of you work out your differences and meet each other's needs. The vitality of your marriage is important. There should always be a dimension of romance and intimacy that sets your relationship with your wife apart from all others.

- Do you make your wife and children a priority? Do you consider them a part of your ministry? Do you spend time with your family on a regular basis? When you have discretionary time, do you choose your family rather than other people or personal pursuits?
- Do you have a ministry partner or some friend or mentor with whom you have developed an accountability relationship?
- Are you in ministry as a professional pursuit? Is it merely a job that uses your giftedness and appeals to your ego? Does it seem to offer the most pay for the least work?

A minister's wife can also take special precautions to remain faithful to her vows of marriage:

- Spend time alone with God every day.
- Have a godly demeanor. You can look attractive and feminine without sending the wrong signals.
- Avoid putting yourself in compromising situations, such as being behind closed doors alone with another man, even in an automobile, for an extended period of time.
- Don't compare your husband with another man in your mind or conversation.
- When you slip into a sinful action or even an improper thought, stop and turn and run the other way!

Ultimately, the only protection for the pastor and his wife is the Holy Spirit of God. You must have a commitment to spend time with the Lord regularly and exclusively. However, your marriage must be important enough that you give time to nurturing it every day. True intimacy is more than flirtatious games and idle words; it is a way of life. An intimate and exclusive relationship between husband and wife is based on devotion and passionate affection. You have to work at keeping the spark in your marriage.

People who are married cannot allow themselves to be involved in intimate relationships with anyone of the opposite sex. Any nonsexual relationship that becomes emotionally intimate to the point that it takes something away from the marriage is a form of unfaithfulness. Words of affection, feelings of longing, looks of desire, innuendoes of intimacy are inappropriate with anyone other than your spouse. The Scripture is clear: If this is a danger, run away from it as fast as you can (Prov. 4:26–27)! Change your location; get another job; walk away from a friendship. The break must be drastic and final.

Although women in the marketplace are more vulnerable to these deadly attractions because of their exposure to more men, homemakers also may be allured by male attention, especially when they do not have the attention and fellowship of their husbands.

When your needs for intimacy and companionship are being met by the person with whom you have linked yourself so that you are indeed one, you will not be interested in unfaithfulness to your spouse because that would mean unfaithfulness to yourself as well! When your discretionary time is spent happily with your spouse and children, you won't have time for pursuing the forbidden. If you are surrounded by a multitude of godly counselors, you have added another protective fence. Finally, if you are seeking to serve the Lord with your whole heart and if your primary desire is to please Him, the boundaries are absolutely clear and will bind you to Him whom you serve.

What do you do when you have evidence that your spouse has been or is being unfaithful? Unfortunately, Jesus has clearly mandated that believers must confront as well as reconcile. In fact, confrontation is often necessary before reconciliation. The Bible offers a pattern for confrontation. You must examine your own life before confronting another. Confess any sin, seek forgiveness from anyone wronged, and be reconciled (Matt. 5:23–24). According to the pattern Christ gave, you first confront one on one. If that does not produce repentance on the part of the erring one, then take someone with you who becomes a witness of the confrontation.

Pastors are given an extra safeguard from false accusation since two or three witnesses are necessary to receive a charge against an elder (1 Tim. 5:17). If still nothing is resolved, then the matter must be taken to the congregation with yet another opportunity for repentance. But some still will not respond, even when fellowship at the Lord's table is withdrawn. Then the congregation as well as the wronged spouse and family must continue to pray and work for the restoration of the errant one. He must be treated kindly and with loving care with the hope that he will be drawn back to the Lord and His church as well as his family.[1]

Divorce: Is It an Option?

In a news clip, actor Ben Affleck commented on the divorce of fellow Hollywood personalities Demi Moore and Bruce Willis: "I hope the tabloid press doesn't make a lascivious deal out of what is a normal situation—a breakup." What a sad day when the breakup of a marriage is touted to be normal.

Someone has said jokingly that divorce, even in the church, is not just being sanctioned; it is being sponsored as an easy out to an unpleasant situation. Even the families of pastors are not immune to this tragic trend. Among professionals, clergy couples ranked third in the number of divorces granted. Perhaps this startling statistic can be attributed to the unique marital stress and strain that seems to come into the lives of those involved in public life and service.[2]

Hear the heart of the pastor's wife who married a divinity student in college and then moved into the life of a pastor's wife. She received many smiles and some words of encouragement but suffered with her own problems and had no one from whom to seek counsel. Her pastor-husband seemed able to communicate with everyone but her. He seldom participated in family mealtime, and his weekends were given to sermon preparation or youth activities. His own wife and children were left to fend for themselves. After a decade of struggle, this pastor's wife walked and got a divorce.

Can you justify this tragedy by saying pastors are human and thus entitled to make mistakes? Or should you take this tragedy as a warning to examine your own life and marriage to be sure you are committed to the priorities God has given? For whatever reason, divorce is tragic. A couple who have become one are torn apart just as in the amputation of a limb. There is no way to explain divorce to children; they experience pure, undiluted pain!

The most basic foundation for Christian marriage is the covenant, the most sacred and inviolable of all pledges and promises and God's way of relating to His people. When God presented His design for marriage in Genesis 2:24, covenant was the heart of His plan. Jesus, when asked about divorce, simply returned to that simple plan presented at creation (Matt. 19:4–6). Unfortunately, the marriage license has been viewed as more a contract for negotiation of beginning and ending as well as who does what than a covenant in which people are totally committed to a permanent bonding regardless of performance or prosperity.

Family breakdown is inevitable if husband and wife do not make couple time as well as family time a priority. Carving out time together is one of the greatest challenges for any ministry family. A minister may be available to his congregation twenty-four hours a day, seven days a week, while ignoring his own family.

Parade magazine posed this question: Can you make a living and have a life? The brief article suggested that spending too much time on the job meant spending too little time with family and labeled this dilemma as a "chronic problem in America." These experts cited alarming statistics: 65 percent of married couples had both partners working; 70 percent of mothers with kids under eighteen are working, and the delay in having children and limiting the number of children is attributed to work goals. Most of you are working harder and longer than your parents.[3] However much you have raised your standard of living, you are probably hurting your family life. Finishing seminary, abandoning bivocational work, getting to a large church with an adequate salary—none of these will solve the problem.

A minister needs to take days off regularly; he needs to take vacation time to recharge his own batteries and renew his energies. He cannot be available to his congregation all the time and remain effective any more than a physician can spend his days around the clock in the emergency room with no rest or time away. Time with family can relieve stress. Boundaries must be set on the time of ministry couples, and your expectations of family needs must be realistic.

Preachers do have to be away from home, and sometimes that means overnight (especially for evangelists, denominational administrators, missionaries). When my husband is away overnight, he calls me daily. When the children were young, he tried to call in time to talk to each of them and hear about what was happening in their lives. He also scheduled his travel commitments around our children's special events. Complicated athletic competitions made this challenging, but with great effort we got the schedules well in advance and coordinated calendars.

Daddy's homecoming should be a joyous time worth adjusting schedules to take advantage of the time with him. When our son-in-love accompanied us to Africa, our daughter and granddaughters prepared little gifts for him to open each day. My sister-in-love prepares cards for my brother, as he does for her, when each is traveling alone. They have no children, but they still nurture each other in this thoughtful way during times of separation.

When my husband was out of town, sometimes for days at a time, I planned my days to be both mother and father to our children. Routine was essential and attitude critical. Keeping yourself well and rested is vital to meeting the needs of your children. Sometimes that means lowering your expectations of what you can do within the home as well as saying no to overcommitment outside the home. I could have done better at fortifying myself with extra rest to have needed energy at the end of the day to prepare and serve a nourishing meal, to give baths and observe bedtime rituals, and to supervise homework for older children.

You can create a warm, comfortable, attractive, and harmonious home for your husband and family, doing this vital task "as unto the Lord." When you neglect your home for whatever seemingly good reason, the Lord's work is being neglected. Devote yourself to the work of the kingdom as much as you can, but remember that your first work in the kingdom is your own husband.

The pastor's closest family tie is with his wife. There is always something important to do in the church, but first you must be the best wife and mother and keeper of the home that you can be. Make your husband happy and content, and you will leave him free to do the work to which he has been called. Pray for him, offer to him godly counsel, love him, share his burdens. In doing so, you will not only meet his needs, but you will also be serving the church and the Lord.

On the other hand, the minister's wife may experience her greatest heartache if her husband places her behind his ministry or even behind their children or extended family. No minister should allow his wife to forget how important she is to him. She should not have any reason to doubt his love, nor should she ever forget that her husband needs her not just for ministry but for his own personal happiness and companionship. Loving devotion has a way of revealing itself through common courtesies, sincere praise, public appreciation, and tender affection. Maintaining loyal love is a job to which every couple must apply themselves.

The husband of a minister's wife will probably be the only pastor she will have as an adult and perhaps even the only spiritual counselor she has. A minister may be able to fool some of his people some of the time, but he can hardly fool his wife any of the time. He will reveal himself to her through his actions and even his thoughts as the daily pressures of life seem to bring out the inner self.

What if you don't have a kingly husband? Beyond prayer, is there anything you can do to help him or to be satisfied and submissive yourself and live out truth as an example for your children?

First, make your husband a priority in your life. Don't be a woman left behind. Study your husband; learn all you can about his ministry; share at least some of his interests and pleasures. Be patient when you have to adapt the family schedule to the conditions of his ministry. When he has to work irregular hours, accept his inconvenient absence without resentment or recrimination. If he has to do his sermon preparation at home, create an environment where that is possible. If you have a career or lifestyle that hinders his ministry, be willing to adapt or even give up your own pursuits to be his helper. Keep a happy countenance and joyful spirit. Be willing to move to a new church field when your husband determines the Holy Spirit is leading to another place of service.

Second, don't underestimate the power of prayer. Society has focused on a quick-fix in which long-term investments are considered inefficient and ineffective. Make your prayers specific. Pray that your husband will be faithful in private as well as public worship (Ps. 17:15). Pray that he will be holy and set apart unto the Lord in every area of life and that he will grow spiritually, bearing the fruit of the Spirit in his life (Gal. 5:22–23). Pray that he will live what he preaches and that he will consistently immerse himself in the Word of God. Pray that he will exercise loving, servant leadership in your family (Eph. 5:25–31).

Third, you can do the right things yourself. If your husband refuses to build a quiet time with the Lord in His life, you can still incorporate intimacy with the Father in your own daily routine. If your husband is pessimistic and bitter, you can refuse to allow him to pull you into these attitudes. You can determine to please the Lord with your own attitudes, which means there will be no pride or vindictiveness or bitterness toward your husband but rather a quiet confidence in the Lord that enables you to rise above your circumstances and respond in Christlike ways even in the midst of hurt and sorrow.

Fourth, you can find a confidential prayer partner—not someone in your church—perhaps a friend from seminary days or a close family member, one who can lift you up and provide a listening ear and godly counsel.

Close all exits for your marriage. Accept the biblical mandate, which says there is one man for one woman for as long as they both live. Pastor Fred Lowery once encouraged a group of seminary students with these words: "Put your mate before your ministry and your children before your church."

Paige and I have continually reminded our children that they have high priority in our lives. Our daughter Carmen has a favorite way to break in any new secretary for her daddy. She can't wait to call his office in the midst of a busy day and see whether the secretary will put her right through to her father! She knows the rule, and she wants to be sure her father's secretary knows it, too!

One way to keep your family as number one is to involve them in your ministry. They need to catch your vision for loving service to the church family. They will learn from your example to love unconditionally and serve unselfishly. Husbands and wives both need unconditional love and complete acceptance.

What's a Preacher to Do?

A minister can lead his congregation to help him protect and care for his family. First, he can set aside a scheduled family evening and let that be as important as a gathering of the church family. He can train his staff to avoid scheduling meetings on that evening. He can put aside telephone calls, dictation, and sermon preparation and let that evening be one for family fellowship and fun.

Second, he can set aside a day for his wife. The illustrious pastor/evangelist Stephen Olford has been noted for his Heather Day, an uninterrupted day each week devoted to his wife and named in her honor. On days Paige has devoted to me, we sometimes work on writing projects or coordinate calendars or talk about goals and projects; but we do these things only as we like, at a leisurely pace and without interruption.

As the years go by, a wife needs to talk even more, and a husband can become more distracted and be less inclined to listen, much less to respond. Paige and I have to work at making time for conversation and to use that time to talk about the things that are important to us. Because we live in a public house, we usually take days for our couple time when we are on the road. Often we decline gracious hospitality in order to have our time together; sometimes we even rearrange ministry commitments in order to have personal time. For a pastor these special days need to be announced from the pulpit or placed in the church newsletter as well as communicated to staff. A pastor sets his priorities as does anyone; and because he is a public figure, it must be done publicly.

Paige and I have had the common goal of working together as a team for the Lord from the inception of our marriage. Accordingly, my husband has not only allowed but also encouraged me to prepare with him so that our ministries could be a successful, cooperative effort. Yet with all the opportunities provided for formal studies, I can truthfully say that the most helpful preparation I have had for spiritual ministries has been my own private study, personal tutoring by my godly preacher-husband, and the unique experiences the Lord has woven into the fabric of my own life.

My spiritual pilgrimage has brought me to the point of a willingness and even eagerness to exchange rights for duties, a desire to turn debilitating frustrations into eternal joys, and a visionary view of extending tragic limitations to triumphant opportunities. I desire to seek fewer self-fulfilling experiences in exchange for more God-honoring obligations. I want to yield personal rights in exchange for God-given privileges. I want to commit my life to begin my ministry for the Lord in my home, focusing on meeting the needs of my household. I want to renew my efforts to be a helper to my preacher-husband in his God-assigned task. I want to expect great things from my preacher-husband and attempt great things with him. I will gladly spend and be spent in all I do for God as the wife of a preacher.

> "To Rose, 'mother' was more than a noun, feminine gender, it was an active verb, 'the greatest career,' which she pursued with prodigious energy. . . . 'I looked at child rearing not only as a work of love and duty, but as a profession that was fully as interesting and challenging as any honorable profession in the world, and one that demanded the best I could bring to it. . . . I have relished my role.'"
> — Rose Kennedy in Bonnie Angelo, *First Mothers:*
> *The Women Who Shaped the Presidents*

CHAPTER 4

Children of the Church—
Orphans at Home

"Except the LORD build the house, they labour in vain
that build it. . . . Lo, children are an heritage of the LORD:
and the fruit of the womb is his reward" (Ps. 127:1, 3 KJV).

The children of preachers face the scrutiny not only of the congregation but also of the community and neighborhood. They are always on display because of the public role of their parents. Everyone knows the pastor's children, and everyone considers himself a surrogate parent charged with keeping the PKs in line. Children cannot conform to the expectations of two people, much less two hundred different people. Although PKs are supposed to be perfect, in their humanity they inevitably fall short. Any trouble they find is magnified. It is also true, however, that occasionally when children are acting up, all are corrected except the preacher's kid. That is just as tragic. The children of the pastor, like any children, need consistency and routine in their daily discipline.

People do expect more of the pastor's children. And they seem to think that however a child turns out is a reflection on his mother. Certainly for a mother, her child becomes the work of her life, her monument, as well as a crown she will place at the feet of the blessed Jesus.

The children of ministers do have a unique opportunity for developing an awareness of the world and its needs. Interestingly, statistics seem to indicate that more persons listed in *Who's Who* come from the homes of ministers than any other single profession. In 1900, A. E. Winship published a study of a Puritan pastor's descendants. He documented that Jonathan and Sarah Edwards produced thirteen college presidents, sixty-five professors, one hundred lawyers and a law school dean, thirty judges, sixty-six physicians and a medical school dean, and eighty government leaders (including a vice president of the United States). The record of public service throughout the generations for this preacher's family was extraordinary. Their offspring seemed to choose men and women of "like character and capacity" as they established their own homes.[1]

Your family is your first and foremost responsibility. Even a baby in the womb is aware of the sounds and movements in the outside world, and an infant absorbs and learns much from his mother, who should be most concerned that the right messages are stored in that formative mind.

Susanna Wesley had a good idea in determining to set aside an hour for each of her children beyond supervising their schoolwork and other mundane tasks. With nineteen children she allotted an hour per child weekly, but you could probably manage an hour a day for each of your children, especially if you learned to operate on some kind of schedule.

Rearing a child demands the best shaping influences you can provide—enriching life experiences and a home environment that provides loving care and discipline. Children require some hovering, much praise, and a few unique challenges, which a mother is best equipped to provide.

One of the best gifts you can give your children is to introduce them to the joy of reading widely and voraciously. You must also continually guide your children through these experiences to be sure that they are turned Godward.

Your children, like you, were created for a relationship with the living Lord, and they will only find ultimate happiness and satisfaction through such a relationship; but they will learn that only through your personal tutelage. You—not the church or the school or any of their representatives—are God's agent for shepherding your child spiritually. You will accomplish this task through communicating the Word of God to your children, helping them to know what He expects, and using the rod of discipline.[2] Guidelines for this awesome responsibility are found in Scripture, especially in the Book of Proverbs.

Mothers are a composite of the artistry and loving touch of God. Their capacity for unconditional love and their modeling of a servant's heart would seem to lift them beyond the trials of life. Yet a mother's suffering does not end in the delivery room when she gives birth in hard labor and great pain. She will suffer with every scraped knee and bleeding cut; she will hurt through her child's foolish choices and rebellious acts; she will suffer with the child's pulling away and eventually leaving the home. In

Dottie's Dictum for Protecting PKs

- Give attention to your child.
- Direct his heart's desire to please Christ, not the church or even parents.
- Present a joyous attitude toward your ministry for Christ regardless of the challenging circumstances in which you work.

fact, every time the child goes out the door, she will feel a tinge of pain and sorrow.

The rearing of children and the accompanying confinement can be a time for preparation for future ministries. Yet mothers and fathers must often be reminded that children always take precedence over any other ministry because nurturing a child is the most precious ministry you can offer to the Heavenly Father.

Children are the next generation of those who will serve and praise Him. They should feel a part of your ministry and will if you communicate to them a sense of gratitude for their contributions. Children need to feel that they are important enough to merit an investment of your time. Perhaps there should be some periods of the day that belong exclusively to them—in the morning before they go to school when you are sending them off in the right spirit—and perhaps again when they return from school to give them an uninterrupted time to tell you about the day with its joys and sorrows. Even bedtime rituals are important.

New studies have confirmed that adequate sleep is essential for a healthy lifestyle. Too many ministry parents drag their children to church meetings in the evening when they need to be supervising their homework and getting the children ready for bed. Avoid making your children feel you are always rushed and overwhelmed. Don't make them feel guilty when they need your time and attention.

Paige and I moved to Arkansas after completing seminary training. With a newborn baby and a toddler, I had something in common with Snow White's dwarfs: Sleepy, Grumpy, Dopey, and Sneezy! I had just graduated with a seminary degree in theology, but I was not asked to teach any important women's class. My life's work consisted of changing diapers and wiping runny noses.

When we left Arkansas and went to Texas, I had a preschooler and a first grader. Again I expected to be asked to teach a women's Bible class, but I was not. In retrospect, God was helping me to make right choices in that season of life. I was able to pour my time and energies into my husband and children, helping them to make transitions and settling our home so that we all had a comfortable and pleasant retreat.

When my children entered high school in Dallas, I was immersed in a schedule of teaching and speaking, especially family life conferences with my husband. At that time I made the hard choice to cancel engagements, and I refused ministry events in order to be available to my teenagers.

Children need time outside scheduled activities. In other words, they need a childhood—time to be spontaneous and to relax. You don't want them to be robots. Rather, you have the responsibility to lead them to do God's best—not just because they are preachers' kids but because it is the right thing to do. That means you praise your children for what they do right and include them in your ministry when it is appropriate. You are not responsible for having perfect children. Rather, you are to respond properly to children who experience the normal ups and downs of life. Making your child feel special is a precious gift.

Building a family requires commitment, expertise, and quality materials. Sons and daughters are building blocks for a household as much as brick and timber constitute a dwelling. The Hebrew word for *son* is *ben*; the word for *daughter* is *bath*; and the word for *house* is *bayith*, from a root meaning "build." The Hebrews looked at their homes as the opportunity for "building" (from *banah*) sons and daughters. Certainly, as the aforementioned psalm suggests, God is the architect; but He has chosen to accomplish His building program through parents, which is why the great nineteenth-century English preacher Charles H. Spurgeon entitled Psalm 127 "The Builder's Psalm." Children must be built well, and that means quality—the best materials—as well as quantity—lots of time. For these two ingredients, mother is the key.

The privileges and dangers for the children of pastors exceed those of other children. The pastor and his wife find parenthood a challenging task. They long to beat the odds and rear happy children who do not harbor resentment toward the church. To do that, family life must revolve around pleasing God and not around pleasing people in the church.

Children should be taught to share their parents' commitment to serve the Lord and His church, but the church should not consume or dictate all of life. You should want your children to love the church. They need to see the good things your congregation does for you and your family.

Avoid speaking frankly and disparagingly of the church and its leaders in front of your children. They don't have the maturity to deal with these situations, and they tend, on behalf of their parents, to take up an offense against the parties involved. Rather, demonstrate your love and concern for the members of your congregation. Let your children see that you have good fellowship and fun among the members of your congregation.

The family of a minister needs a break from the church to enjoy normal family activities. Of course, even playtime should be marked by talking about and to the Lord in a natural way. Be sure your children understand that you do not go to church and serve the Lord just because Daddy is a pastor. The godly choices you make for your family come out of a heart commitment to follow the Lord and obey His Word, enforcing boundaries and following standards set by God for all those who follow Him.

Get Me to the Church on Time!

One challenge for the minister's wife is getting to church on time with her mind in gear and her attitude in check. Although no one has any better excuse for being late to church than the minister's wife (she doesn't have a husband's help on Sunday morning), no one's late entry is any more scrutinized. Think through your routine and get a plan of action.

If you really want to be on time, you can use your time and creativity to make it happen. For me, that means having clocks (set correctly and synchronized) throughout the house and especially in the bathroom and kitchen. I set the alarm clock for the time I need to start my day lest I decide to relax a bit longer and return to sleep.

How do you know how much time you will need? Sit down and list everything you have to do with the approximate time it takes to do it. If you find yourself continuing to fall behind, adjust the schedule. It doesn't hurt to add fifteen minutes to your day once you have set your schedule. When I prepare a budget for an event, I always add approximately 10 percent as contingency just in case something has been overlooked or some inadvertency pops up. Many times I have wished that I had transferred that excellent emergency procedure to my time budget!

You can also set your arrival time at church fifteen minutes early rather than the time Sunday school begins. You must deliver children, perhaps check with your husband for any emergencies he may have encountered (split pants, loss of a button, coffee on his tie, misplacement of a typed illustration he wants to use), and get yourself to your appointed place of service. Give yourself some extra minutes for the unexpected, which you can expect will happen!

Preparation is everything. Gather Bibles, purse, hat, coat, gloves, umbrella, diaper bag (when appropriate), and place these items by the exit to be used or in the car. Then select clothing for you and the children (until they are ready to select their own—still to be done the previous evening). Even my husband came to see the wisdom of this advance preparation. This efficient plan also works for the two of us. It narrows the margin for crises. If a garment needs pressing, is missing a button, has an unexpected soiled spot or if a vital piece of your ensemble is missing, at the cleaner's, or in the clothes hamper, you can regroup in the midst of relative calm.

My preparation also included setting the breakfast table. I like an inviting table—even for meals that are not leisurely. Now I prepare breakfast trays since Paige and I choose where we will eat—on the deck or in the prayer garden, weather permitting; at the breakfast table; on trays in the family room or bedroom or library. Not only is the menu decided, but tableware is arranged, and prepping for meal is completed (washing fruit, setting up tea or coffee service, selecting condiments). Simple breakfast menus are best on Sunday. If I want to serve something hot (for a preacher with two sermons to preach back-to-back, a hot breakfast means a lot), I do oatmeal with brown sugar and raisins and cinnamon toast or waffles (batter can be mixed the night before) with fresh strawberries (washed and cut the evening before). I do not like doughnuts on the way to church or Pop Tarts in the car!

Before retiring on Saturday evening, even more than other nights, work your way through the house to pick up the clutter and put your house in order. Sunday should be a day free from all but essential daily chores.

What about the Sunday morning countdown? You've prepared; you are up on schedule; you have allowed some extra minutes for emergencies. Work smart; follow your planned schedule; adjust as you go. Plan to put the dishes in the dishwasher—it's neater and more efficient for the rest of your day. If you have fallen behind, leave them on the table. Of course, you want to answer a ringing telephone, especially if you do not have an answering machine; but sometimes in a busy parsonage without a switch-board operator, it just isn't possible to do so and get out the door. My family has an emergency code—ring twice and hang up and then redial. Only our family is aware of the private SOS. On Sunday morning I didn't answer the telephone—except the emergency code!

Finally, the First Lady must be working herself into the proper mode for worship and praise. If you can't get your quiet time before you leave, try laminating special verses for your bathroom mirror. You can at least be reminded of an encouraging word from the Lord as you apply your makeup.

Begin on Saturday evening to prepare your children for worship. Let the time for laying out their clothing be a happy time of talking about the Lord's day. Remind them of their schedule for the next morning. You might even make a Sunday chart using pictures and simple words to instruct them on how they can help with Sunday morning chores. When you load up the car, tune in some spiritually uplifting praise songs, use the time to recite the week's memory verse, or combine the two. Make happy faces for you and the children standard fare on the Lord's day!

What minister's wife doesn't pray that her children will one day say, "I'm glad my dad was a pastor"? Children need to be reminded that their pastor-father has a wonderful job. They need to know the perks it brings, such as some flexibility in scheduling even though he works long hours. Mothers can downplay resentment over demands on father's time by portraying service to the Lord as a privilege and by speaking lovingly of the church and its members.

Children should not feel that they must solve church problems. You cannot shield them from problems and concerns, but you can teach them to depend on the Lord for solutions. You can make sure they do not feel you love them only when they live up to the expectations of the congregation. Rather, you can teach them to be concerned about God's expectations. Their conduct is not as important as their character. How they reflect on parents is not the issue but rather how they represent the kingdom of God. Their respect for the Lord's house and their self-control in conduct are set to please the Lord.

Encouragement by example and admonishment by words to participate in church activities and organizations is also imperative. The pastor's wife must help her children love the church and feel concern for the members of its congregation. Children have an uncanny sense of evaluating the moods and attitudes of their parents. You must resist a downtrodden spirit concerning church and ministry. Rather, your children should sense a happy spirit in your attitude toward ministry.

Whatever is said by way of instruction is overbalanced by the automatic and unconscious influence of what a child sees and hears. No creature is more imitative than a child. How tragic in the portals of heaven that the sins of children must be cross-referenced to parents, who in reality are the offenders.

What would I do differently in the rearing of my children? Without contemplative reflection, I know that I would spend more time praying for them! After all, parents do have twenty-four-hour access to the Parenting Expert of all time, and He faithfully responds to those who seek Him. The forces of evil assaulting our children are beyond anything you can imagine.

If I were the devil, that's exactly where I would target my attack—upon those who are most vulnerable and yet most valuable, the next generation.

The children of preachers become even more of a target because when they make wrong choices, the consequences affect not only them personally and their families but also the kingdom of God. Satan has a way of making a child's personal failure seem to be the responsibility of his parent and thus the evidence of the inadequacy of biblical principles.

How can you pray effectively for your children? I have recorded prayers and answers to those prayers in prayer journals. God has not always responded as I asked Him to do; but He has been there, pulling me through and teaching me in the process. I have also become convinced that some of my most effective prayers are those I take directly from Scripture. When I use God's words, I am confident that I am praying in His will. Prayers that get to heaven start in heaven! I use Scripture from my daily readings—always something from Proverbs, usually words from the psalmist, and then whatever passage is part of my devotional time.

Certain givens should be included in your prayers for your children. I am already praying for the salvation of my preschool granddaughters. I still pray for my adult children, not only for physical protection but also for a spiritual arsenal that will protect them from evil.

My husband and I selected Ephesians 6:10–18 as life verses for our son at the time of his birth. These verses detail the weapons needed in spiritual warfare. I want my children to have a love for righteousness and hatred for evil. When they sin, I pray for mercy; yet I still want them to be accountable. I have always prayed that my children would have respect for the authorities in their lives—parents, baby-sitters, teachers, civil authorities. These who were a visible presence in the lives of my children provided a training ground to help them recognize the authority of the Heavenly Father whom they could not see.

Not only must you pray for godly friendships for your children, but also you should begin praying from the moment of the child's birth for the spouse God has for each child. God has a perfect mate for every individual, and to make that union according to God's plan brings the greatest happiness and least turmoil. Already I am praying for the little boys who will grow up and become the husbands of my granddaughters. I pray that they will adore their mothers and admire their fathers and that most of all they will have hearts for God. I prayed that my children would remain pure until marriage and would conduct their lives as a testimony to that purity.

Finally, I continue to pray that my children will be sensitive to going God's way in every area of life. I will never cease to pray for my children and my grandchildren. As long as I have breath, I will consider it to be my most important responsibility and greatest privilege.

Throughout history from the establishment of the home in the garden of Eden until this present day, women have uniquely shared in producing the successive generations, nurturing and sheltering the fetus until its birth, training and caring for the child through childhood, supervising the molding of the youth through adolescence, supporting and loving the offspring into and during adulthood. There was a time when being a wife and mother was considered a craft or trade. Single young women often worked and received wages as "apprentices" for a family in order to learn homemaking skills.

Model Christian Marriage

A foundational principle with which parents rear their children in the Lord is their responsibility to show their sons and daughters in lifestyle a pattern for Christian marriage (Eph. 5:21–33). In fact, it is more important for a child to see his mother and father loving each other than to experience an outpouring of parental love on him personally. This statement may seem reckless until you consider that the greatest tragedy of this generation is the lost pattern for Christian marriage. The breaking of homes by divorce, the multiplied blendings of families by remarriages, and the disruption to family life when mothers are forced from the home to the marketplace have all taken a toll upon the family.

Somewhere in the midst of all this upheaval and change, God's pattern of one man bound to one woman forever (Matt. 19:5–6) has been lost. Even a child who feels unloved can continue the pattern and establish his own home, making corrections through his own observations and experience; but if he has no concept of the basic family unit, there is little chance of his building a successful marriage.

The Creator designed communication to be part of the foundation for the family unit. This basic ingredient nurtures the one-flesh relationship He designed. For example, the "nakedness" described in Genesis 2:25 was not only physical but must also suggest an absence of any coverings that would hide or conceal or mar complete openness between Adam and the woman created to be his helper. Communication is also essential in parenting. Children must be heard as well as seen and lectured.

Children must see their parents show affection one to the other—with a touch, a hug, a kiss—not the passion reserved for the deepest intimacy but loving that shows. This touching and tender affection should extend to the children as well.

Headship and submission must also be worked out in home life—a loving and serving leadership interwoven with a willing and respectful submission (Eph. 5:21–33; 1 Pet. 3:1–7). All of this living interaction should portray vividly and clearly femininity and masculinity and their complementarity within the role assignments given by God. Regardless of the respective sexual identities of children within the home, gender in its fullness must be a part of their understanding.

Mold a Child into Going God's Way

The second principle for parents is to lead children to go God's way via discipline (Prov. 22:6). Discipline runs parallel to love just as limits must accompany freedom. Rules must often be backed by the ruler!

You must be clear and specific in telling your children what you expect of them, what they should or should not do. Threatening a child with angry words or striking a child with heavy blows is not productive. If you make threats that both you and your child know you will not keep, you are teaching him not to take you seriously. Don't expect perfection from your children. Everyone, even you, makes mistakes. Allow your child to fail and be willing to forgive a repentant offspring. Use pleasant and gentle words to draw him to obedience, but he must see your displeasure with quarreling and contention or angry temper tantrums and especially with disobedience. How can a child ever learn to obey God whom he cannot see until he learns to obey his parents whom he can see?

Godly discipline demands the breaking of a child's determination to go his own way, not a breaking of his will or his spirit. A parent does not show love for a child by overlooking the child's faults and disobedience and neglecting to discipline him but rather by influencing him to go the right way, thus prohibiting the child's determination to go his own way from gaining control over his life.

According to my paraphrase, Proverbs 22:6 reads, "Train up a child according to his own way, and he will never depart from wanting to have his own way." The verse is not only a promise of reward for parental faithfulness but also a warning to parents that a child must not be reared with the freedom "to go his own way," a dangerous spiritual condition (see Judg. 17:6; 21:25; Prov. 3:5; 12:15; 21:2; 29:15; Isa. 53:6). Even a child who chooses for the moment to be attentive to the things of the Lord may later be pulled away by Satan and reject the godly training of his youth unless his will has been exchanged for God's will.

The child must be dealt with tenderly, yet firmly, with a clear understanding of the offense (Prov. 4:3–4, 11; 15:32). The parent must reflect grief with and for the child over his transgression (Prov. 17:25), and he should remain with the child until the relationship between parent and child has been restored (Ps. 51:7–12). Nevertheless, the Scripture clearly states that the "rod" is God's way of exercising physical punishment for the offense. I used the cardboard tube from a suit hanger for physical punishment of my children because it was firm, inflicted a stinging reminder that punishment was the fruit of disobedience; and no matter how many my son destroyed or hid, there was always another in the closet!

With teens discipline seems to be a bit more challenging. Pastor Fred Luter, Jr., suggests several options. As long as the child is under your roof, you determine what he can and cannot do. "There's the door" method uses tough love just as God did with Adam and Eve when He forced them out of the garden. Or, you can compromise your preferences, but beware of compromising biblical principles and your personal convictions. Finally, love the child unconditionally and patiently wait for the Lord to work. Sometimes your disappointments become God's appointments—with you or with your child.

Unfortunately, one of the greatest challenges in rearing children is sibling warfare. A child can bring out every single trait in a family member that ever annoyed him, especially at family mealtime or holiday celebrations. Often siblings are close but competitive. What you must instill in your offspring is the fact that even if family members do fail him in some way, they are still the greatest influence in his life. Building strong connections with your family will generally stand you in good stead throughout your life. Independent and unique siblings can be taught to function efficiently by learning to work together in order to become an interdependent and loving family unit.

Parents, too, can perpetuate bitterness and rebellion by unrealistic expectations from their children. What you expect from a young child is different from what you expect from your teenager, and your interaction with adult children is different still.

Personal hurt is at the heart of every family estrangement. As a spiritual leader, you know that ultimately only God can heal hurts, but He works through individuals. If you love your child unconditionally, then you will want to try to work through the difficulties. It may be that you have happy memories and positive situations to which you can look for encouragement, and these can serve as the foundation for restoring fellowship or enriching a relationship.

Just an Idea

- Don't wait for a crisis to communicate your love for your family—parents for children and children for parents.
- Don't ignore memories of past expressions of love and gratitude when a drought of communication comes.
- Don't stop calling and writing just because children or parents seem too busy to respond or even care.
- You do what is right, and let God take care of the rest!

My daughter Carmen is a godly young wife and mother, who as a pastor's wife takes seriously her responsibilities to home and church. When she graduated from high school and again at the time of her marriage, she prepared some precious journals for her daddy and me. If I ever feel neglected by Carmen, I can pick up one of those journals, which I keep in my bedroom by my favorite chair, and read words of loving appreciation and encouragement penned by my daughter.

As a family, sit down and talk, not to attack or defend but to enjoy conversation and interaction with one another. Share happy memories and update one another on what you are doing. One of the greatest tools Satan uses to attack and destroy families is to entice them to withdraw and refuse to share what is happening in their lives. I talk to my parents every night I am at home and many nights when I am traveling—even if I am overseas. My mother loves to hear what Paige and I have done that day, and she is eager to know if I have any news to report from her grandchildren. She likes to tell me about her day.

Paige and I have tried to make it easy for our children to communicate with us by having a toll-free number because we, too, like to hear what they are doing. They have been so much a part of our lives and hearts that they remain central in our busy world. Ministry continues to offer its fulfillment, but nothing can take the place of hearing the voice of a child or grandchild and knowing what they are doing.

When I leave the city, my schedule goes to parents, siblings, and children. I want them to know exactly where I am; I want to be available if one of them should have an emergency; I even like to think that there might be a time when someone would want to talk to me so much that he can't wait for me to get home.

How to Resolve Family Conflict

- Don't wait for someone else to do it.
- Gather the family in the security and comfort of home.
- Reconnect with one another through neutral conversation.
- Then bring the conflict to the table. Define it; determine how it started; let each person express himself.
- Ask each family member to try to stand in the shoes of the other.
- The solutions may well come naturally, but perhaps the pastor-father needs to look for an appropriate Word from God.
- Pray together and for one another. Recommit yourselves to one another and to the Lord.
- Put the matter behind you, forgiving as God forgives—as if it never happened!

With so many means of communication, there is no excuse for a family not to keep in touch via telephone, E-mail, letters, cassette tapes, videos. Newsletters are great even when it isn't Christmas! Some families create a round-robin letter that moves from person to person with each one adding his news and then forwarding it to another—a wonderful option for E-mail!

Motivate by Teaching Spiritual Truths

Finally, parents are responsible for teaching their children spiritual truths through family worship and private instruction (Deut. 6:1–15). Praying together as a family provides spiritual unity. A time for family devotions provides a natural slowing down and can give a pause that refreshes all. It also offers a setting for family discussions. There is no greater vehicle for spiritual teaching. No parent will be successful in molding the life of a child without giving special attention to the roots (the foundation of faith) and the stem (the road to be traveled) as well as the blossom (the mature life of service). A set time for meaningful and creative family worship at least five days a week is absolutely essential for preparing your children for the world.

The preacher-father is extremely important in family worship. If he is to be the shepherd and spiritual leader of his congregation, he must be the spiritual leader of his own family. In Puritan homes one chair with a high back was always reserved for the father. The Puritans had almost perfected the discipline of family worship.

Pastor Jonathan Edwards saved an hour at the close of each day to spend with his children in addition to the tutoring he did as part of their education. He gave his full attention to answering questions or simply engaging in conversation. Edwards also tried to take one of his children with him on every trip he made. His mode of travel was horseback, and the child had to ride behind his saddle, but each looked forward to the honor with great anticipation. Having time with each child alone was essential for getting to know the child and his unique personality and dreams.[3]

Bishop Gottlieb Spangenberg exhorted Moravian parents in 1756, "To love their children as souls of the Savior, to set a perfect example for them by walking closely to the Lord." Many accolades have looked to Susanna Wesley for her commitment to her children and her investment in their lives. She did indeed pour herself into her children, and her sons had a mighty impact on the kingdom of Christ across the centuries. However, Susanna did not have the same commitment to her marriage; and only one of seven daughters who reached maturity had a long and happy marriage. Some would attribute this tragedy to her husband's inadequacies, but in fairness you must consider that daughters should receive an even greater impact from their mother. Would her daughters have turned out differently if Susanna had invested more in her marriage? Could she then have left a godly heritage in her daughters as well as her sons? Only God knows, but ministers' wives would do well to consider the matter with open mind and heart.

The lives of your children need to be anchored in the truth of Scripture. This truth not only gives husbands and wives clear instruction on their roles, but it also provides to parents their responsibilities for rearing children in the Lord. These truths also include God's purpose for the family and its role in producing a nation whose God is the Lord and a culture that honors the Creator.

Parents need to take time to list the main values and principles for living they want to pass on to their children. By doing this exercise, you will gain insights into what you consider to be of greatest importance. What specific positive character traits do you want your child to have? What unique personality traits does each child possess that you want to encourage? Are there traits you need to discourage? If you have developed a loving relationship with your child, you will find the child eager to please you, especially in the early years. You must stand in the shoes of your child and see things through his eyes, being careful to respect his feelings and thoughts. It doesn't hurt to remember how you wanted to be treated as a child or teen. Avoid giving your child negative labels or allowing siblings to give one another negative labels.

Clearly the nurturing of a child was not primarily the assignment of the Christian school or the church; it was to be done by the parents day in and day out as they walked, stood, sat, or lay down (Deut. 6:4–9). Life situations are excellent tools for teaching children how to solve their problems and live their lives according to biblical principles. There is no better method than the ever popular "show and tell." More effective than any admonition is the example of parents in personal quiet time, praying and reading the Bible daily.

A weekly family evening, during which telephone calls and meetings are suspended, can create bonding and memories never to be forgotten. The time appointed for this family gathering may need to be shared openly and unashamedly with the congregation from the pulpit and via the church paper in order to protect its sanctity. The time should be chosen so as to fit into the church schedule; but once chosen, it should be honored except in emergencies.

Family worship and family play are both important, but family activities cannot be a substitute for individual attention to each child. Ministry parents must carve out time alone with each child weekly. That means learning to say "no" and disciplining yourself to plan carefully for the apportionment of time.

Parents must set boundaries on family gatherings, refusing to squander that precious time on ministry data. Reporting, decompressing, and evaluating the day's ministry can eat away at the time you have reserved for family. If children have concentrated time when parents ask questions about their activities and answer questions they have, then they will feel that they have the place of priority in the lives of their parents.

The best gifts parents can give their children are wrapped in their smiles, tears, hugs, and examples. Giving your children your time and faith is a gift that keeps on giving. Pass the faith that has been a guiding compass in your own life to your children as a sure direction on the path of life. Give them a love for the Lord and for His church. Going to church should make you glad!

The Gift of Sabbath Rest

Give your children the gift of Sabbath rest by making Sunday a day of rest as well as worship. In Puritan homes no one worked after sundown on Saturday—not even making up the beds. Mothers cleaned their houses on Saturday and prepared wonderful delicacies to be eaten on the Lord's day. The mood of expectancy began to build as everyone in the household focused on the coming Lord's day.[4]

W. A. Criswell, long-time pastor of the First Baptist Church in Dallas, Texas, did not accept engagements on Saturday evening. On Sunday he did not even take a bath. He had special clothes, including shoes, to be worn only on the Lord's day. He preached, ate lunch in his home, rested in the afternoon, and took care of any pastoral emergencies; but the Lord's day was devoted to worship and rest.

Sunday should be different from other days. I don't shop or participate in entertainment options or clean house or even do laundry. My happiest years in ministry were those when the family returned after Sunday services for a lunch at home. I set the table and prepped for our special meal on Saturday and then had my final countdown carefully planned so that the family could enjoy mealtime. Then I did the clean-up afterward so that my husband and children could take the naps they enjoyed. I finished in time to put my feet up and read the Sunday newspaper cover to cover!

Give your children the security and confidence of traditional family life in which parents and children enjoy fun and fellowship on a regular basis. Help them through relocation challenges by using your creativity and energy to nest into a new situation.

Nowhere in God's creation should there be a more precise and vivid theological textbook than the Christian home. Every day should reveal to those within the family circle and to the world looking in "a word about

God." Just as grandmother Lois and mother Eunice diligently and zealously taught the young Timothy, the pastor's wife must pass on to her children "the unfeigned faith" (2 Tim. 1:5 KJV).

There is a difference between being immersed in the life of the church and having your own faith. Your child may be involved in all the activities of the church and yet be unable to articulate reasons for the faith of his father and mother. You need to let your child know about your own personal testimony—how you came to Christ and what difference that made and is making in your life. You need to encourage your children to witness to their friends by sharing their own testimonies.

Children should be taught how to pray about what concerns them. It is never too early to teach your children to pray. Even babies are much more aware than you would think. Children learn by example. Reading Bible stories, singing gospel songs, and praying with your children will create an environment in which your children can grow spiritually. When something good happens, a child should be taught to thank God for that blessing, regardless of how small and insignificant it may seem. You should share with your child answered prayer and let the child observe your praise and gratitude. Children should be encouraged to pray in words they can understand. They need to be reminded that no petition is too small for God.

Help your child become aware of the gracious beneficence of the Lord by teaching him to observe the beauty of God's creation—lush greenery, beautiful flowers, breathtaking sunrise and sunset, unusual and varied animal life. Even a storm can be a reminder of God's marvelous works. Children should be taught early that God answers prayers according to His own pleasure and their best interest. They need to understand that the answer may not be yes or no but could be "wait" or something else never imagined. You might also begin praying special prayers for birthdays, holidays, and other occasions. Prayer should accompany mealtime, begin the day, interject the day in times of trouble or crisis, and end the day at bedtime. Every celebration should be accompanied by prayer and by an acknowledgment of God's presence.

Children need to be encouraged to talk about spiritual matters, asking their own questions and learning to formulate their own answers. They need to learn to ask God's forgiveness even for small transgressions. They need to be reminded that their assignment is to find what God wants them to do rather than what parents or members of the congregation see as their destiny.

The Gift of a Name

Names have always been important spiritually. Every minister's family ought to have some tool for recording the birth and name of each child. Perhaps a family Bible or a journal or even a book with the structure for family records—whatever the means, the task is an important one. Throughout Scripture meaning and challenge is associated with names. Before choosing names for our son and daughter, Paige and I prayerfully considered the meaning of each name. I have pursued the significance of names even when parents gave no particular thought to the meaning. Divine providence seems to ensure that the name assigned a child fits his unique personality and gifts and presents an appropriate challenge for him.

Paige and I also assigned to each of our children a passage of Scripture as a personal challenge for their respective lives. Armour's verses were from Ephesians 6:10–18, reminding him to put on the "armour" of God as he faced the battles of life. Carmen was challenged with the Proverbs 31:10–31 passage about biblical womanhood. In each case we found a way to display these verses. Armour has a wall hanging in calligraphy; Carmen has one done in cross-stitch.

In the midst of nurturing your children physically, mentally, emotionally, and spiritually, don't forget to include a sense of fun and play within the family circle. Don't make the mistake of leaving the impression with your children that all the fun is on the outside. Recreation is a necessary diversion for bringing balance to work and ministry. Laugh together;

Dottie's Dictum for PKs

- Develop your own personality and discover your own giftedness.
- Understand that your parents don't just have a job; they are following a divine mandate.
- Realize that you must establish your own personal relationship with God and sustain it.
- Attend church happily and participate. Accept the challenge to be a role model—it comes with the territory!
- Be friendly with people in the church. Many think you are special. They provide the wherewithal for supporting your family.
- If you don't like for your father to use you as a sermon illustration, tell him; or set boundaries on what he can use.

create your own insider communication as a family; learn to make light of trials and difficulties when that is appropriate; don't be afraid to put aside your dignity and let your hair down. My husband often laments that the greatest fun for our children seems to be at his expense, and they do love sharing stories about Big Daddy—like the time he locked the keys in the car twice in the same day!

The children of ministers are special, and often they feel special because they are in the limelight. They get unusual attention because they are loved in a special way. They are welcomed into homes in the congregation. Even moving from one church field to another is not so bad because it introduces your children to many different communities and their cultures. They learn to be more independent, to make friends more easily, and to adapt to change. I've always tried to be a friend to the friends of my children and to invest in their lives. I sought to use my mind and imagination to stimulate theirs and to introduce them to godly fun and fellowship. I wanted my children and their friends to be introduced to my faith and the moral framework in which that faith was embedded.

Prodigals and the Hearts They Break

One of the most heartbreaking aspects of parenting a prodigal who seems to reject you, your faith, the family, the virtues you implanted from youth, or all of the above is that it seems to make your investment of selfless nurture null and void. You feel that you have failed and that you are responsible for the path your child has chosen. Parents of prodigals carry a massive burden of self-condemnation.

Satan knows that there is nothing more destructive and debilitating for a mother—nothing that saps her spiritual power and emotional health any more. This kind of guilt is more difficult to shed because you have no specific behavior or deed that violates God's Word to which you can point. As you question every decision you made as a parent and even reconsider the biblical principles you tried to use, Satan uses your confusion to increase your hurt and despair, wearing you out and weakening your faith. Instead of praying, you mourn; instead of moving forward, you are immobilized. Instead of remembering God's blessings and what He has already done, you are questioning His goodness.

Sometimes the exemplary life you think you lived was not viewed as Christlike. Whether you were not faithful in your living or your child was not faithful in observing and learning is really not relevant when you are crushed and beaten in your most important assignment. You feel totally alone. You can't really talk to anyone else about what is going on in your family or the pressures you are under. It is as if you are in the midst of a hurricane, being uprooted and twisting in destructive winds, without any help.

Preachers are supposed to have perfect homes and perfect kids. You are so beaten by the elements of destruction that you cannot see the road, much less the end of the road. A day may come when your child will see a more balanced picture of his life in the home of a pastor. Some busy pastors do keep balance in their lives and make time for their wives and children. If your child seems to have bitterness toward you, a day may come when your child will decide to forgive you for what he perceives as your imperfections and inconsistencies. After moving through his own personal failures and recognizing some personal shortcomings, he may decide you deserve mercy and forgiveness for those imperfections he attributes to you.

Dottie's Dictum for Parents of Prodigals

- Love your children unconditionally.
- Serve your children creatively and diligently.
- Maintain a balance between family and ministry. Spend time with your children.
- Relate to your children as a caring mother, not a Sunday school teacher or pseudo-Holy Spirit. Let them be children.
- Study your children and their unique needs.
- Protect your children not only from worldly influences but also from members of the congregation who seek to crush them with unjust criticism and unrealistic expectations.
- Communicate with your children. Listen to them and talk about what they want to talk about.
- Pray, pray, pray, and pray some more.

He may even find that you rated higher than he first estimated on the scale of maternal skills and spiritual disciplines.

What can parents of prodigals learn? You can learn from mistakes. Legitimate guilt turns an inward look to what went wrong. This introspection can be helpful in repairing a broken relationship with your child or removing the wall between you and your child. God does not leave you without a plan for winning back and welcoming prodigals.

In Luke 15, the heartbroken father waited expectantly for his son to return. He was not unaware of the wrong choices made by his son, and he knew too well the destructive habits that controlled his son. But he also knew that the emptiness of the world would not ultimately satisfy his boy.

One of the most important things for mothers who feel rejection from a child for whatever reason is never to give up seeking reconciliation. There is no statute of limitations for motherhood. You don't help your child by lowering your standards, losing your convictions, ignoring his disobedience, or making light of his dishonoring of you. Rather, you pray more than ever for your child that God would pursue him with the hounds of heaven.

God can bind Satan from the life of your child, but you have the responsibility to ask Him to do so, never giving up your intercession. The importunate woman in Scripture finally got what she wanted by her persistence (Matt. 15:21–28). She was a pagan woman, and she was making her approach to an unjust ruler. You are a believing woman committed to the Lord Jesus, and the One to whom you appeal is the essence of justice and mercy. You must keep your personal devotional time, and you must make family worship a priority.

Ten percent of what happens to you and 90 percent of how you respond to what happens determines your success in life. You should be inspired not to give up on an indifferent or wayward child, if for no other reason than what is at stake for your child. You may be in your senior years; if so, your grief will last for a season. When you go to meet the Lord, the memory of that sorrow is gone forever. On the other hand, your child probably has many more years, if the Lord delays His coming; and for his personal peace and happiness, he needs to resolve this matter so that he can enjoy your nurturing wisdom and counsel and your loving touch in his life even in his adult years, as did Solomon with his mother Bathsheba.

God takes seriously the assignment for children—whatever their ages—to honor and appreciate their parents. God designed this special relationship so that an offspring never reaches an age when he doesn't need his parents. Duties are yours, but events are God's. Do your duty as a mother, and let God direct the events of life while you rest in Him. Out of the ashes of rebellion, God can build a man or woman of strength.

A Forever Friend

Parents must live their lives in practical ways that show a faith that works. Children must see you reading Scripture, praying regularly, and attending church joyfully; but even more they need to see that these spiritual disciplines make a difference in your life. They must see fruit of the Spirit in your life. Family devotionals, bedtime rituals, mealtime, holiday celebrations—into the living of life you must weave fun and fellowship in the family circle.

You must have expectations for your children, but they must be reasonable, and they should be based on God's Word. Recognize that there will be problems and consider biblical solutions. Put your focus on the positive aspects of your ministry experience.

Busyness is not godliness. God is not impressed with your production capacity as much as He is concerned that the product of your home—your own children—be chiseled and molded and perfected to the best of your ability. You may tire of this mundane task, but the Lord admonishes you not to grow weary and promises to supply the energy and strength as needed in this all-important task (Isa. 40:28–31). God's strength is for what He plans for you to do—not stamina for everything you might want to do!

Explain to your children the truth about living in a fishbowl. Help them know that they are not the only children living in a glass house. In a school the principal's child has careful scrutiny from both teachers and students; the coach's son is expected to be a star athlete. Let your children get a glimpse of the challenge for their entire family—the opportunity to show other families how to live and interact.

A minister's wife has no more important opportunity for service in the kingdom of Christ than nurturing her own children. She must become a forever friend to her offspring, being committed to listen attentively and talk openly, studying her child and spending time with each child. She really lives with her children, creating precious memories and fashioning their lives. A preacher-father is no less important. For him to treat his wife with tender courtesy sets an example for the children to follow and reinforces all she tries to teach them.

For every mother, releasing her child begins at birth when the umbilical cord is cut. As Hannah so poignantly expressed, a child is loaned to his mother by God. A mother must be willing gradually to release the child without pushing too hard or holding back too tightly. Biblical guidelines for mothering are clear: teaching your child God's Word, leading him to a personal relationship with Christ, molding his character, making his worship experience special, and giving him a vision for missions and evangelism. Instruction and example are both necessary in the "show and tell" methodology endorsed in Scripture (Deut. 6:4–9), encouraging your child with affirmation of what he does right and gentle correction when he is wrong. Respect and praise are important in making your child confident and effective in life.

> "She spared no pains in conforming to his inclination and rendering everything in the family agreeable and pleasant; accounting it her greatest glory and there wherein she could best serve God and her generation, to be the means in this way of promoting his usefulness and happiness."
>
> — Samuel Hopkins about Sarah, the wife of Jonathan Edwards

CHAPTER 5

Home—a Prepared Place

The home of the minister is in a peculiar way a public house. The pastor's home does not need to be a showplace, but it should be furnished with taste and creativity. The church should be able to point with pride to the parsonage regardless of its size, design, or location.

How do you learn good taste? If you were not reared in an environment that would make such second nature, you can learn by watching others who obviously have the kind of taste and sensitivity you desire. You can read books and magazines, observe how things are done in the homes of others, and seek a mentor who is willing to invest some time in your life.

Home is a place where people live, play, and even where they are allowed to make messes. Home should welcome the family and others whom God may send through its doors. If a minister never knows whether he has clean clothes to wear or if he has to wash his plate before dinner, he is defeated before he begins. Someone laughingly said that "a sink full of dirty dishes at the parsonage may not be anyone's business, but the report will soon be everyone's gossip!"

Household management comes naturally to some, but there are opportunities to fine-tune that skill. Literally hundreds of volumes in my personal library—some of them dating to the late 1800s and many from other countries—are in the area of homemaking, food preparation, interior design, gardening, floral arrangements, hospitality, table setting, and napkin folding. I clip or photocopy helpful hints for cleaning and organizing my home. I file these hints in three-ring binders and index them in handy reference sections so that I can quickly access the information when needed.

When Paige and I moved into a new living area, I reorganized cabinets, closets, and a pantry dozens of times until I had everything arranged efficiently. Then I added labels, and someday I plan to complete an inventory on the computer so that I, and anyone, can immediately find whatever is needed. A student from a homemaking seminar thirty years ago recently reminded me of my kitchen tour, during which she was introduced to label organization of the kitchen. It does work!

Meal planning is just as important. For years I had no help with my hospitality functions. I prepared about a dozen menus—luncheons, dinners, teas/coffees, receptions—and attached the recipes to each menu. I practiced until I could prepare those recipes efficiently and serve them attractively. If guests did not seem to enjoy something, that recipe was scratched and another put in its place.

In order to gain confidence in hospitality, you can create a "company" box into which you place necessary ingredients for a quick and easy meal or refreshment break appropriate for guests. Especially should you learn to brew a good cup of coffee and, if I'm coming, a wonderful cup of tea.

The pastor's wife, and every member of the family, should form a habit of keeping at least the entry and living room presentable and ready. Such commitment does not mean the family cannot relax. Quite the contrary, relaxation is much easier in a clean and orderly environment.

Not only should your entire dwelling be a warm, safe, and secure place, but also you should create a smaller space that is buffered from the outside world. The mother of former president Franklin Roosevelt had a small sitting room she called her "snuggery," and indeed such a special place is one for snuggling! Mine is a corner of the bedroom with a platform rocker and easy chair, each with a hassock; a soft cashmere blanket for covering your feet; excellent reading light; piped-in music; scented candles—everything you need within easy reach.

The home should be a haven where familiar traditions and rituals reassure its residents that life, even with its turmoil and difficulties, is indeed worth the effort. Those traditions that make your family unique will go with you wherever you travel and be the human rock to which you can cling. Home should be a source for gathering strength for the challenges of life, a living album for remembering the past and your heritage, an oasis for finding joy to celebrate the present moment, and a reservoir of energy and optimism that enables you to recharge your batteries to go out into the future highways of life.

Home should be where the heart is, but too often it becomes the place where the hurt is. Life in the parsonage has never been easy. While wives sleep, it seems that the sheets are wrinkling, the dust is scattering over the furniture, the dirt is gathering on the floors, the cobwebs are forming in the corners, and the family is getting hungry.

When Paige and I began full-time pastoral ministry, the church-owned dwelling was common. The church to which we were called decided to get rid of its older property because of the need for repairs and updating. Paige and I had some input on the house they purchased. The biggest downside we found to living in a church-owned property came in the tax consequences, which almost destroyed us financially. Our salary had been adjusted down from the compensation of the former pastor, who had been at the church for a number of years. It was about the same salary we had in seminary, with the added benefit of the parsonage and its upkeep. Our Social Security taxes were figured on the value of the large home, which we could never have afforded, in addition to our salary. Be sure you understand the total picture before you agree to benefits. We would have been better off to ask the church to choose a much smaller home, given our salary and circumstances.

Paige and I have lived in church-owned housing next door to the church as well as housing located in a residential neighborhood away from the church. When we lived next door to the church, we had many interruptions. Because the house was owned by the church, some people felt they could come and go as they pleased. If someone in the church kitchen needed a cup of butter, she walked across to the parsonage and asked for a handout. If a teenager needed a ride home after the youth meeting, he knocked on the door and expected one of us to provide transport. We also had an unusually high number of transients who approached the parsonage for food or money.

When you do not have a voice in choosing your dwelling, you may find it hard to fit your furniture into its rooms. It may be even more challenging to bring harmony between furnishings and permanent draperies, wallpaper, and other unchanging features of the church-owned property. You also lose the opportunity to build up equity so that upon retirement you can purchase your own property. If the church provides a housing allowance, you purchase your own home and have tax advantages. By the time you complete your ministry, you should own a home free and clear.

On the other hand, to live in church property can have the advantage of repairs and improvements being done in a timely way—depending on who is in charge of the property! To have housing and maintenance of that housing could give you an opportunity to put aside some money for a down payment on a future home. When God leads you to a different field of service, you do not have the pressure of selling a house to add to the other challenges of moving.

If you are in a church-owned parsonage, especially if it is adjacent to the church, you must graciously draw boundaries to protect your family. Perhaps a plaque on the door could indicate whether you are receiving guests. You may even need some guidelines carefully formulated and graciously shared with the congregation. Whatever you do should be bound in ribbons of love and service.

What are your options in negotiating for housing? My philosophy is that it never hurts to ask. If you make your requests humbly and graciously, you may be surprised at how helpful a church will be. If God has directed you to go and directed them to receive you, then together you should be able to work out what is best for both.

My husband and I have never let salary or housing or any other benefits determine God's will for us. We try to discern God's will before we begin to talk about the logistics involved. A minister needs to meet the needs of his family, but that does not always take the same salary or an increase. To refuse to talk to a committee unless the salary starts at a certain point is to deny the providence of God and tarnish the testimony of one of His servants. The bottom line should be deciding what God wants in service from you, not what a church will do in compensation for you.

Living with a Flourish

The preacher's home should be a place of refuge, a sanctuary to which the family can go and close the doors when they need time to heal and renew. People used to take the time to bring a flourish to everything. First Ladies, you could revive that idea by adding your own unique signature, with a flourish, to whatever you do!

My mother paid me a high compliment one Sunday when I flew to Dallas for a twenty-four-hour visit. No one was serving afternoon tea on Sunday. After taking my parents to lunch, I settled them at home and went to three grocery stores in my effort to find what was needed. I returned with specialty breads, tomatoes, cream cheese, cinnamon biscuits (alas—no scones or Devon cream to be found in DeSoto!), and the fixings for banana splits (not usually served at teatime, but a favorite of my daddy's). I put everything together and tried to come up with a presentation plate appealing to the eye as well as the appetite. I went through all the rituals for a wonderful pot of tea with a makeshift cozy to keep it hot.

How to Serve with a Flourish

1. Be alert to what is around you. If you have no tea cozy, pick out the prettiest dishcloths and wrap them artistically around the teapot.
2. Lower your expectations to suit reality. If you have no napkin rings, use a scrap of ribbon, embroidery floss, or common string.
3. Pull out what is normally unused—china, silver, cloth napkins—and add it to your table.
4. Create your own centerpiece with fruit or vegetables or some unique accessory in the room.
5. Adjust your menu but try to include something that is out of the ordinary.
6. Create your own atmosphere—candles, music, or special conversation topic.
7. Time, energy, creativity, a servant's heart, and unconditional love are ingredients for a flourish!

As I invited them to the humble table, my mother remarked with delight, "Oh, everything Dorothy prepares is special!"

Home Away from Home

Familiar objects, small treasures that are special to members of the family—not necessarily expensive or valuable to anyone else—are essential for creating the comfort of home. People frequently ask me how I manage to travel and happily live out of a suitcase. My answer is spontaneous: "God gives you contentment in whatever His assignment is to you." Yes, my husband and I do miss our home, especially since the seminary has added a private living area with a library large enough to hold our personal collection of books! However, long ago I learned to nest wherever we are and make it home. I add to my suitcase a few items that bring home to me. For example, both my husband and I have small leather double frames with family photographs. I also have a traveling scented candle and a CD in my computer to provide easy-listening music. I have learned how to brew the best pot of tea on the road: Wash the coffeemaker carefully; fill it with bottled water; place loose tea in a filter or put tea bags in the carafe. You have brewed tea. Having tea will not change your circumstances or solve your problems, but it can bring comfort and beauty into your world when everything else seems to be falling apart around you.

Unpack your suitcases—even if only for one night. Settle your clothing and treasures and projects appropriately so that the room becomes your home away from home—a retreat that can renew you between your responsibilities. If Paige and I have a car or if our hosts have asked about special needs, I stock Perrier water and spring water as well as fruit and pineapple juice (a natural antibiotic for the throat and a good antidote for coughing). With these few items, Paige and I can be quite at home.

Treasure Boxes

Every family member should have some space to call his own, and each should have special treasures that move from place to place. Ministers, as other public servants, do seem to move more often. Such a move can be traumatic for children and teens. You can ease the pain by being sure that the first boxes opened in a new location are each family member's "treasure box." Family photographs should be a centerpiece for your home decorating. They are memory builders of the people you love most and reminders of happy family times from the past.

How about ministers' families who are uprooted for overseas assignments? A treasure box suddenly becomes all the more important. Add boxes for seasonal decorations to help your family through holidays and to arouse curiosity among the local people, giving you an opportunity for a natural witness. You might also pull together some odds and ends that can

a meal in the freezer, setting aside a day to prepare food for the coming month, developing simple menus with tried and proven recipes that can be prepared in minimum time. However, beware of making your primary goal preparing a meal in less than thirty minutes. If you do, you will gravitate to convenience food, increasing cost and lessening nutritional value.

Even with an empty nest, Paige and I enjoy a leisurely meal at home in considerably less time than we would spend going to a restaurant. The joy for me continues to be found in preparing the meal (yes, I still love to make my biscuits and popovers and even an occasional angel food cake from scratch), serving with love, and savoring the family mealtime.

Hospitality

Christian hospitality is distinctive from worldly entertaining; it is a command from the Lord and not an option reserved for those with the gift of hospitality. As you consider your ministry of hospitality, determine what occasions you want to celebrate—seasonal festivities, functions for different groups in the congregation, special events coinciding with revivals or conferences, neighborhood or community outreach, or simply being able to offer light refreshments to those whom God might send to your hearth. For each occasion you will need to know the budget available. Big events will surpass your household food budget. A portion of our personal budget is designated for entertainment (meals, gifts, equipment). Sometimes in larger churches the pastor is given an allotment for this purpose.

Consider the resources available for executing the event. Is it small enough for you to do yourself? Do you have friends, family members, or coworkers who can help? Do you have the space in your home to set up needed tables and chairs? Do you have the needed equipment?

Selecting a menu is another important task. This job is made easier if you keep a file on menus with which you feel comfortable for different occasions. Attach recipes for easy reference. For a touch of elegance, carefully write out the menu on a nice card that could be placed on an easel on your table to announce the menu du jour.

Dottie's Hospitality Staples

- Several folding tables with round tabletops that double seating and some chairs. (My first tops were plywood—heavy and full of splinters; now we have lightweight synthetic ones, easy to store.)
- Tablecloths (including round ones for extra tables) in white or ivory (showers) and forest green (holidays) and cloth napkins (inexpensive and may include contrasting colors to cloths).
- Assorted candle holders, especially small ones for votives, plus lots of candles.
- Baskets for bread (line with colorful napkins coordinated with table linens).
- Table mirrors (round, rectangular, and small beveled mirror coasters) to reflect the unfolding scene.
- Mini clay pots and a dozen bandannas for informal occasions.
- One to two dozen glass plates and cups to be used in connection with china or alone for receptions.
- Punch bowl and ladle (I have enjoyed having two sizes).
- Coffee service (mine is silver, but you can get nice ones in porcelain as well).
- Condiment servers (salt and pepper shakers, sugars and creamers, bowls for sweetener). I prefer glass to blend with any tableware.
- China, stemware, flatware, including a few serving pieces, according to your taste and budget. If you do not have a supply of these basics, let your family, and perhaps your husband's secretary, be aware of your selections in case someone asks for a suggested gift.
- Glass casserole dishes (round, rectangular, square) in a variety of sizes.

Plan your linens and table accessories well in advance. If you are not sure of yourself, prepare a table-setting card with information on linens, centerpiece, tableware, as well as details and a diagram for setting your table for a particular season or occasion.

Your table arrangement can also be done in advance. Will you have the equivalent of a head table? Will you use round or rectangular tables? At Magnolia Hill, once tables and chairs are in place, I have actually used a tape measure to allow enough room for guests to get to and from the table and for servers to move among the tables. Because place cards are used for almost every occasion, I use small boards to arrange the seating in advance.

How do you set a table? The dinner plate is at the center of the setting. Add flatware, keeping in mind that you will begin your meal at the outside and work your way in. The knife is on the right next to the plate with its blade facing the plate. To the right of the knife is the teaspoon for coffee or tea service at the end of the meal and the iced teaspoon to the right of that. The soup spoon is to the far right since soup is usually one of the first courses. On the left, the dinner fork is closest to the plate (assuming you have placed the dessert fork and spoon at the head of the setting). To the left of the dinner fork is the salad fork. (In many etiquette books and at very formal dinners, the salad is served after the main course, reversing this formation; but unless you go to a state dinner at the White House, you probably won't see that setting.)

The napkin should be placed to the far left with its fold away from the plate unless it is on the plate or in a glass. The salad plate is to the left of the forks and outside the napkin and the bread plate above the forks. (If you don't have bread plates and your table is tight, salad plates can go in this position.) The butter knife is placed across the bread plate with the handle to the right and blade facing in. The water glass is placed above the knife, and the optional iced tea glass is to the right of the water glass. The cup and saucer are to the right of the spoons. I like to have the handle in three o'clock position so that there is a smooth line as you look down the table. Above the plate and centered are the dessert spoon with handle to the right and dessert fork with handle to the left. Your place card can be centered or placed to the side.

Magnolia Hill tables are set early to allow for finer touches. I like to walk into a room and sense what the response of my guests will be. Is there order, beauty, coordination, elegance? Have I succeeded in preparing my guests for the occasion—casual supper, formal dinner, intimate luncheon, quiet afternoon tea?

Atmosphere is important in making your guests feel welcome and comfortable. On a cold winter evening, would a fire in the hearth give warmth to your hospitality? Would a pitcher of lemonade on a hot summer afternoon refresh someone's spirits? Would a centerpiece featuring the newly released book authored by your guest encourage him? I also want to contemplate whether the occasion will accomplish a spiritual goal—to make my guests feel loved, cherished, and even edified during their time in my home. For a buffet table, cards are put on the table where food is to be placed to be sure the plan is workable.

Most events call for a receiving line of some sort—the host couple and perhaps the honoree(s). Every minister's wife will doubtless do her duty in receiving guests—often a contest in physical endurance. For receptions you will be on your feet a long time. You will be entrusting your hand to everything from an anemic touch to an iron grip. Avoid wearing a ring on your right hand unless you know it will not add to your pain. Although elegant and stylish shoes may appeal to your vanity, be more concerned that your shoes are sensible and comfortable!

My husband stands first in line. In theory, he should introduce himself to the guest, who then announces his name. My husband then presents the guest to me, repeating his name. I extend my hand and give my name only if my husband has forgotten to do so or if he is distracted when I greet the person. If the guest does not give you his name, you are under no obligation to try to extract it. However, I usually make an attempt: "Tell me your name again and where you are from." I then turn to the person to my left and present the guest using his name and any brief bit of information that might help the person to whom I am presenting him as well as indicating to the guest my interest in him.

Use the names of your guests whenever possible because it makes the person feel important to you, and it helps you to identify him with his name in future references. Try to give your guests an opportunity to greet you as they enter and then express their appreciation for your hospitality as they leave. For large receptions my husband and I divide these duties. I will be at the front door as guests enter, and he will stand at the side door where our guests exit.

As you continue to extend hospitality, you will collect seasonal decorations in the process. If you organize them and take time to store them away carefully, these decorations can be recycled. To prepare your house for each holiday and season says to your family and guests that they are important enough for you to prepare for them in a special way.

You also need some reference works to help you along the way—an up-to-date etiquette book,[1] a cookbook with creative and tasty recipes, a book on hospitality with ideas for centerpieces, place settings, and menus, and your own file of ideas. The only fixed etiquette for me is biblical loving-kindness. Learn the rules; most of them are based on what is most efficient and effective. Nevertheless, let your actions be courtesies common to those who would put others before themselves. You may find yourself doing something inappropriate, and even silly, to avoid embarrassing or hurting your guest. Queen Victoria once entertained a guest who by mistake identified his finger bowl as soup. She noticed the faux paux and immediately did the same so that all the other guests followed suit.

If one of your guests brings you a hostess gift, be certain that a card is attached or make note of the name on a piece of paper or the package itself so that you can acknowledge it as promptly as possible. If possible, open the gift in the presence of the giver so that she can enjoy your delight and receive your thanks. Then you can quietly tuck it away so that others who did not bring a gift are not embarrassed. If you cannot open it due to a long reception line or other circumstance, at least express your gratitude for the thoughtfulness. In every case you should send a note later.

Another challenge for the pastor's wife is using the women in the church to serve tea, coffee, and cake. This service is considered an honor. I usually assign women to do this duty in thirty-minute increments. If you have different factions or groups within the church, you will want to choose carefully from all groups. If someone cannot stand for a long period, assign pouring coffee since this task is done while seated.

The minister's wife is also called upon to assist in social events. If you are asked to pour, ask your hostess for any special instructions. Then do the job in the most efficient way for you. Survey how the serving pieces are arranged as well as the cups, including the source for additional pieces and refills as needed.

When I am pouring coffee and tea, I seat myself comfortably in front of the coffee/tea service and place the two pots to my right on a diagonal so that I can reach either easily. I put the sugar and creamer to my left. Before pouring a hot drink, place a silver spoon in the glass cup (a precaution against breakage), fill it, add condiments, and remove the spoon while it is on the tray to avoid any drips on people or cloths! Then place the cup on the plate of the guest, using your right hand to hold the cup's handle and your left to steady it when necessary. I also ask the hostess to give me an extra napkin or tea towel for any emergencies.

For punch, stand in front of the punch bowl. Before beginning, arrange the cups for your convenience and determine a procedure for getting more cups and refilling punch (more challenging than refilling coffee or tea). I grasp the ladle with my right hand and hold the guest's cup in my left hand over the bowl. I always need an extra napkin or tea towel for this job as it is almost impossible to dip punch without some drips. Holding the cup over the bowl, reach for the plate and bring it to the cup. For serving coffee, tea, or punch, your greatest asset is a smile and pleasant word of greeting to each guest.

You will also find harmony and order when you give attention to your meal service. Plates are presented from the left of each guest and removed from the right. Pass all food to the right. When I have food at each end of the table (bread, butter, or other condiments), this plan still makes things move more smoothly because items start at each end of the table, making quicker service for everyone, but by following this guideline there is no confusion in the process.

Individual table etiquette should be followed by the minister's wife not only for personal satisfaction but because she is a role model to others at the table—perhaps even to the minister himself! You should sit upright without elbows on the table and with your hands folded in your lap except when using your eating utensils. You should not begin eating until everyone has been served, and as the hostess, you should be the last served. Never talk with food in your mouth. Keep used flatware on your plate and place it in the four o'clock position when finished. Flatware should not be propped against the plate. Used flatware is not placed on the table but kept on your plate until its removal with each course. Even in some highly respected restaurants, a server will occasionally remove a piece of flatware from your plate for you to use for a future course. Such is unsanitary and inappropriate; don't do it! If you do not have enough to provide a utensil for each course in your table setting, simply wash these carefully between courses and replace what is needed for each course.

A faux paux is all too common even among well-educated people. Here are some practices to avoid. Do not handle your flatware by the end to be used (i.e., the tines of a fork or blade of a knife). Even when I place my flatware in the dishwasher, I leave the handles up (that's a Health Department regulation for restaurants). Never use your personal fork or knife in a common serving dish. In the kitchen never use your stirring spoon for tasting, and be sure everyone helping you is aware of this important rule. If someone keeps the serving fork by mistake, be prepared to replace it with a fresh one without returning the one inadvertently kept. It is rude to comb your hair or even apply lipstick at the table. Excuse yourself and find another spot for your grooming. Don't blow your nose into the napkin! In my house you are never more than a reach away from facial tissues.

For a minister's wife hospitality may be extended from her own home, from some setting in the church, or even from a community center. When you invite church members to your home, you are safest in inviting an already existing group—the deacons and their wives, the senior adults, the college department. When I host events in my home, I enlist help— whether paid or volunteer—to assist me in the kitchen so that I can spend time with the guests.

My favorite venue is the home, and most of my suggestions have focused on that setting. However, the First Lady in some sense is expected to preside over churchwide events just as the nation's First Lady would preside over White House-sponsored functions. You are not responsible for the planning and execution of all these events nor perhaps for any particular event, but rather you should be attentive to final touches and most of all be present to welcome guests and notice any special needs they may have. Others may help in greeting and making guests comfortable, but the minister's wife is the appropriate person to preside over churchwide hospitality events.

Sometimes it is expedient or appropriate to have a church-sponsored event away from the church. For an event sponsored by the Applewood Baptist Church in Denver, pastor's wife Diane Wittman was at the heart of preparations for their Colorado Christmas Afternoon Tea. A group of ladies from the church decorated and hosted tables. The room became a treasury of creativity and splendor. Many had a part, but at the heart of all was the smiling and gracious pastor's wife. She greeted women, was the troubleshooter for a few catastrophes, and was a radiant First Lady, whom the ladies of the congregation were proud to present to their community friends!

Afternoon tea is a favorite family gathering and one we love to share with friends or even strangers who cross our paths. Coming apart for a cup of tea lifts my spirits more than any human event. In fact, I launch my day with a cup of tea, the culminating touch for my breakfast. I take time for a morning break with tea. I travel with a small pouch filled with tea bags and a tiny canister filled with loose tea, which I can use if the coffeemaker has filters!

The Duchess of York has said in several media interviews that she travels with her own tea kit (shortbread, loose teas, Irish linen napkins, a silver spoon with her signature bumblebee, a thermos reserved only for tea, and her own special teacup and saucer). When Paige allows me space for a tea kit in my limited luggage allotment, I will know that I have truly arrived!

The cup of tea is not the only part of the equation. The perfect setting—the library, the garden room, the small morning room decorated with a tea motif and even a teacup chandelier, the living room, the bedroom, the family room, the deck, or the prayer garden—is also important. Even though our best teas are in the intimacy of our home, a small hotel room will do in a pinch.

My first task is to create an elegant atmosphere wherever we are—china cups and sterling flatware, candlelight, soothing music in the background, fresh flowers or a potted plant, a touch of lace as a table topper or a special doily. When we are on the road, I have to lower my expectations, but I still try! The whole point is to spend a bit of time and energy and creativity to show that teatime is special! The tea service can be a china or silver teapot or even a terra-cotta vacuum pot (not so pretty but it keeps the tea piping hot). However, I adore tea cozies and have collected quite a variety of styles and fabrics, which I love to interchange in order to create a new and fresh look.

Preparing the tea is a ritual in itself—heating the pot (and my friend Ruth Hunt always had the cups heated as well), pouring the boiling water directly over the loose leaves, waiting in anticipation while the tea steeps, and at last pouring the golden liquid into a beautiful teacup.

Side dishes may include small and dainty finger sandwiches (cucumber, tomato, and egg salad are my favorites), a homemade and freshly baked scone with genuine Devon cream and a special jam, and perhaps a selection of sweets.

My menu is arranged on a tiered serving stand for convenience, although there is nothing quite as elegant as serving each course separately and allowing time to savor and enjoy. But all this elegance and appetitive delight would be in vain if it weren't for the people. Teatime can be enjoyed by one alone, but it is perfect for enjoying with your family and friends and acquaintances who may join you. Tea is about reflecting on your own thoughts, relating to those whom you love and know and those whom you want to know. It may be the ultimate communication among friends because it takes time; it is best observed in a private and uninterrupted setting; it speaks of comfort, rest, and relaxation by its very nature.

Whatever you do in the way of extending hospitality to family and friends or to special guests and acquaintances, don't feel that you have to

Dottie's Best Coffee

- Brew six ounces of water per two level teaspoons of coffee.
- Use freshly drawn cold tap water or bottled water if desired.
- Use the correct grind for your coffeemaker.
- Don't reheat coffee. It can be kept warm about twenty minutes on the burner and then should be placed in an air pot or vacuum server.
- Store unused coffee in an airtight container for two weeks. For longer storage, keep in freezer. Do not return to freezer once removed.

Fergie's Tried and Proven Cup of Tea

- Boil the water.
- As it begins to boil, pour some into your teapot and leave it a few minutes to warm the pot.
- Bring water to a boil again and toss water from teapot.
- Put one teaspoon of loose tea for each cup of tea into the teapot.
- When the water comes to a boil again, pour a little over the tea to warm and soak it.
- Top off the pot with the rest of the boiling water.
- Let it steep for three to five minutes.
- Pour into your teacup using a strainer or infuser.
- Neither Fergie nor I add lemon, milk, or sugar—just tea.[2]

do all the work, especially at the last minute. I like to set my table(s) early—for a large group, sometimes several days ahead. The wide selection of elegant paper products means you do not have to use fine china. Cloth napkins add an elegant touch. Select a fabric that does not require ironing and use a napkin ring (as simple as ribbon or raffia or elegant as silver). I bought our daughter-in-love Rachael silver rings with mini frames into which I placed a series of photographs of Armour. Or just use some inexpensive dish towels in the small size or terry facecloths to which you could glue or stitch some trim.

Putting together centerpieces using accessories from our home gives me great pleasure. Lemons, limes, and pumpkins can be gutted to use as vases or candleholders. Clear, inexpensive vases can hold rock or marble gardens. Terra-cotta flowerpots of all sizes, trimmed with ribbon and lined with colorful napkins, can be commandeered to hold chips, pretzels, or

> ### Dottie's Dictum
>
> Avoid using paper
> plates for a buffet
> unless you have some
> sturdy baskets in
> which to place them;
> or you might also use
> your everyday plates or
> inexpensive glass
> dessert plates to sup-
> port the paper or plas-
> tic plate. With paper
> alone, your food may
> end up splattered on a
> special carpet.

nuts. Baby-food or jelly jars are wonderful for vases, candles, or even beverages. Clear spice jars and inexpensive salt and pepper shakers can hold individual flower buds. Seashells, pinecones, rocks, and moss can create wonderful atmosphere for your table. I've used beach buckets, boots, books, dolls, fruits and veggies, and accessories from throughout my home to build an appropriate centerpiece.[3] I work hard at creating an atmosphere of relaxation and warm comfort.

Culinary excellence evolves more from caring than from talent or training. When best and most enjoyable, cooking is a creative pursuit. I try to keep "company meals" simple, using easy-to-prepare recipes with which I am familiar and some of which can be fixed in advance. Plan to spend some time in the kitchen and slow down to savor the process. Flavors and ingredients need time to mingle and blend. People enjoy simple home-cooked meals, and they will love being in your home, which makes them feel special and close to you.

Don't hesitate to accept help if offered or even to ask someone to bring food or assist in serving or cleaning up. However, if you do request help, think through exactly what you need done. I make lists. You may also find it possible to hire some help—perhaps a resourceful high school or college student or someone who likes to do odd jobs.

Find ways to maximize the fellowship for your guests. Arrange the seating thoughtfully. My husband and I sit opposite each other. I try to select

> **Dottie's Dictum**
>
> For tender meat, marinate; cook slowly and long. Cut boneless chicken breasts into thin cutlets (or ask meat counter to do so); pound even thinner between sheets of moistened wax paper. What flavor and fork tender!

someone who is outgoing and a strong conversationalist to sit midway between us on either side of the table.

- The female guest of honor (or wife of the guest of honor) sits to my husband's right and then the woman with seniority of years or position to his left.
- The male guest of honor sits to my right and the next man in seniority or position to my left.
- I try to alternate the men and women.

All of these guidelines evolved in order to keep conversation flowing among the entire group. My husband would be delighted if I seated the guest preachers next to him so they could huddle and immerse themselves in solving the theological problems of the age. On the other hand, I would like nothing better than to have a circle of women with whom to discuss children, shopping, and recipes. However, to divide this group by gender or to place all couples side by side or those who work together every day adjacent to each other would tend to create little cliques around the table.

Arranging the guests around the table is an art. Those who love

> **The Big Daddy's List**
>
> - Prepare offices and library for viewing.
> - Get fireplace ready to light.
> - Select CDs for background music.
> - Settle Noche—the Big Daddy's dog!

to talk must be mixed with the shy ones, or the cross-pollination of ideas and exchange of information among all would be lost. There are times when an exception is made. If someone is especially shy and not in sync with the group in background or lifestyle, she may be seated next to the only person she knows; or if colleagues don't see one another often and need some interaction, the rules are set aside. I look carefully at the seating for every function at Magnolia Hill.

My husband has icebreakers ready to start the conversation flowing—a current event, a trivia question, or an opportunity for each guest to introduce himself. Once the conversation is started, you can usually depend on your carefully chosen and placed people to keep it going. Occasionally I find my attention being monopolized by one individual, in which case I may say graciously, "Let's bring Pastor Jones into this conversation," or, "Pastor Jones, what do you think about this matter?" Your purpose is to stimulate, inform, and entertain all your guests, making each feel special and a part of the circle.

Is There Room at the Inn?

How about guests who sometimes need overnight lodging and/or meals? I recommend that you sleep in your guest room occasionally to be sure you have everything needed by your guests. Select a bed with a good mattress. You can add attractive bedding with whatever your budget allows. Every person needs access to two pillows. I never buy queen or king pillows because they don't stack well.

A bedside table is needed to hold a lamp, preferably with a three-way bulb (be sure you can read in the evening with whatever lighting is available), a clock, and facial tissues. Even if you must get by with an orange crate draped in fabric or a tray balanced on bricks, try to have a small table for each person sleeping in the bed.

A comfortable chair, suitable for relaxing conversation or reading should be available for each guest. A small desk or table with a straight-back chair should be ready for your guest to write a note or work on a project. Again, a lamp is helpful as is a wastebasket.

A dresser or chest enables your guest to unpack clothing. A mirror, too, is needed. Add whatever extras you can—a Bible, reading material like a novel or magazines (daily newspaper privilege is also nice), pen and paper, perhaps even notecards, adequate hangers in the closet for skirts/dresses/suits, a flashlight in case of electrical outage, a radio, an assortment of pins and safety pins, even a few over-the-counter medications like aspirin or throat lozenges.

A vase of fresh flowers or small potted plant, potpourri, a bowl of fruit or a plate of cookies, a bottle or a carafe of water with a fresh glass, and fragrant candles add a nice touch as do amenities for the bath—shampoo, bubbles, conditioner, lotion, Q-tips, cotton balls, nail file, and perhaps a supply of sample sizes of other toiletries that may be needed upon request. If your bath facilities only include a shower, don't forget a shower cap! I have also found that my guests enjoy information packets on the area and a schedule of events planned during their visit.

From Pigpen to Paradise

Whatever your expectations for keeping your home, you must have some schedule and plan for orderliness.[4] Meals should be served at regular times for health as well as morale. To be sure, any plan must be flexible, but at least you need some realistic goals. Walk through the house before going to bed at night, especially the living room and family rooms to be sure there are no remnants of food or beverage. Then put dishes in the dishwasher and leave your kitchen clean and ready. I prepare for breakfast by setting my table and doing preliminary work on the breakfast menu.

When you get up in the morning, make your bed. Your children can be taught the same routine. If they oversleep and don't get it done, do it yourself after they have left for the day's activities. Opening doors and draperies prepares you for the day's challenges. As soon as your family is out the door, you can clear the table, fill the dishwasher, and put the kitchen back in order. I set up for the next meal as well.

Financial Accountability

The whole matter of fiscal responsibility is intertwined with stewardship. You can become proactive in managing your resources effectively and prudently. You can take a little and make it go a long way. You can multiply a few things and accomplish a lot. You may feel frail and inadequate, but you can have the touch of an angel and the grip of someone pumping iron. You can take a rustic cabin or shabby apartment and make it house beautiful for your family. Your entering the room can be like turning on the lights—a warm, radiant, comforting presence.

Financial woes seem to be a source of family tension and anxiety in the parsonage as well as in other homes. Many pastors consider leaving the ministry just to get a better-paying job. Most pastors are hesitant to ask for an increase in salary, but many are anxious about their future and concerned about caring for their families as well as preparing for their own retirement. Although the surveys I have seen in recent years indicate that many pastors are still tithing their income, some do not and simply give what may remain after other needs and desires are met.

The starting place is your own attitude. You can be pessimistic and resentful, adopting the attitude of self-pity and the feeling that you don't have what you should have. On the other hand, you can be grateful for what you have and optimistic about how God is going to use you and your resources.

The throwaway mentality of this generation has created enormous waste and poor stewardship. Before you discard a possession, consider whether it may be useful as you have been using it or in some other way. You don't have to buy everything you think you need. Something you need today may be useless tomorrow, which means you probably could have gotten along without it today!

Focus on the given instead of the not given. Concentrate on managing carefully what you have instead of coveting what you do not have. Do more services yourself—doing simple repairs, making centerpieces and catering for your own hospitality, and creating your own gifts.

One of the most overwhelming jobs I ever accepted was typing my husband's doctoral dissertation. With two preschoolers and the responsibilities of a pastor's wife, I felt completely inadequate to tackle a document with four languages other than English, technical documentation, and strict guidelines; but we did not have the money to pay someone. I was a trained typist, and my graduate training was in theology. I studied the guidelines and tackled the assignment. I not only successfully completed that task, but two decades later I typed my own—even when I could have paid someone else to do it. Create your own resource list of people who work effectively and economically. You can willingly accept the most menial and thankless task not to win approval but just because you love the Lord Jesus and His people.

You must also determine what you actually have: property, earnings, investments, insurance, collections of value. Especially do you need to know what is available in case of emergency—illness, death, termination, or disability. Few families consider the necessity of keeping cash and the possibility of quick liquidation to cover several months' salary. No family can survive unless they discipline themselves to spend less than they earn. You live within your means by buying only what you can afford. Don't go shopping unless you really need something. Even if you use credit cards for purchases, don't purchase what you don't have money in hand to buy. This discipline will save you oppressive interest charges. Plan ahead for your shopping in order to give yourself time to search for bargains and compare prices. Of course, you can't do this unless you know regular prices for what you need. Research items you need to be sure you get the most efficient and durable model. The lowest price is not always the best buy. Quality merchandise will outlast cheap knockoffs.

One of the greatest challenges for a ministry family is the pressure of accommodating yourself to the expectations of others. Because you are a family in the public arena—your husband is a community leader—you may feel the need to look the part, keeping up with others in similar positions. In fact, this attitude may not be yours but that of the congregation, who would expect you to represent them well even when they do not pay you enough to do that! At this point you need to remind yourself that the best and most long-lasting impression you can give is to model good stewardship according to biblical guidelines.

Living below your means is not easy in a culture that entices you to find every possibility for extending credit and using plastic to purchase what you will someday have the money to afford. Most financial advisors suggest living on 80 percent of your income, giving 10 percent, and saving 10 percent, which fits biblical guidelines well. Many people are already so strapped with debt that they cannot even imagine where to begin. But if you start by cutting what you can cut—soft drinks and fancy beverages, entertainment with a price tag, restaurant meals and convenience foods, late-model automobiles, appliances and gadgets, subscriptions—you will be amazed at the dent in your outflow.[5]

By refusing to build up credit card debt, you minimize interest and finance charges; that means you can work toward paying down your mortgage as quickly as possible. Can you get by with only one car? Can you extend the ownership of your car as long as possible by keeping track of preventive maintenance and watching for warning signs of problems? Can you cut back on medical expenses? Avoid the use of tobacco and alcohol. Even life insurance for Paige and me has been cheaper over the years because of our abstinence policy. On the other hand, ministers need to be reminded that eating healthily, having a consistent exercise program, and getting enough sleep are also safeguards that help avoid medical problems.

Another challenge for ministers' wives is managing their hospitality budgets. The parsonage seems to be an attractive gathering place. There are some cost-cutting possibilities that don't demand eliminating events as much as managing them well. For example, perhaps you will substitute a potluck for a dinner party; you might settle for a dessert party instead of a full buffet; you can collect some good down-home recipes, like beef stew, chili, chicken and dumplings, soup and bread, which are cost effective as well as easy to prepare; you can also cut back on eating in restaurants as a family, which can increase your meal's nutritional value as well as cut costs drastically. Although being hosted for dinner usually calls for reciprocation, a preacher, as other public servants, is not under obligation to host a return dinner in the parsonage for every church family who invites him to dinner.

Gifts are another high-budget item for the minister's family because of the many celebrations within the church family. With your own children and grandchildren, you can set an example of cutting back on the number of gifts and concentrating on one special item packaged with loving care; you can watch throughout the year for bargains in retail outlets as well as visit garage sales and discount stores and keep your own gift closet stocked for the occasional gifts you wish to give; you can give yourself and your special services instead of things.

Retirement planning is as essential for ministers as for everyone else. If you and your husband start early, you will have more years to accumulate earnings large enough to make a positive impact. Contribute regularly, monthly if possible, and work up to at least 10 percent. If you have the amount deducted from your salary before your paycheck is issued, you are less likely to allow something else to take that money. Obviously the money saved must earn interest to be effective. Consult your CPA or denominational retirement office to investigate tax-sheltered income and various ways to make your investment in retirement grow and prosper.

Cutting your outflow is merely the starting place if you are consumed with unsecured debt. The worst sinkhole is credit card interest. Do not rely on credit cards for daily purchases and low-cost items. Record your credit purchases so that you always know how much money you are paying out in interest.

Dottie's Dictum for Saving

- Save your coins. Use bills to make purchases; empty your purse into your stash each evening. Regularly roll coins and deposit in your savings account.
- If you get unexpected income—honorariums, refunds, or coupon savings—deposit it in savings.
- Put 10 percent of your household or personal budget in your personal savings account.

To work your way out of serious debt, read the best of financial advisors and seek professional help if necessary, remembering that not all help is created equal! If something sounds too good to be true, it probably isn't! Avoid scams and anything that promises instant wealth with little investment of resources or labor. If you borrow, get your loan with the lowest true annual rate, even if it takes longer to make the arrangements. Never borrow one penny more than you actually need. Pay back your loans as rapidly as possible; include additional money to be applied to the principal each month.

The minister's family should be exemplary in managing their resources—another way of equipping your congregation for productive family living. If you have prepared a bare-bones budget and your salary will not cover necessities, if your salary is far below those in your church family, if you have already removed all the fluff, then perhaps you need to talk to a godly deacon and ask him to pray for you and your family and see if he has any counsel for how you are to meet your family's needs. Most important, you need to put your needs before the Father.

One of the poorest testimonies for a minister is to appear always with a hand out—requesting discounts or gratis service, whining about money, allowing himself to be absorbed in the materialism of the age. Often the minister is given a discount or gratis services. If that happens to you, never fail to write a note of appreciation, and don't expect it to be true evermore. Expect to pay and be surprised and grateful if grace gifts come. When you are out with parishioners, expect to pay your share. If, again, they interdict and insist on paying for your share, express gratitude in writing, but don't expect the same again.

The minister's compensation includes several distinct parts, and churches would do well to divide these into distinct categories of financial support. As the minister's wife, you at least need to be aware of these divisions: church ministry-related expenses required for the minister to do his work (distinct from personal income and family budget), protection coverages (insurance and retirement programs), personal income and housing. Churches sensitive to these divisions may be surprised at what they are actually paying their pastors in personal income.

The minister and his wife would do well to get tax consultation from someone familiar with the unique rules and regulations that apply to the income taxes for ordained ministers. As you can imagine, some are helpful, and some are not.

The areas of concern with which you need to be familiar are these: housing allowance (excluded from income taxes if the amount is properly designated by the church and actually spent to provide housing), reimbursements for church ministry-related expenses (these amounts spent are not reported to the IRS and are not subject to taxation if the church has a properly designed reimbursement policy rather than merely an allowance to be used by the minister), insurance payments (if term life, medical and disability premiums are paid directly by the church as a protection benefit instead of being paid directly by the minister, they are not reported as taxable income, with some limitations), retirement contributions (also subject to favorable tax treatment—ask about a salary reduction agreement)—and any contributions made by the church to retirement are tax deferred.[6]

A minister's library also has special considerations in taxation. Books purchased as well as subscriptions to journals and periodicals are tax deductible. One of the budget considerations for a preacher's family is how much income is to be allotted for the purchase of books for the preacher's personal library. Commentaries and other appropriate volumes are indispensable to a preacher who conscientiously prepares for biblical exposition. A wife who is interested and willing can help her husband catalog his library as well as file and index articles, illustrations, and quotations. A user-friendly library will be helpful to a preacher and his wife throughout the years.

You do have a choice concerning participation in Social Security, but get wise counsel before making your decision. Do not depend on Social Security alone to finance your retirement years. Insurance is absolutely essential. Again you need counsel from experts, but the areas in which you need adequate coverage are these: medical plan, disability plan (often overlooked but important), and life insurance (amount may diminish as your children are reared and leave home). Take your time and evaluate your personal needs, but don't delay in settling these vital issues. Wives, be sure you understand thoroughly what kind of coverage your family has. Where are the documents? Whom do you call in time of emergency? How are payments made?

Another often overlooked matter is the necessity of an up-to-date will. Everyone—husbands and wives—should have a will, regardless of the size of your estate. Each state has different requirements. For Paige and me, moving from Texas to North Carolina called for redoing our wills. Yes, it does cost money, and what you spend will depend on the resources you have and how they need to be protected. Don't try to do it yourself; seek a qualified attorney to help you. If you do not follow all the directives properly, the will may be declared invalid.

If you have minor children, a will expressing your clear desires is necessary for naming a guardian for your children. If you don't have your own will, the state will use its formula for distributing your assets and rearing your children. Even if your resources are limited, a will may actually save resources that would otherwise be lost in court costs and taxes. Paige and I also are using our wills to extend our Christian testimony and influence because a portion of our estate will be returned to the Lord's work.

Homemaking—an Artful Ministry

A minister's wife must remember that her home and family are ministry in the church. When any woman chooses to marry, she accepts the responsibility of helping her husband, nurturing her children, and keeping her home. Effective service where God places you is an assignment from God and not a choice for you. The keeping of a home takes time and energy and creativity. Homemaking is an art, and fashioning any piece of art takes time.

The minister's wife is part of the church family and should attend the regular services of the church unless providentially hindered by personal illness or crisis or that of her children or extended family. You should choose some area in which you are gifted and feel comfortable serving the Lord within the church. This commitment provides you a platform for influence within the church family and gives encouragement to your husband and others. However, you must also be careful not to overcommit yourself to church programs, remembering that life has its seasons. You cannot do as much outside the walls of your home when your children are infants and preschoolers as you can when they are attending school. Whatever responsibilities you accept outside the management of your home must be secondary because home management is in itself a ministry to your husband, your family, and to the congregation.

In a heavenly match the minister's wife will complement the minister. When he is serious and even sullen, you can respond with happiness and bubbling joy. When he is abrasive and angry, you can be gracious and diplomatic. When he is harsh and cutting, you can be warm and loving. You can determine to put aside your own dreams to make his dreams come true, or more importantly you can help him fulfill the calling God gave him.

The minister's wife can be content to stand in the background and yet always be ready to step up to the plate when her husband needs her. You can pour your life into the people in your congregation, crying with them, helping them solve their problems, laughing and celebrating with them in their joys. Unrewarded work and fruitless investment of time and energy, despair and discouragement, heavy burdens, and challenging trials do not deter her from her task. You consistently stand as an example to the congregation, a steady rock of strength to your husband, and a guiding light to your children.

The Taj Mahal was built to honor a wife. It took twenty-one years to complete this magnificent structure. Nothing any woman has ever built for herself will equal it, which has a lesson for women. If you seek to build your own monument, you will fail miserably, but if you serve your husband and family and the Lord, they will build your mansion in heaven; and it will go far beyond the gem-studded marble Taj Mahal built for the Pride of the Palace.

For your husband and you to have the greatest productivity, your home must provide comfort, order, relaxation, peace, and renewal. A wife is the one to provide the perfect atmosphere, appropriate setting, and best environment for a loving place to which each member of the family wants to come. There should be no place like home!

Home is the place you want those you love to find when they need comfort and care. However, you cannot give genuine comfort until you receive it yourself (2 Cor. 1:2–3). When the Great Hills Baptist Church finally entered their new sanctuary after seven long years of difficulties and construction, a large cross was placed atop the edifice. An airline pilot who happened to be a member of their congregation was coming into Austin's airport one foggy evening. The air controller who was guiding him in to safety said, "Line up with the cross, and it will lead you home!" If wives and mothers line up with the cross, they become a bright beam to lead the family home.

CHAPTER 6

Defining Your Ministry from a Biblical Perspective

The First Lady is the model or example to whom the other women in the church will look. Your presence, if not providentially hindered, is expected in church services and for special events. If you have no interest in participating in the programs of the church, neither will the other ladies of the church. You need to go in and out among the people, and you should be available by telephone within reason. A pleasant and helpful telephone personality is a plus.

Second, as your husband's helper, you will be watched to see what kind of confidence you have in his leadership. If you ignore his pleas for workers in the vineyard, so will the rest of the congregation. Ultimately meaningful service to the church will not be rendered because the church expects it or even because your husband expects it but because you love Christ and want to serve Him!

139

Your work in the church begins in the home. Once the home base is covered, a preacher's wife is ready to take her place at her husband's side as a coworker in the church. Whatever you do in the church should to some extent depend on your personal gifts and interests and the opportunities and needs for exercising those gifts in your congregation.

Team ministry is a pattern found in Scripture, especially in the marriage and ministry of Aquila and Priscilla. Although there is not much information about them and their ministry, they provide a worthy New Testament pattern to consider. Team efforts require time together. You must begin with commitment to your spouse and shared goals of ministry.

The minister's wife makes some choices up front. You can view your husband's ministry as a job and resist being a part. You can be merely a spectator. Or you can immerse yourself in his ministry as a martyr with no initiative for using your own gifts and skills. Another extreme is to take over your husband's ministry, determined to manage him and the church. The pattern of Aquila and Priscilla is one of partnership by design. They work together and complement each other, but clearly they follow the biblical guidelines for Christian marriage.

Are there any limitations for the minister's wife? There are some jobs in the church a minister's wife should decline. I say that with the understanding that neither I nor anyone else can be a clone for the Holy Spirit, but with almost four decades of ministry in the kingdom, perhaps my warning is worthy of consideration.

The minister's wife can offer special encouragement to the women's work and should be an active part of this program in the church. If there is a planning council for women's work, I strongly suggest that you be an ex officio member. Some ministers' wives assume the presidency or directorship of the women's ministries program or of the women's missionary organization. On the other hand, to direct the women's work officially may strain your relationships with the women you are enlisting for various responsibilities and rob you of the time to be an encourager and mentor to all the women in the congregation. You also could find your time totally consumed by one assignment without the opportunity to be a part of the broader ministries to women. If you are not tied to a leadership position in one organization, you may be better able to visit and assist with all.

Leadership training is one of the most important things you do. Your position, and often your experience, will be invaluable in equipping the women of your congregation for work in the church and in the kingdom. You certainly will not have all knowledge, but you will do well to know where knowledge about a variety of subjects and tasks can be found. Women you train will continue to serve the Lord long after you have gone. Often you can accomplish more by working through others than by doing it yourself. That means a willingness to accept the failures of others and patiently try again. Your ideas may be shelved for a time and then be embraced as coming from someone else. Much can be accomplished for the kingdom of Christ if it doesn't matter who gets the credit. Allow the women who work with you to share, or even receive totally, the credit for the work done. Your willingness to work with many different groups in the church will endear you to the congregation, for they will feel that you esteem them all.

You may have a personal library of books that offer instruction and encouragement to women. You are familiar with the denomination and wider work of your church and have contacts that may be helpful in securing speakers and workshop leaders for conferences. Few can be a better liaison between the women of the church and the staff. If you have church-related activities on your personal calendar, you can help coordinate dates for women's ministries in order to avoid confusion. You can also serve as a troubleshooter and peacemaker when there are misunderstandings and difficulties. One thing you should not do is handle the monies of any group within the church.

A Call to Order

Even if you do not assume the presidency of an organization within the congregation, you ought to be aware of some basic parliamentary skills.

You may need to preside over a group in business session, and even more likely is the possibility that you will be called upon to advise various groups.

- Honor the call to order—no undercurrents of conversation when the body is trying to transact business.
- To make a motion, you must address the chair and be recognized; then the motion is made and seconded before discussion is allowed and the vote taken.
- You "rise to a point of order" by so stating and then being recognized by the chair before you actually state the point of order. If the chair does not rule the point "well taken," the woman raising the point can only be sustained by a vote of the body.
- Time limits for motions or speeches from the floor must be strictly observed, or the chair is obliged to drop her gavel.
- The chair must maintain neutrality by speaking only briefly to restate the motion or to announce "common consent."
- If the chair has something to share, which is not covered by the rules but will be a benefit to the group, she may call for a "point of personal privilege" as can anyone else in the body. Otherwise, the one presiding should pass the responsibilities of governance to someone else while she enters the discussion as any other member of the body, resuming the chair only after she has yielded the floor.[1]

Paid Staff Positions

Another even more challenging area is to decide if you should be a paid staff member, whether a music director or worship leader, the children's director or youth director, even a secretary or office manager. In every case you are faced with the potential for upheaval. If that should happen, you could place your husband in the position of seeming to exercise nepotism (favoritism extended to an employee because of familial relationship rather than expertise or training). Sometimes reality has nothing to do with perception.

Many women whose husbands are in ministry are not only highly gifted but also well trained, and they have the advantage of knowing the minister and sharing his vision more than any other person in the world. However, to become a salaried church staff member means that you should accept regular office hours, a set job description, and be treated as other staff members. These terms in themselves will sometimes inhibit you from meeting the needs of your family and from being the minister's helper. For example, during the Christmas season the First Lady is expected to attend a myriad of social events, and you will want to plan personal hospitality opportunities in your own home.

As her husband's helper, the minister's wife is just as valuable as any staff member, and she can and should work within the church to use her gifts. However, to do so does not demand a salaried staff position. For example, if she is a gifted musician, under the direction of the responsible staff person, she can use her talent in organizing an ensemble, working within the music ministry, using her musical gifts in worship, or using her music in community ministries. If she is skilled in organization and management, she can work on projects for her husband behind the scenes.

On several occasions Paige invited me to hold a workshop for secretaries in which he asked me to use my experience and skills as an executive secretary to share techniques for answering the telephone, guidelines for making appointments, for filing, and for opening and sorting mail. Almost without exception he has asked me to help train new secretaries for his staff since I know him and his expectations better than anyone else. However, because I am not the paid secretary, I do not have to worry about when I want to have lunch with him or when I want to take my vacation. When we do things together, we don't have to coordinate with other staff members.

When a problem arises, the minister's wife needs to be free to comfort and nurture and sometimes to make peace. A public example of this matter is found in contrasting two American First Ladies. Hillary Clinton, although not on the payroll, sought and took prominent, official positions.

In every case a disaster followed. On the other hand, Laura Bush, who was not considered a candidate for any public service, has come to the public arena as her husband's helper in a time of crisis. In so doing, she has won the hearts of Americans, and she has proven invaluable to her husband. She has accompanied him to disaster sites and memorial services; she has represented him at schools and public events; she even did his weekly radio address on an issue to which a woman needed to speak.

Sounding board, companion, friend, and confidant— presidents and pastors have a lonely position and a heavy load. They need First Ladies who are committed to loving support and willing service without the restrictions resulting from their own private pursuits. Although not a paid staff member, the minister's wife should be a person on whom the church should be able to depend as a partner to her husband. Others in the congregation may be able to do the prescribed tasks, but you cannot be the First Lady without making your place by doing some task in the church.

Find what suits you best and then give your best to the task, while being careful not to spread yourself too thin throughout the entire program of the church. The pastor's wife cannot hope for perfection, but you can be working toward that goal. One thing you can control is your own attitude toward the members of the congregation. Whatever you choose to do should be done with joy and enthusiasm and not just because it is expected of you.

The counseling ministry is another in which it is expedient and natural for the preacher's wife to share. In preparation for this task, you need to saturate yourself with Scripture in order to discern biblical principles, helping people solve their problems by turning to the Lord and His Word. You might also read some books on biblical counseling. You may need to be available to counsel with women in worship services. You should know how to lead someone to Christ and how to help a sensitive heart find its way to decision time.

The minister's wife may also have times when her husband can profit from her counsel. God often speaks to a wife. When He does, you must prayerfully ask the Lord's guidance in how you approach your husband as Esther did with Ahasuerus. The most important ingredient is your own spirit and attitude. Respect for your husband and a humble demeanor set the scene for you to share with him your intuitions and concerns. These conversations should be done in private and without distraction. You should speak sincerely and plainly. Once you have presented your case, perhaps you should ask your husband to pray that God will give you both peace in the matter, but then you must be willing to release the matter and leave it before your husband (your counsel is your gift to him) and in the hands of the Father. The hard part is not in sharing counsel but in releasing that counsel with no strings attached.

The minister's wife should believe in her husband. Expect great things from him; attempt great things with him. Cooperate with him in all he undertakes. Be patient with him when things go wrong, and praise him when things go well. Confide in him; pray with him and for him.

Counsel for the Counselor

Where does the pastor's wife go when she feels the need for counsel? If she suffers from the effects of a dysfunctional childhood or if her marriage is on the rocks—if her problem *is* her pastor—to whom does she turn? If she does not feel she can talk to her husband, then she should find a proven friend from her ministry circle, or she could get a recommendation from her denominational pastoral care department for someone who could offer help.

Every woman needs a safe person. Mary, the mother of Jesus, had Elizabeth, a distant relative but a mature and godly woman whom God placed in Mary's life to listen and encourage her. Jesus had an inner circle and then three within that group who filled a special need in His life. Yes, a living and breathing person is needed, but you should never underestimate the listening ear and healing balm of the Heavenly Father. Pouring out your heart to Him and immersing yourself in His Word (especially the wisdom literature—Psalms, Proverbs, and even Ecclesiastes) will reaffirm His power to restore and renew.

Here are some boundaries for personal intimate friendships, especially within the congregation you serve.

- Before sharing information, assume that what you say will probably be spoken to someone else. With that assumption you can decide in advance what is safe to share.

- Decide upon subjects that are appropriate for close friends within the church family. You can talk about your hobbies, health and nutrition goals, current events, books you have read, movies you have viewed, recipes you have found, menu ideas, home decorating hints, family activities you enjoy, community and church service projects, and—with careful discretion—prayer requests, personal struggles, and parenting problems.

- Some subjects are best off-limits in conversations with church friends: salary and financial matters, confidential counseling information from members of the congregation, conflicts within the church and among its staff members, your own marital problems, confidential prayer requests from members of the congregation, and personal spiritual conflict that might be hurtful to your future ministry. These are subjects for which you need a confidante outside your congregation with whom you can share your burdens—someone you know will listen and pray and not talk to others.

Perhaps the Lord is prompting you to begin a support group for ministers' wives. Such an organization should never be the focus of your life, nor should it become your security blanket. But it could be a channel for ministry. You might develop friendships and fellowship not otherwise available. You could find some meaningful bonding with women who have similar situations and challenges. You may learn from women who have worked through the problems you are now facing. You could observe leadership qualities and self-confidence in others and share ideas with women who have your focus.

A Potpourri of Ministries

The hospitality ministry is a natural one for every wife, but again it behooves the preacher's wife to make herself an example. Of course, those women who have a gift for entertaining will give more time and energy to using their homes in this way. Nevertheless, every preacher's wife ought to find some way of extending Christian hospitality, which is in itself a broad field. As you practice hospitality, record the events—names of guests or identity of group, menu served, occasion celebrated. This record gives you a tangible way to remember who you are including over a period of time; it helps you to vary menu and table decorations; it provides a means of noting food allergies or other information about those to whom you extend hospitality.

Food and deeds of kindness for the sick and elderly are always needed. Carolyn Rouse had a neat idea for responding to emergencies. Her First Response Box is designed to respond quickly to needs. She has a large picnic basket in which she keeps paper products and plastic flatware, packages of popcorn, hot chocolate mix, tea bags, instant coffee, condiments for hot drinks, peanut butter, jelly, crackers, and cookies. You could add canned soup, assorted cereals, milk that does not have to be refrigerated, canned juices. Tissues, wash-and-dry pads, and Clorox wipes are also helpful. Then grab your basket and rush out the door to be the first on the scene to offer comfort and care.

Serving as hostess for special events at the church is not merely standing in the receiving line but also includes overseeing details of the event and helping in preparation and cleanup. Letters and cards to the sick and hurting and to those who have excelled or who celebrate special occasions are a wonderful vehicle for showing that you care. Hospital visitation and making home visits to shut-ins are other avenues of service.

The pattern for womanhood, the design for marriage, and the blueprint for the home have been greatly distorted through the years. Able Bible teachers are needed to share biblical truth. Especially in recent years women are clamoring for greater authority and more leadership roles in the church. However, in Scripture, the role of the woman in the church is clearly based on God's divine order for the home—submission to and honor of the husband by the wife. Certainly, unless the direction of womanhood is turned back to the divine design, the home stands to lose. What greater reward could a spiritually mature woman find than passing on to other women lessons in godly womanhood (Titus 2:3–5), including the boundaries God has given in Scripture. Water with boundaries is a running river, but water without boundaries is a stagnant swamp. The boundaries add vitality and purpose.[2]

The teaching ministry demands prayerful study and meaningful meditation upon the biblical guidelines for exercising this meaningful gift. Even if you feel inadequate for what is considered a public ministry, don't let your lack of confidence and fears keep you from doing your best to rise to any occasion. You can prepare yourself by reading books or attending workshops to help you learn the rudiments of public speaking.[3]

Speak in a voice that can be heard, and use language that can be understood by women in the pew. Plan interesting subject matter, and prepare a clear outline of what you want to present to your audience. Illustrations, especially personal ones, and humor help with application. With a spiritual message you need to appeal for a response from your listeners. Someone has quipped that you need only something to say and the determination to say it! Staying within your time limit, whether five or fifty minutes, is a courtesy to others on the program as well as to your audience.

The preacher's wife should be familiar with library and study tools—from the library of her husband or the church. Develop your own method of preparation of study notes and outlines and a plan for filing these for future use.

Ministries to Individuals and Families

One of the occasions for greatest ministry will be when a death occurs.

- You need to be there if possible. A loving touch says more than eloquent words. A hug or even a gentle pat is a way to express your loving concern.

- What do you say? "I am praying for you" or "I love you" or "I am hurting with you."

- Sometimes it is impossible to go. The death may have occurred in another city. You or your husband can make a telephone call; you can send a handwritten note of comfort, including an appropriate verse of Scripture (Isa. 43:2; 2 Cor. 1:2–3).

- Determine what the grieving family may need. Don't expect them to ask for help. If you go to the home, look around and take a mental inventory. Do they have a good supply of tissues, napkins, and paper/plastic products for mealtime, paper towels, toilet paper? Do they have a guest book or paper for people who come by to sign and enter a record of food, floral arrangements, and small gifts that are received? Are there young children who need care—perhaps even during the funeral service? Has someone volunteered to stay at the house during the funeral (security issue as well as practical help for receiving flowers or food while the family is gone)? Has someone arranged for meals at least through the day of the funeral? Have all the family members and close friends been notified? Do they have laundry that needs to be done or linens that need to be changed in preparation for out-of-town guests? Does the house need some straightening and cleaning—to be discreetly done, of course? This is a time to look and see what needs to be done and get it done! Of course, the minister's wife cannot and should not be expected to do it all. You may be so overloaded in your own life that you really cannot do anything other than write a note, but you can get the ball moving through notifying the church secretary or a Sunday school class teacher of one of the family members or some godly woman in the congregation who has the gift of mercy and service.

- Should you send flowers? To send floral tributes or even potted plants becomes expensive for a minister's family. You are faced with determining what criterion would dictate such expense. I have used several ideas when I am especially close to a family and want some type of floral tribute: a simple carnation boutonnière for a man or a small corsage for a woman (often fashioned by my own hands) can be attached to the clothing of the deceased with the family's permission; I have also picked up a bouquet of fresh flowers or a mini potted plant at the grocery store and dropped it by the residence rather than the funeral home. There may be times when a death within the immediate family of an active and faithful church member occurs out of town and the church staff or congregation need to respond. In this case I have always signed the attached card with the names of my husband and me and the church or institution.

Paige and Dorothy Patterson and the Southeastern Seminary Family

- The bereaved need to feel the warmth of being remembered by real people; and if they want to respond with a note of gratitude, they need a person to whom they can address their thanks. Even if the flowers are purchased by a corporate account, the name of the pastor and First Lady should appear on the card for the reasons already stated.

- What do you do when you know that any contact with the family and certainly attending the funeral will awaken your own emotions? I have always been prone to tears. I cry when I grieve, and I cry when I am overwhelmed with joy. Never be ashamed of your tears. The psalmist speaks of putting them in a bottle (Ps. 56:8). Do you have a tear bottle? You should. People realize a measure of comfort in shared tears. Of course, you should pray that the Lord will make you a tower of strength for those who are hurting and minimize your tears, but never let your sensitivity to the hurts of others keep you from ministering to them.

- Give those who are grieving the opportunity to talk about the one they lost, and perhaps you will even sense it appropriate to talk about that person's impact on your own life. At the funerals for my husband's mother and father, many shared how our godly parents had impacted their lives. T. A. and Honey Patterson had been retired for almost two decades. It may have seemed that they and their service for Christ were forgotten, but it was not so! Even in the midst of our great loss, Paige and I actually rejoiced to be reminded of the contribution this godly couple had made to the kingdom of Christ as well as to the personal lives of our family.

- Don't forget about those who have experienced the loss of a loved one. Remember to continue to pray for them; write their names on your personal prayer list. If you send notes to those for whom you pray, do so for these hurting ones. Handwritten notes are personal and precious. Whether a note of sympathy or an expression of appreciation, avoid general notes in the church bulletin. Take time and make the effort to respond personally. If the expense of postage is a problem, deliver by hand as you pass in the church corridor. Perhaps your greatest ministry to one who is grieving will come weeks or even months after her loss when everyone else has forgotten. Then you can send a note, drop by a casserole or dessert, deliver some hand-picked flowers, or select a meaningful book to say you are remembering her pain. Pastors may select an inexpensive book to be used for those going through the grieving process. In that volume the pastor or his wife can inscribe a note and then mail or deliver the volume to anyone in the congregation who suffers a loss. If the church budget does not allow this expense, perhaps the pastor can write a brief devotional on death to be printed for grieving families, or he could preach a message of special comfort to families who are hurting, and duplicate copies of the tape could be distributed as appropriate. Another possibility is to produce a comforting verse of Scripture on an attractive card stock to be sent to the grieving family.

- Respond in some way, even if you are not close to the family. The presence of a First Lady or some communication from her will be a comfort to the family; especially is this true if your husband is unable to respond personally.

Weddings are another event important to members of your congregation. Are you aware of the tradition suggesting that all fees or honorariums received by the preacher go to his wife? I think it is a delightful custom. On more than one occasion, I have returned the cash to the couple as a personal wedding gift—if I am especially close to them or if their humble situation makes me feel they really need the money. If you keep the monetary offering, you may want to begin a tradition of using the money for something special—home furnishings, garments for your wardrobe, or a special trip.

Often the minister's wife is called upon to serve as a wedding consultant.

- Where do the families sit during the ceremony? The bride's family sits to the left of the aisle, as you face the front of the auditorium, and the groom's family to the right. Mothers occupy the front pews and other family members sit nearby.
- Where do the attendants stand? The ushers can all stand on the right side and the bridesmaids to the left as you face the platform, or they can divide with half of the ushers going to each side and the bridesmaids taking their places slightly in front of them. As with everything about the wedding, the bride's preferences should be honored without question.
- How do they enter the auditorium? The officiating minister, bridegroom, and best man enter from the right side together, followed by ushers (from side or rear), then junior bridesmaids if there are any, bridesmaids, maid or matron of honor (if both, maid comes just before

bride), flower girl, ring bearer, and last of all the bride on her father's arm.

- How do you select the music? The bridal couple may choose to seek counsel from musicians, but the choice is theirs. They should share their choices with the minister in case there is some question on the propriety of the selections.

- Who pays for what? The bride's parents send wedding invitations; take care of flowers for the ceremony and reception except the bride's bouquet, some corsages, and boutonnieres for the ushers; fees for musicians and for use of the church facilities; the bride's wedding gown and personal trousseau; expenses of the reception; and photography of the wedding. The groom's parents take care of their own travel and hotel and traditionally host the rehearsal dinner in honor of the couple. The bride and groom are responsible for their rings and bridal gifts for each other as well as appreciation gifts to their respective attendants. The groom also pays for the marriage license, bridal bouquet, flowers for the mothers and grandmothers, honorarium to the clergyman, and the honeymoon trip.

- Who stands in the receiving line in the reception? The mothers of the bride and groom respectively, the bridal couple, and the bride's attendants. The bride's father may join the line, but usually the fathers, as well as ushers and best man, mingle· with the guests. The bride's mother receives each guest and then presents him to the groom's mother, who announces the guest to the groom and he to the bride and on down the line to her honor attendants and the bridesmaids.

When invited—if possible—the pastor's wife should attend wedding ceremonies and receptions and even the rehearsal dinner (during the rehearsal she may be most needed for her expected expertise). On the other hand, the pastor's wife may go to a great deal of trouble and the expense of hiring a babysitter to be a part of this special occasion. In return the mother of the bride may introduce the pastor to her guests and family with great pride and effusive praise, while ignoring his wife standing beside him. Although such behavior is the height of rudeness and shows poor taste on the part of the offending party, you can be gracious in a way that will be noted by others!

Be sure your etiquette book has a good section on weddings, or purchase a volume on wedding celebrations to give you needed information and ideas. Sometime along the way you may have a wedding in your home. Make some basic preparations ahead of time, and you will find that it can be a happy occasion for you as well as the bridal couple.

Keep at least one room of your home presentable for unexpected guests. I store my seasonal decorations and accessories in large plastic containers, carefully labeling each as to season and contents. My wedding box included white tulle, the white Bible I carried in my own wedding, a bridal veil (your own or one easily made with a quick visit to the craft store), the ring bearer's pillow used in our family weddings, and bridal "bears." You might also include a CD of wedding music and your notes of instruction concerning wedding protocol. All of these accessories also come in handy when preparing a centerpiece for a bridal shower.

Many preachers' wives will want to reach beyond home and church in their ministry. Especially after their children are reared, they will have more time for creative pursuits. Choose an area of service in which you have interest, expertise, and opportunity. It could be political action on moral issues—abortion, voluntary prayer in schools, homosexuality, scientific creationism, or sex education. It may be a project in the arts—opera, symphony, the art museum, or the theater. It may also be institutional service in a hospital, retirement facility, juvenile detention center, home for unwed mothers, or a jail. There is also the option of school projects in athletic programs, booster clubs, parent-teacher organizations, or service as a teacher's aid. There is no end to the possibilities for civic and community service, and such ministries can be blessed of the Lord, especially if you determine to use the avenue of service for an opportunity to witness and share your faith or to help hurting people in the name of the Lord.

The Challenge of Multiple Jobs

What about the minister's wife who is gifted and equipped to have her own career? Or what about the minister who does not receive compensation adequate to meet the needs of his family? These are difficult issues, and whether the minister's wife pursues a career or takes a job to supplement the family income cannot ultimately be decided by anyone but the ministry couple. It is not the business of the congregation, although integrity would suggest that this issue ought to be on the table for discussion with any pulpit committee.

Let me address the issue from two viewpoints: my own understanding of Scripture and my personal experience. Scripture does not specifically address the issue of wives with careers or jobs beyond their family circle. However, since the Lord does not leave you without what you need to find His will in any important matter, there are clear principles to be considered in making this decision.

The design and plan of creation was for the wife to be a helper to her husband in all to which he would put his hand. The gift of maternity and a nurturing assignment would certainly suggest her willingness to bear and rear children. The examples of women in Scripture overwhelmingly place wives and mothers in the home.

The ideal woman in Proverbs 31:10–31 is clearly pouring her energies into her home, the management of her household, the rearing of her children, the helping of her husband. Whatever she does relating to property transactions or producing and selling merchandise is obviously secondary and related to the bartering common to that time.

The curriculum for the spiritually mature women who would be teaching the women who were new and fresh to their responsibilities is clear on what was most important (Titus 2:3–5). Character qualities to emulate are described, but the skills and assignments are centered on work in the home, ministries to husbands and children without apology or deviation.

The ornament of a woman, from God's perspective, is not her productivity in the marketplace or even in the church but rather the "gentle and quiet spirit," which helps her relate to her husband; and 1 Peter 3:1–7 obviously describes a woman whose priorities are in her home.

In passages like Deuteronomy 6:4–9, Psalms 78 and 127, the family setting is elevated, and the responsibility for rearing and nurturing children in the Lord is an overwhelmingly important and consuming task.

Can you be a godly woman and seek employment in the marketplace? Certainly. Is how you spend your time and energies your choice? Yes, but if you are totally committed to the Lord Jesus, then you will be most interested in knowing His guidelines. You can be certain that His thoughts will not be yours; His ways will not be the same as yours, according to Scripture (Isa. 55:8).

If a minister's wife is employed, she cannot share as fully in the routines of her family or her husband's ministry or the life of the congregation. She cannot spend as much time in personal Bible study and prayer, nor can she have the time for personal ministries in the church. For these reasons the matter must be carefully considered.

The question is not one of finding an outlet for using a woman's talents, training, and energies in a worthy way or merely opening a channel for pursuing personal interests. There are always ways to do this without the bonds of structured employment. There are outlets for using talents and skills beyond the walls of the church that do not require position and salary. Nor is the question about the greatest opportunity for witnessing to people who would not cross her path except in the marketplace. The marketplace is open, and she can have ample opportunities to share her faith in the community. The decision should not be a cop-out because of unfulfilled expectations in church ministry and resentment toward an unthoughtful congregation.

Churches do not always pay a living wage, and this injustice is not easily solved. However, first be sure that your financial needs are not the result of poor money management or a discontentment with what God has provided for you and your family. Also, consider carefully whether the salary is inadequate for basic necessities or if it simply does not provide the level of affluence you want for your family. Two-income families incur many hidden costs. You cannot evaluate monetary success by income alone; rather, what comes in must be offset with outgoing expenses—everything from extra clothes, convenience foods, child care, second car, and taxes.

Every woman must distance herself from her own desires, solutions, and plans and come to Scripture with a blank slate, asking the Lord to reveal to her what He wants. Then and only then can you step forward in faith to bring that to pass. The walk of faith is a mere farce if it works only when you can see clearly what is ahead and receive solutions before problems are unfurled.

My personal experience responds in two ways. First, my husband served a rural church, which required his service only on the weekend. He has also been the pastor of what might be called a village church—larger in size and definitely more complicated in its problems—with a parsonage next door. He then went to a fussy church in a heavily Roman Catholic community of a large metropolitan area. He finally reached a full-time and full-salary congregation, a First church with respect in the community as well as throughout the state.

In every one of these pastorates, from the smallest to the largest, my husband needed a helper. My opportunities for service in the kingdom of Christ were there, but I discovered that my enthusiasm for keeping my home, caring for my husband, and nurturing our children were the big factors in enabling my husband to do his job. In none of these positions did my husband receive anything other than ordinary compensation. Even in the full-time position, the salary was little more cash than our seminary church had provided. A spacious parsonage was added to the package, but that turned out to be a mixed blessing. We struggled to stretch our furniture and purchase appliances (for the FBC pastor to make daily trips to the laundromat might have caused a stir), and we were taxed on the value of the home we could not afford to purchase or keep up! Our financial pressures in many ways were just as pressing as they had been in school! We had a little more income, but it was quickly eaten up in the overhead of a large pastorate!

God does not give any woman a blank slate and tell her to write her own job description—to do as she pleases with her life. She is not simply to consider her gifts and training and make her own choices. Rather, He gives you a road map in Scripture with the fixed boundaries and general guidelines and lots of crossroads with choices to be made. Fortunately, however, He also furnishes a guidance system for finding and redirecting you when you get lost along the way. The Holy Spirit is on call twenty-four hours a day, seven days a week, and He always knows your location and the proper destination. If you let Him, He will get you there!

The Investment of a Letter

Writing a letter in your own hand allows you quiet reflection as you compose thoughts and feelings. This handwritten communication can become an emotional centerpiece into which you pour your most intimate feelings. You are expressing yourself not only in what you say but also in how you say it—what paper, card stock, writing tool, or decoration you may choose. I have chosen to select note cards and postcards personalized for me with the imprint of our home Magnolia Hill. Instead of looking over a large selection of possibilities, I like having something quickly available for my pen. When I go overseas for an extended trip, I take address labels for family and friends that can be applied to postcards as well as a glue stick for affixing stamps.

Florence Littauer uses the metaphor of a silver box to describe encouragement. No commodity is more scarce, nor is any ministry more needed than that of lifting up another. One of the best ways to encourage others is through personal notes and letters. Unfortunately, we have become accustomed to electronic transmissions that require little time, effort, or expense. Didn't the psalmist say that he would not give God something that cost him nothing? Perhaps you need to rethink how you communicate with your family and friends and those whom you want to encourage.

For months I searched for a small writing desk for my bedroom. It had to be small to fit the wall space and too small for a computer. I wanted it to be light in color and so feminine my husband would not want to use it. I really dreamed of a desk that was simple but unique with serene elegance, one that would draw me to its surface and away from the fast-paced, frenetic lifestyle into which I had fallen.

There is something special about a place that clearly says it's time to slow down, have a cup of tea, and write a note to someone you love without having to be hooked up or plugged in. I did find the perfect one in Dallas. It is white with blue trim (matching my walls). Its surface is adequate; it has one center drawer and a chair that fits its scaled-down size. A workman lifted it a few inches so that my knees would fit perfectly. I have already found the perfect desk accessories and put them on my wish list, together with a hand-painted teapot lamp.

Dottie's Dictum

One of the most priceless gifts you can give friends and loved ones, including those in your congregation, is an annual family Christmas letter. Modern technology enables you to include a family snapshot with little extra cost. The photograph can be seasonal or portray a favorite family memory. In the letter you can reacquaint readers with your family and convey your holiday greetings, together with a testimony of the reason for the season! If you don't have money for postage, deliver by hand the Sunday before Christmas.

What am I going to do at this bedroom desk beside French doors overlooking our prayer garden with rays of the sun pouring into the room? This desk draws me to the oasis of a kinder and gentler life, even if only for a few moments. I can dream; I can plan my week's schedule; I can pour out my heart in personal notes. I will stock it with different note cards (I love to tie them in bundles with my Magnolia Hill ribbon), letterhead, envelopes, postcards, stamp art, pens—including my favorite fountain pens—with different colors of ink, address book, prayer box, postage stamps. All my correspondence, and only my correspondence, will be done from this lovely spot. I can send off a note of thanks for a gift or special treat; I can draft a note of encouragement; I can send an assurance of prayer; I can write a newsy letter. When I want to send any written communication, I know where to go—a place that has everything I need.

Frustration or Fulfillment

Often the minister's wife receives the brunt of criticism directed against her husband. People will say to you what they don't have the nerve to say to your husband. You must sift through the debris and evaluate what is important for your husband to know. Sometimes it is hard to see your husband through the eyes of another and even harder to see him through God's eyes. Your first response is often to the person delivering a stinging criticism. Whether just or unjust, you need time for prayerful consideration of the matter before delivering the rebuke you instinctively want to unload. As a First Lady, you are to model graciousness and restraint. Your parishioners have a better chance of learning how to behave in Christlike ways themselves if you and your husband teach them to do so. Perhaps an appropriate first response would be something like this:

> Your words concerning my husband will be carefully
> and prayerfully considered. I am confident that he wants
> to serve you and our congregation in the best possible
> way. If he errs, it is a head mistake and not a heart

decision. You would understand that neither you nor I should order his life and make his decisions because ultimately he is accountable to God. Please pray with me that God will give my husband—our pastor—clear direction and true discernment in this matter.

In your response, make clear that you are listening but not making a judgment. Avoid casting blame on the one delivering the criticism. Put the matter in a spiritual setting and be clear that God must ultimately adjudicate the matter and give direction. Never fall into the trap of becoming a conduit to deliver complaints to your husband. In fact, you may want to include in your response, "You really should speak directly to the pastor about this matter."

Once you have made an initial and innocuous first response, you should consider the matter prayerfully and determine if indeed your husband might have a blind spot, which opened him to the criticism. Some rebukes should be taken as reminders of human frailty and as a means of refining life and testimony. Another lesson to be learned from endured criticism is to curb your own critical spirit. Try to avoid even listening to criticism about former pastors and staff members, and certainly you should not participate in talking about the faults and failures of these who have gone before. They are now gone; let the matter be closed.

When it comes to receiving personal criticism, learn to listen attentively, sift through for any lesson to be learned, and then move on. Let your response be one of graciousness. Perhaps in the end you simply think or even say, "Let the Lord judge between me and thee!"

The Giving of Gifts

Most ministers' wives are faced with wanting to give more gifts than allowed by their budget. You must determine guidelines from the beginning of your ministry to a congregation and then be consistent with how you handle this challenge. You can always use personal notes and cards (computers make this option a creative one) to express congratulations and participate in celebrations. Don't ever underestimate the most important gift you give, which is to present yourself in loving service to your congregation.

When tangible gifts are given, ministers' wives must learn to be creative and frugal, while at the same time making each gift personal and special. Presentation is a vital ingredient. Set out to make the ordinary extraordinary. Tie everything with ribbon! Add buttons to a dreary sweatshirt; attach bows to a plain ponytail holder.

If you keep your wrapping paper plain, you are free to use whatever trim you have on hand. You will achieve a professionally wrapped look if you first carefully measure and cut the length of wrapping paper needed, leaving at least a two-inch allowance for finishing the cut edge with a fold. Secure the wrapping with double-sided tape to give a clean look and prefold the paper where it wraps around a corner of the box. I learned how to do this by dismantling a professionally wrapped gift and then practicing until it became natural.

To bind and garnish the package, raid your sewing basket, the seasonal decorations you are ready to recycle, your kitchen cupboards (cookie cutters or measuring spoons or some small gadget you've never used), and assemble these items in a box, basket, drawer, or on a closet shelf. For years I recycled every piece of paper, each gift bag, and most strands of ribbon. Often I used the iron to revitalize the worn stock, and I used bits of other decorative pieces like twigs of holly or pinecones, rickrack, and millinery flowers, as accents. Now I purchase forest green bags (from a wholesaler), a coordinating color of tissue, and personalized ribbon. This two-color combo streamlines my storage area and is a wiser budget decision for the large number of gifts I am giving in our present ministry. But for more than two decades, I gave a number of gifts with little financial investment, lots of recycling, and some creativity (Saran Wrap, foil, brown grocery bags cut open to use inside out, or butcher paper with stamp art can be used effectively).

An imaginative, caring heart can indeed come up with the appropriate pizzazz for the perfect gift. The way you give is far more important than the gift itself. A worthy presentation does not have to be different for each gift you prepare. You can work on several unique packaging ideas and then reuse them again and again. Concentrate your energy and creativity for a moment "outside the box," and you will be surprised with the result. Whether your presentation—the outer wrap—or the gift inside, it is the thought that counts! My daughter Carmen lets Abigail and Rebekah decorate paper bags for their daddy's presents—not just for birthday and Christmas but even when he goes on a trip!

Creativity itself is a gift that has a certain magical quality about it. When nurtured, disciplined, and expressed regularly, creativity will grow. It can never be used up. This phenomenon is personally satisfying, and yet it is also other-person oriented, resulting in the overwhelming urge to share with and give to others of yourself—your time, your energies, and your creativity!

Stockpile gifts for various occasions in a drawer or on a closet shelf. You will probably need certain categories of gifts: new baby, graduation, wedding, birthday (especially if you have young children who are being invited to peer celebrations), staff, hospitality. You can shop garage sales, watch for sales at retail outlets, prepare culinary delights in your own kitchen, go to your craft corner—whatever avenue suits your own giftedness. Are you

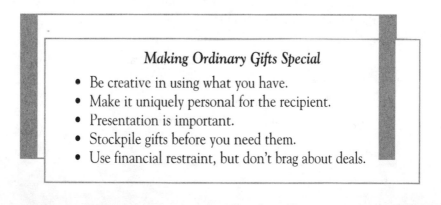

Making Ordinary Gifts Special

- Be creative in using what you have.
- Make it uniquely personal for the recipient.
- Presentation is important.
- Stockpile gifts before you need them.
- Use financial restraint, but don't brag about deals.

gifted as a bargain reaper? Do you have a treasured family recipe? Have you developed some special crafts? Or do you have a friend with whom you could collaborate on any of these suggestions? For example, you furnish supplies and your friend does the labor. You both get your own supplies and you baby-sit with the children or assist in the projects. By the way, if you do get a good deal, don't brag about it. Let that bargain-to-die-for be your own little secret!

Another item to stockpile is greeting cards. I have a deep card drawer that is full of special occasion cards. Perhaps a box or an accordion file works better for you. Some cards are free, tucked in a catalog or mailing; you can pick others up in sales; you may simply assign a small monthly budget to purchase some greeting cards. Better yet, produce your own, whether through a computer program or simply with whatever art supplies you have on hand. Recycle cards you receive by cutting off the cover or verse and using it to make your own custom card for someone special.

Some of My Favorite Occasion Gifts

The arrival of a new baby is one of the most important events in a family. It is an event that has the potential for spiritual encouragement as well as congratulatory greetings.

- Many pastors give a small New Testament (pink for girls and blue for boys) during a baby dedication ceremony within the worship service. In this case a church usually purchases these Bibles in quantities, and the gift is from the church and the pastor.

> We rejoice with you!
> Paige and Dorothy Patterson
> and the SEBTS Family
> Psalm 127:3–5

- Since coming to the seminary, I designed a computer-generated family tree. I send parents with a newborn this family tree parchment suitable for framing, together with a work sheet for gathering information—an inexpensive gift easily mailed!
- While traveling I also found at a very good price a cotton envelope pouch with a small bib tucked inside. This unique gift could be easily and economically duplicated with fabric remnants by someone who sews.
- One of my students designed a three-by-five baby dedication booklet, using overruns from a printing company, for which she paid nothing. (Some print-

BONUS: Neltia Henderson also uses her idea for wedding gifts. She invited my class to join her in producing such a booklet to honor my birthday. Each student wrote me a personal note. With her hole puncher, Nelita prepared each card for binding with a coordinating ribbon. What a treasure for any occasion!

ers give leftover paper to churches and nonprofit organizations at no cost.) On her computer she developed some appropriate artwork and then placed Scripture on each card—verses a mother might use in praying for her baby.

The number of high school graduation invitations, especially in larger churches, can be overwhelming. Often invitations come to the pastor just because he is an important figure in a student's life, or at least his parents want the pastor to be important to their child.

- The card booklet is an option with appropriate artwork and Scripture that will be encouraging to the student. If you use this option with male graduates, be sure that the artwork is masculine and appealing to a young man.

- A good book is another option. Perhaps the pastor will write a booklet to be produced by the church with words of challenge for students getting ready to move to a new season of life. Computer-generated artwork makes this a nice possibility.
- You might also design a packet of IOUs as postcards requesting home-baked goodies. If so, be sure the postcards are easy to complete with postage already in place. Another possibility is to get the student's college address from his parents, and midway through the semester send a box of goodies (I use popcorn for packing to keep cookies from crumbling).
- Another option is to prepare a "college" basket. You might include note cards and postage stamps, pencils (even personalized ones are inexpensive), pens, candle or incense, small packages of tissues, a few quarters for doing laundry, a small box of laundry detergent, Post-its of different sizes (buy these at discount centers), some long-lasting goodies like cheese crackers or candy bars, etc.
- Birthday in a box is another option for a student with access to a kitchen. Send card, cake mix, icing, party favors, paper tablecloth, cups, plates, napkins, plastic flatware, greetings on tape or video, and a small gift. I have also baked and sent a pound cake by priority mail. I recently heard about a lady who makes decorative cake-shaped gift boxes and fills them with healthy munchies, scented candles, specialty teas and coffee, current magazines, small books.
- You can also get cassette tapes, CDs, periodical subscriptions, or books on sale. Or prepare a movie night basket with video store gift certificate for movie rental, microwave popcorn, boxes of candy, and cans of soda. Don't forget napkins and straws!

Weddings are again benchmark occasions in which the participation of the pastor not only in officiating but also in sending some remembrance may give him an opportunity for influence with the couple in the future.

- Neltia's booklet of celebration is a wonderful option, especially if you have computer skills.

- Basket ideas are endless. You could use themes like romance (sparkling cider or grape juice with two glasses, candle, cassette or CD of easy-listening music, boxes of dry pasta, jar of spaghetti sauce, can of Italian breadsticks); family worship (devotional book, prayer journal, pen, and perhaps a computer-generated, personalized prayer card booklet with photographs of family members and their birthdays and space to write specific requests); correspondence (stationery, greeting cards, post-cards, pen, postage stamps, and perhaps return address labels with the couple's new address); kitchen (assorted utensils, recipe cards, apron, spices), bath and beauty (bubble bath, powder, body lotion, candle, sponge, etc.).

- Personalized calendars—purchased or generated by the computer—can be prepared with family birthdays and holidays marked and with photographs or special artwork added. Such calendars can become family history.

- Brides can also enjoy a gift wrap basket into which you place wrapping paper with color-coordinated tissue, gift bags, an assortment of rib-bons, double-sided tape, scissors, and gift cards. You can follow a seasonal theme or choose items appropriate for any season.

- I also have two favorite publications appropriate for starting a new home. Both have the theme of Christmas and give the couple an opportunity to record Christmas memories. One is a hardback with space for twenty years of memories, and the other is a paperback one-year album. I love doing a first Christmas basket with the album, an assortment of ornaments, a tape or CD of Christmas music, and perhaps a small nativity.

Dottie's Favorite Christmas Memory Book
CHRISTMAS MEMORIES BOOK
Published by Mystic Museum Stores in Mystic, Connecticut

Birthdays are another special occasion for which you need to be prepared, and that means all ages. Again, I think your creativity will give you a head start.

- The card booklet is easily adapted to this occasion. The cover might be an acrostic using the honoree's name. You could use the card series to express what you appreciate about the birthday honoree, or you could use various Scripture verses to challenge and encourage.

- The birthday box described for graduates could also be adapted for anyone celebrating. If the person is local, you could bake the cake and deliver the celebration box yourself.

- Cookie bouquets can be fashioned using Popsicle sticks. Balloon bouquets can be designed with small gifts placed inside the balloon before they are inflated so that when the balloon is popped something falls out.

- Books appropriate for every age can be purchased when on sale or in bulk. You can also select one of your own favorite books and inscribe it, including what the volume meant to you and why you think your friend will enjoy it. They are easily mailed as well. Or you can prepare a book lover's basket with a few books, a mug with packets of hot chocolate, instant coffee or tea bags, a tin of cookies, and a distinctive bookmark.

- Why not be really creative and give what you do! Design a gift certificate with your name and the service you are giving—calligraphy, graphic design, typing research papers, baby-sitting, errand running, car washing, house cleaning, or scrapbooking. Or give an excursion for coffee or tea—your treat of an aromatic beverage and some time for conversation!

- How about using cartoons from your daily newspaper or magazines or creating your own humorous anecdotes on the computer to share with a friend? You could even compile a group of these into a small album or booklet—customized for someone special!

You should enjoy giving gifts to members of your church staff or other groups with whom you work closely. Perhaps you can choose individual gifts if your budget allows, but you again may need to decide on a gift appropriate for all. When my husband and I started traveling internationally on a regular basis, I discovered that I could pick up small remembrances as a trip gift for our personal office staff since they always seemed to have some extra tasks to do in our absence.

- I have made or purchased napkin rings (shells from Hawaii, carved animals from Africa, Christmas ribbon or tassels from a sale bin, stenciled paper). Sometimes I find inexpensive cloth napkins I can slip into the ring, or I find fabric within my budget that can be made into napkins. If we have a staff Christmas dinner, the napkins and rings double as a service item and place favor/gift.

- I have used Christmas ornaments more than any other gift. In Bethlehem I purchased olive wood ornaments at an excellent price. I ran a bright ribbon through the loop and then attached them to a tree in the living room and let each person pull one off to take home. I have also used crocheted doilies from the English countryside with a ribbon slipped through the cutwork. I have used area postcards with a hole punched for the ribbon. I have picked up ornaments at the end of one season and then used them the following Christmas. I have used a favorite recipe printed

A *Quickie for a Special Occasion*

Spray a mini loaf pan with Pam into which you layer a can of biscuits after dipping each in melted butter and a mixture of cinnamon and sugar. You can add toasted pecans or almonds, candied fruit. Bake according to directions; deliver hot from the oven.

on a card with colored ink and some computer artwork with a hole
punched for matching ribbon.

- I have also enjoyed giving gifts from my own kitchen—Christmas
cookies, fruit breads, spiced tea mix, cinnamon popcorn, snack mixes.
Wrapped up in Saran or cellophane gift bag, and tied with colorful ribbon, food always delights, especially when it is the fruit of your own
hands. Even something easy to prepare can be a cut above the ordinary
and bring loving greetings with each bite!

- I have purchased loose teas, especially from Africa and Asia, poured
the tea leaves into small fabric bags and sometimes added a tea infuser
to make a neat gift. I also have purchased fresh spices and small clear
bags in the Indonesian grocery market. The spice packets fit nicely
into small baskets from the open-air market.

Giving is a gift, and some people will stop at nothing when there is an
opportunity to give. What a precious way to show love. Wasn't it Eliza
Doolittle who responded to Professor Higgins on the silver screen, "Don't
talk of love; show me!" Jesus commended the widow who gave all she had
at the temple (Mark 12:41–44).

Gifts are great fun to prepare and give. For me, gift selection and preparation have usually taken more time and creativity than money. I have discovered that the number of gifts I give demands that I plan carefully. I
choose gifts by category and then personalize with notes and some adapta-
tions. If you cannot afford a gift, you can always send a handwritten note of
congratulations; and if you cannot afford a postage stamp, you can hand
deliver the note to the individual. If you cannot even come up with a card
or paper, use the telephone or extend your heartfelt congratulations in person. Just knowing you have taken note of a special event and care is most
important.

When I was fresh to the ministry, a veteran senior pastor's wife happened to be on the same trip we were making. While we were shopping, I
was struggling over choosing a trip gift within my budget for our personal
staff. When I asked her opinion on the choices before me, she shocked me

with her response: "Don't get into the habit of giving gifts to staff members. It will cost you too much!" I'm glad that my first mentor was my mother-in-love who was a creative genius when it came to choosing and wrapping gifts and who had the gift of giving. She was never wealthy, but she was generous and thoughtful. I personally don't think you can ever do too much for your colaborers. They

> ### The First Lady should keep gift ideas for:
>
> - Birthdays
> - Weddings
> - Graduations
> - New babies
> - Staff members

often enable you to do your job and sometimes can help you do it better. They seldom get any credit as most accolades go to the pastor. They are paid less than you are. You need to find a way to express your gratitude to each one. Spend time and energy and creativity, and it will return to you above and beyond all expectations.

Social Events—Hostess or Attendee?

As a hostess, I have found some extras that turn the ordinary into something extraordinary. I love using small place favors at each plate or having something for each guest worked into the centerpiece. For example, I have used mini easels to hold cards with recipes, Scripture verses, poems, miniature drawings, or photographs of the honoree. I have also used tiny terracotta pots to hold flags, sticks bearing candy, or plants. I have placed small scented votive candles from a sale bin on cardboard rounds covered with foil. I gather place favors on trips—Christmas ornaments, handkerchiefs fashioned into dolls, crocheted coasters, mini baskets filled with candy. For the centerpiece I have used a collection of mini vases with flowers and greenery from the garden or a basket overflowing with Christmas ornaments or goodies from the Magnolia Hill kitchen, which then became a small gift for the guests to take home.

Dottie's Dictum

- Place favors
- Menu card
- Place cards
- Talking with each guest

Above all, you want to be a warm and sensitive hostess, showing interest in each person. That means making eye contact with the guest and really listening. This kind of concentration will make a few minutes of greeting seem like an hour of conversation! Focus on the person. Instead of chattering away about yourself, ask the guest about herself, her family, her current projects, her workplace. Look around for your wallflower—one who is shy and retiring—and draw her into your circle and connect her to someone for the evening.

Menu cards suggest planning and even a touch of elegance. You can print the menu on the computer or write it out with a flourish in your own hand and then place on an easel at each end of the table or at each place setting. Stamp art, computer graphics, or free-handed design can accent these cards.

Place cards also give you a chance to seat your guests appropriately. I choose to use the traditional seating in which my husband and I sit opposite one another so that we can each give attention to a different group of guests.

When you are invited to someone's home, take a small hostess gift—gourmet coffee or specialty tea, rich chocolates or something from your own kitchen, a book, cut flowers, or a potted plant. If it is a large party hosted by someone you do not know well, as you approach the hostess, identify yourself clearly so that she does not have to struggle for a name.

Being helpful to a hostess is a precious gift in itself. Offer your services. If she declines, don't try to elbow your way into the kitchen and take over, but do remain alert for a way to help that might unfold in the course of the evening. Perhaps used cups or plates can be taken to the kitchen or paper napkins can be retrieved from the floor. Most hostesses have a plan for serving and cleanup. If they are using fine china, stemware, and sterling silver, you want to be careful how and where you stack and arrange the used pieces.

Do your part in keeping the conversation flowing. Introduce yourself to newcomers and help in introducing guests whom you have met to others. If someone seems uncomfortable and ill at ease, take special time to show an interest in her. While you are seated at the dinner table, try to get to know the people on either side of you and across the table. Divide your attention as equitably as possible. Pick a topic for conversation that is inclusive for all.

If you have a cell phone, turn it off for a few hours. If you have young children, leave the telephone number of your hostess with instructions for your sitter to use only in an emergency.

What Did I Do Right as a Minister's Wife?

In considering my years as a minister's wife, I have thought through some of the things I did that have proven right for me, helpful to my husband, and honoring to Christ.

- I have tried to be myself—genuine, sincere, and without pretense. I have lived my life, loved my family, and done my ministry with passion. If I've had no other impact on others, perhaps my enthusiasm will be remembered.
- I have spent, and do spend, my life learning. I read; I observe; I listen to what others are saying; I try to take note of feedback especially helpful to me.
- I have tried to keep at least the living room always ready for guests and light refreshments readily available.
- I have sought through the years to acquire a measure of flexibility and adaptability in my life and ministry to enable me to be as much as possible all things to all people that the gospel of the Lord Jesus Christ might have an impact on some through me.

- I accepted Christ as my personal Savior.
- I completed educational pursuits open to me.
- I married a godly man. God prepared us one for the other.
- I struggled in the path to obedience and standing under Scripture.
- I've had the joy of bearing children and chose to pour my life into them.
- I've been content in the seasons of life and venues of ministry.

- Sometimes I have to trust my instincts in settling problems, in protecting my husband and children, in balancing all the balls I have in the air.
- I have also given our home to the blessed Jesus. I have learned to hide the car in the garage because sometimes we need our space! Most of the time the doors are open, and we are ready to receive graciously whomever the Lord sends; but I have not forgotten that the Lord Himself created the solitary in families, and I cherish an occasional time-out for savoring the small pleasures of life and creating memories.

Unfortunately, I did not do everything right. Perhaps you can learn from my mistakes. When we first entered seminary, I tried to balance three part-time jobs plus a full load of studies, including Greek and Hebrew. My husband didn't really want me to seek employment, but I couldn't see how we could live otherwise since he didn't have a church. As a result, I completely broke my health and still bear in my body the scars of that crushing load.

Unrealistic expectations have plagued me all through the years. I had to learn that you can't live your life to meet the needs of people as you perceive them; rather, you must ask God what He wants you to do (1 Cor. 3:6).

I also have learned that I did not ultimately hide my weaknesses and short-comings. Not only were these known to our congregations, but most tragically they were also observed by our children. Why is it that your children are not drawn to your strengths instead of your weaknesses?

For too many years I compared my effectiveness to others instead of looking to divine standards. I am surviving shark-infested waters a bit better now, but I am probably still too sensitive to criticism and negative responses. Someone said you should bless those who curse you because they may be right! I am trying to consider all criticism constructive—to make me better and to make me more sensitive to others.

- I rejected solitude for many years. My quiet time was brief and perfunctory. I loathed being alone.
- I embraced anxiety because of failures.
- I abused the temple of my body with neglect and unrealistic expectations.
- I abandoned Sabbath rest and spent that day as others—worship services plus working on a myriad of projects.

Questions on Women and Their Roles in the Church

1. How about the idea that headship and submission come only after you are filled with the Holy Spirit? *Answer:* What happened to the assignments given by the Creator in the beginning when He formed the man and the woman (Gen. 2:18–25). Obedience is the way you become filled with the Spirit.

2. Do the guidelines for women found in the Pauline corpus apply to organizations not in existence in the first century? For example, Sunday school and parachurch organizations. *Answer:* The

guidelines for women in relationship to men are not only in the Pauline corpus but in Peter as well. Jesus Himself in the Gospels refers to the creation design for men and women. When foundational principles are given and supported by theological underpinnings, as with Paul's directives to women, which he carefully anchors to creation, they are not to be limited by time or circumstance but rather are to guide in all faith and practice.

3. Is the restriction directing women not to teach men a reference to teaching in a usurping manner? *Answer:* Would the Lord have a man teach in a usurping or "lording it over" manner?

4. Are there many deaconesses in Scripture? *Answer:* Only one woman is identified as a deaconess—Phoebe. Even in that case there is a question as to whether the identification is simply labeling her a servant, which is the meaning of the transliterated Greek word *diakonon*, or a reference to an officer in the church. Clearly in the New Testament those called deacons were not a ruling body but a group devoted to serving the church, a function that does not violate in any way the Pauline directives to women.

5. Should a minister adjust his own assignment to allow his wife to get professional training or accept a position to which she feels God is calling her? *Answer:* I've heard many variations of this problem for the two-career couple. A wife is offered her dream position—whether ministry or secular—and her husband wants her to have an opportunity to exercise her gifts. He's willing to do anything to make that happen. He begins looking for work to facilitate her move, but he is not successful. The doors aren't opening, but still she knows that God is in it. After all, if God weren't in it, she would give up. What does God say about a husband's work? In Genesis 2:15, he is admonished to tend the garden or provide for the family; and in the New Testament clearly the husband is to be the head and thus the one responsible for leadership, provision, and protection of the home. Pastors are directly admonished to

provide for their families (1 Tim. 5:8). All decisions concerning location should be in the hands of the minister himself. Of course, if he is wise, he will take seriously any counsel his wife may have; but the final decision must be his.

6. How do you prevent or heal staff tensions among wives of staff members? *Answer:* Only the Spirit of Christ can supply the balm needed for this task. The pastor's wife, however, can do much by loving all and giving special attention to each staff wife—affirming her strengths and encouraging her to develop the fruit of the Spirit. Nourishing ungodly feelings is hard when you are on your knees praying for one another.

> "The *role* of the pastor's wife is being a helpmeet to her husband, whether in the home, personally, or in the church. . . . The *duties* of the minister's wife constitute what the couple themselves, or the church members, think is the work that she should do in the church or for the congregation. The *image* of the wife is the preconceived picture in the minds of the church people of what the wife should be from her personality to her activities in the church."
>
> — Dorothy Pentecost, *The Pastor's Wife and the Church*

CHAPTER 7

Blessed to Be a Blessing

Why do you live as you do and do what you do? If your answer is, "Because I am the pastor's wife," then you are in trouble. You had better be doing what you do because you love the Lord! Everything you do for your family or for members of the church should be "as unto the Lord."

What does a preacher's wife do about personal rights? That depends on your mind-set. If you are trying to develop a Christlike spirit, then you do as Christ did: you choose to yield your personal rights to God and let Him return them to you according to His plan. Genuine joy is found when you lay down your rights. When you do, the Lord will give you what you need, and you will come under the umbrella of His protection.

Through the years I have asked my classes for ministers' wives to suggest qualities characteristic of the model pastor's wife. These are some of their suggestions: sincere, perceptive, sensitive, gentle, cheerful, discerning, comfortable with her role, well-read, supportive of her husband, organized, a good listener, a leader, well-groomed, stable—that's a pretty good start! However, my personal list takes a little different turn, beginning with a genuine experience with the Lord and setting up priorities according to biblical guidelines. Nurturing a relationship to the Lord on a regular basis, serving her husband and children, and only then turning to outside activities or ministries, she must have a hunger for God's Word and a desire for fellowship with God's people.

An effective preacher's wife will also believe in what her husband is doing; she will support his ministry. She must develop a love for her husband's preaching. She must delight in serving the congregation with her husband despite the inevitable frustrations that come. She will learn to love the people. One pastor's wife shared her custom of moving about the congregation, sitting in a different place in each service. She looked for a lonely person or someone who seemed to be hurting and sat beside that person. Another woman wanted her husband and children to know exactly where she was sitting; she asked different people to join her on an assigned pew.

Katherine Zell was an extraordinary wife and helper to her Anabaptist husband. She thrived on hospitality, cooking meals, serving tables, while also discussing theology. She even compiled hymns and wrote tracts of encouragement, which were published and distributed to those facing persecution. She always maintained that she was not "usurping the office of preacher or apostle."[1] Being a strong woman and thoroughly prepared gave her the opportunity to help her husband and contribute to the kingdom of Christ in marvelous ways.

In serving as a helper to her husband, a wife can be constructive or destructive. God has called wives to be counterparts to their husbands rather than opposers. The First Lady should add to the effectiveness of the pastor. With this reciprocity the pastor's wife complements her husband rather than competing with him. If you are not one with your husband in doctrinal commitment, if you seek to pursue your own gifts rather than help him, if you are constantly trying to draw attention to yourself, you will set yourself up as a competitor.

The First Lady, rather than pursuing her own interests, should be committed to team ministry. A God-centered woman responds to situations in God's way; a selfish woman responds to circumstances.

A godly preacher's wife should be a comforter to her husband, not an antagonist trying to expose his weaknesses. You can question your husband's decisions privately in a gracious way, but you should not question his motives. You should be a rewarder, doing everything in your power to make your husband's life fulfilling and not a robber seeking personal gain at his expense.

The minister's wife must be willing to forgive her husband. Rather than criticizing or ridiculing him in public or nagging him about changes he should make, you should look for and believe the best about your husband. Nothing is more damaging to a marriage than for one spouse to utter biting criticism of the other before a third party. It is the height of disrespect. The preacher is God's messenger to his wife, even if he lives imperfectly at home. You would do well to respect your preacher-husband and honor him before others.

The greatest tragedy for a preacher's wife who becomes destructive rather than constructive is that she is helping to create in her marriage a vacuum into which a counterfeit woman can and often will move. Preachers have great burdens to bear in addition to the inevitable criticism that plagues any public servant. A. W. Tozer said, "God never uses a man until He hurts him greatly." You can be sure that your husband will be hurt, but you are the one to encourage and lift his spirits. You can be the conduit for bringing him full circle. As both of you work hard, you can take comfort in knowing that your work is worth doing. As you sacrifice your personal desires and suffer injustice and pain, you can rest in knowing that you are drinking the cup of the Lord's suffering. When the Lord is all you have, He is all you need!

Ministry Setting

One of the greatest dangers to a gifted and successful preacher is to think more highly of himself than he ought—an affliction I call "blind ambition." One who seeks public venues for his spiritual gifts, one who praises his own ministry achievements, one who extols his own personal virtues, one who believes he must be advertised to be known is in danger. Oh, for a preacher who would allow God to be his public relations agent. God would then decide when his deeds are to be proclaimed and when his light is to be noticed. A person is also free to see and affirm others in their accomplishments—the other-person focus that is so much a part of the New Testament teachings (Phil. 2:3). In competitive situations, you can then rejoice when others excel; you can offer sincere praise and appropriate encouragement.

When your hearts are attuned to service to others, you can enjoy your ministry and work, because the burdens of ambition, jealousy, bitterness, and resentment have been lifted. Serving others is never easy, especially when you are in a position of influence and power, but loving servanthood is essential to effective leadership.

At some point your greatest challenge will be to determine what you will not do. Only then can you escape from the ongoing busyness that has become the curse of life, and especially so in ministry!

Don't Be Left Behind

Although I led a rather sheltered life before I married a preacher, I must have had some sense of adventure in my soul. Or perhaps I just wanted so much to be a part of Paige's life and ministry that I determined to be ready to try anything.

My first trip overseas was to the Orient in the early 1970s. I was thrust into the use of chopsticks and dealing with a meal of chicken's feet—a favorite delicacy of our Asian host! I read somewhere that Princess Anne of the British royal family had lunch in a traditional nomad tent in Alma-Ata, Kazakhstan. According to the account, the princess was spared the boiled head of a sheep—a traditional Kazakh delicacy for honored guests. Paige and I must have been more "honored" because during our visit there we were served and did "eat" the sheep's head presented to us by our hosts.

The First Lady of the parsonage is catapulted into a position of influence by virtue of the fact that she married a minister. None are born to the position, and few volunteer for it. In any case, because you are the minister's wife, many doors are opened to you. You are invited into private homes, asked to participate in public events, pulled into personal celebrations and private grief and suffering. You are usually pulled into the hearts of members of your congregation and into the lives of residents of your community. This burden of public scrutiny can become an incredible opportunity to influence an entire generation of women. No woman has any greater responsibility for making a difference in the world.

Rewards

On more than one occasion, I have had beautiful young women say to me: "I don't want to marry a preacher. That life is not for me!" I am sure there have been days when I would have chosen almost any other life, but they have been few and far between. When I take time to reflect on almost four decades as the wife of a preacher, I quickly come to the conclusion that I have been greatly blessed.

First on my list would be the spiritual rewards. There is accountability in ministry that nudges you along in your personal quiet time. A busy lifestyle frequently pushes aside any time with the Lord. However, the setting in which I live as the wife of a minister has ways of drawing me to the feet of the Savior. After all, I have nothing to offer others if I myself don't take time to fill my own cup again and again.

Second, I have met some wonderful people. Some of the missionaries who have come to our table have awed me as much as heads of state, government leaders, educators, and religious leaders. The people in the congregations we have served and the students and faculty in the institutions with which we have worked have encouraged us, ministered to us, invested in our family members. We are frequently hosted for meals; we have been given event tickets we could never have bought ourselves; we have been taken on trips we could not afford; our children were educated with scholarships. We have been loved and honored—not by every church or ministry we have served, but by some. We have had the privilege of a sustained association with some of the finest people in each community in which we have lived, and in the process we have been invited into their homes and hearts.

Third, I have had some flexibility. My husband has always been busy. He has meetings and functions to attend, sermons and lectures to prepare, visits to homes and hospitals to make; but often he has been able to adjust his hours to help with family emergencies. He is inevitably working on Saturday and Sunday, but often he chooses Monday as a day for relaxation.

Fourth, I do not see how any job could be as varied and adventuresome as that of a preacher. I consider it a privilege to walk beside a God-anointed minister, sharing his sorrows as well as his joys, having the opportunity to pray for him, encourage him, even protect him by extending his usefulness and strength through sharing his load. Interceding on behalf of your husband is one of your most precious ministries. His duties are manifold and his burdens heavy. He has administrative responsibilities, a commitment to study and prepare for messages to be delivered, an assignment to shepherd his people by listening to their hurts and walking with them through the waters of difficulty.

You cannot predict the happenings of tomorrow much less next week or a few years down the road. I never knew that there were so many opportunities to serve. My husband has always had to travel, and that does have its downside. However, we have been to a lot of interesting places, experienced a myriad of cultures, and met some amazing people in the process.

Fifth, I have had the privilege of rearing my children in a genuinely Christian setting. Unconditional love, vibrant faith, and humble service were woven into the warp and woof of our home. I cannot help but believe that the lives of my children were enriched by being at the heart of a ministry home.

Sixth, at this stage in life, I am more and more conscious of the stewardship of influence. It is a privilege to share the trust of hurting people who look to you for help. It is awe-inspiring to see the Lord intervene in hearts and lives that cry out to Him. To see the Lord gain a foothold in a hopeless life is humbling. The ability to touch lives through what I say and do is an awesome privilege.

My husband and I have files full of letters of appreciation for the investments we have made in the lives of people in our congregations and students in our classes. I have had the opportunity of comforting those who are grieving, counseling those who are confused, and encouraging those who are discouraged. I have had the joy of loving people freely, impartially, and unconditionally and then experienced the delight of having that affection returned. I have been able to use the curiosities about and interest in the preacher and his family to set the scene for sharing the gospel with those who are lost and equipping those who are saved. In most cases the people we have served have allowed me to make mistakes; and for every person who is unduly critical of me or any member of my family, there are many others who will readily forgive our mistakes and love us despite our clay feet!

Finally, there is satisfaction for my husband and me. We take joy in serving the Lord by ministering to His people. The environment in which we live and work is a blessing. We love and respect one another. My husband has drawn me into his life and ministry. He not only knows my name and presents me to his coworkers and friends, but also he has studied me to determine my gifts and skills and helps me use them in the kingdom. Yet he still is willing for my work in the kingdom to be limited and voluntary because my primary energies are devoted to the home and family. If I need to be excused from ministry responsibility for a reason, I can state that reason clearly; but if I cannot do a requested task, I can simply decline since impossibility needs no excuse. My husband honors my priorities and supports my personal responsibility for ordering my life.

Spiritual Mothering

Do preachers' wives need spiritual mothers? One of my students responded: "I want someone to show me every little detail of the godly woman's life. I want to know how she does her quiet time, reads her Bible, and studies God's Word."

Women are looking for someone to listen to their hurts. Many of them call 900 numbers and pay someone they don't know and can't see just to listen. If you want to invest in the lives of hurting women, you must learn to give them what you know they need, packaged the way they want.

Few women realize the powerful potential in those who have gone before and those who are walking alongside you in life. Believers are instructed to seek godly counsel on a regular basis. Godly counselors are a wonderful source of wisdom. The discernment of friends and spiritual advisors can save much heartache and clear many obstacles in your spiritual pilgrimage.

In counseling with women, first you listen. I try to make the person who has come to me at ease by encouraging her to talk about herself in a general way. I look for a common interest. A certain measure of healing comes from sharing your burden with another. Sometimes this self-cleansing confession is all that is needed other than a prayer for forgiveness and the encouragement to continue seeking the Lord.

Confrontation can be necessary. Tact is a worthy tool. It gives you the ability to deal with others on sensitive issues without being offensive in doing so. Nothing is as important as preparing your own heart with prayer and meditation in Scripture. In fact, you need to be familiar with the Bible and its timely principles. Only God's wisdom will provide the answers you need. Most difficulties in life are rooted in spiritual problems. The Bible has the answer, and you need to be familiar enough with God's Word to turn to the appropriate passage and show the woman you are counseling what God has to say, leading her to accept a Word from God instead of her own way. You must also mold your life and attitudes to the model given by Christ.

Loving concern must characterize your attitude, whatever the person has done or however profligate she might be. There are times when you must present a Word from God, whether a rebuke or encouragement. The key is to let God deliver the warning or judgment. When a woman accepts the Word from God and sees her shortcoming before Him, then you must gently lead her to ask the Lord's forgiveness. Share a positive Word from God—a spiritual exercise in what to do to obey Him. You may prescribe Scripture to read or even a devotional book that will address the issue of concern, but always encourage the troubled woman to find a congregation of believers for fellowship and accountability and to discipline her own life for time with the Lord in personal prayer and Bible study.

However much you prepare, no matter how saturated you are with Scripture, and however much time you have spent in prayer, you will have limitations. God alone has the resources for meeting needs and solving problems. You may see much, yet say little, and in the process help some.

Choose a time and a private place to connect with the woman. Have an open heart, and be sure that your own heart is right, free from bitterness or indifference. Finally, women who are willing to give biblical guidance must count the cost—damage to personal friendship, the target of personal attack, a victim of misunderstanding.

One of my students described a fulfilling ministry, which she called RSVP, for sharing biblical guidance with women. On the same day each week, she prepared a large pot of soup, made some coffee, and opened her door from 11 A.M. to 2 P.M. During that brief time she was available for any woman who wanted to stop by for a bowl of soup and a listening ear.

> "A joyful servant of God is a net to catch souls for God."
>
> —MOTHER TERESA

Relationships to Women in the Church

The question arises concerning how you respond to other women in the church. Do you pull them close—especially those with whom your spirit resounds—or do you keep them at a distance? In other words, can a First Lady afford personal friendships within her domain?

Close ties to others are essential for everyone, but it is hard to know with whom you can trust your feelings and frustrations. The pastor's family is revered and popular. Everyone is vying for social engagements, fellowship, and conversation with the pastor and his wife. Isolation seems impossible in such a setting; yet it is inevitable when you do not build intimate friendships within the setting where you spend most of your time.

Ministers' wives usually leave not only family but friends as well when they move to a church field. Even holidays find them separated from extended family and close hometown friends because they are expected to plan and execute holiday celebrations for the congregation, many of whom have their families nearby. New surroundings, new environment, and new people sometimes become a dreaded way of life.

Female companionship for a minister's wife is a natural desire. Women friends serve as comfort and even temper your reaction to stressful situations. A certain confidence and strength come from feeling you have someone on your side. When you share your worries and problems with a sympathetic soul mate, they suddenly seem easier to bear.

Some say that the presence of a friend will stop the rising blood pressure that usually accompanies stressful tasks. My husband tells me with confidence that even petting his dog will keep his blood pressure down! Researchers have suggested that people with friends have lower cholesterol and stronger immune systems and live longer.

Jesus had friends. He had an inner circle of twelve men, and within that circle He had three to whom He was especially close and whom He called out for special intimacy. His intimate friendships were not without some negative consequences—jealousy, backbiting, pettiness. Yet Jesus depended upon friends to meet His personal needs, and He did move away from the multitudes and even from His inner circle in order to enjoy rest and fellowship with these intimate friends. However, there is no evidence that He drew these intimate friends into what would be defined as a clique or exclusive group that would build a barrier between Him and other

friends and associates or even between Him and the multitudes He came
to serve. Quite the contrary, His times with intimate friends served as
refreshing and reviving interludes to prepare Him for more effective service to others.

The wives of ministers need special friends. Each friend is different in
her own unique way; each one blooms in her own time and place; but they
seem to come together to make a beautiful bouquet. Keeping friends is not
easy. You must work at it or lose them. Tended friends will in turn tend
you. They seem to comfort you in a miraculous way. They share both joys
and sorrows.

For women who have public roles and a myriad of responsibilities to
their respective constituencies, there are several types of intimate friendships. While my husband and I were in the midst of our academic preparation, I made some special friends with whom I have continued to
interact through the years. One of my closest friends in seminary has been
serving the Lord in Asia for more than thirty years. We have seen each
other infrequently—during her stateside visits and a few times when my
husband and I were in Asia—but through letters, and now E-mails, we stay
in touch and keep up with family and personal struggles. Joy Cullen is still
one of my closest friends.

Edith Neal and I were childhood friends in Texas. We attended different universities; we met again during seminary and continued times of fellowship; we served on the church field together briefly; then we parted to
pursue different ministries with little contact. Finally, a decade ago Edith
and her husband joined us at Southeastern Seminary. I had just come
through a heartbreaking experience, which involved the betrayal of
friends in ministry; and I had determined in my heart that I would have
no more close friends other than my husband. I didn't want to walk
through that kind of hurt again. But God had other plans, and He in His
mercy and grace brought Edith to me. What a delight it is to have a friend
and kindred spirit so close by!

These special friendships formed early in life and ministry and sometimes challenged by distance and circumstances do not exclude other

intimate friends. When we were serving a church in Arkansas, one of our church members was a single woman who served as a bank officer. At the time I met Judy, she was not attending church regularly. In fact, you might say that she was running from the Lord. But God allowed me the privilege of making her my friend and watching her return to the Lord. I've never had a dearer friend than Judy Robertson. Even though our lives were very different, we found wonderful opportunities to have fun and fellowship. She never seemed to mind that I usually had two preschoolers in tow as we went out to eat or to shop or simply to the park. Just before we left Arkansas, Judy went off to seminary and then to the mission field, but our friendship continues.

In Dallas my husband was an associate pastor of the church with his major assignment as president of the Bible college. I thought one of our staff wives to be my closest friend—she seemed to fit all the rules of a colaborer who understood the challenges of ministry—but the friendship ended in great hurt to me.

On the other hand, I had several other friends who didn't fit the usual criterion because they were not only members of the church but they had also made large donations to the college. However, this mother-daughter duo have been a powerful presence in my life. They loved me as much when we served a Bible Institute with a dozen full-time students as they did when we served a college with five hundred students or a seminary with twenty-five hundred students! They listened, prayed, encouraged, and loved me even when I wasn't really lovable, wallowing in my self-pity. Ruth Hunt has gone to be with the Lord, but June remains a forever friend. Again and again through the years, I have reached out to her for hope for my hurting heart. She is always there with godly wisdom and healing comfort.

At this stage in life, I am blessed with intimate women friends on several different levels. I delight in friendships with women whose husbands also serve Southern Baptists. Our paths cross throughout the year; we keep up with family news; we share challenges from our ministries; we pray together for our husbands; we are indeed kindred spirits who share fun and fellowship as well as kingdom ministries.

Then I have precious friends among our inner circle of administrators at Southeastern Seminary. These women are always there; they anticipate my needs; they respond lovingly to my difficulties and hurts; they work shoulder to shoulder with me in extending the kingdom here on our campus; they are good listeners and prayer warriors and wonderful playmates as well.

Also I am blessed with students—young women who have been in my classes or entered into mentoring relationships with me through the years—who have become special and intimate friends. Heather King graduated and lives in another state, but she faithfully calls me and visits when she is nearby. She seems to anticipate when I am hurting and can endure a lengthy conversation with an old lady graciously. Joy White and Betsy Sibley are still in degree programs and have worked with me in women's studies, lifting burdens, sharing vision, and just being there for me to lean upon.

Bobbi Moosbrugger is on staff at Magnolia Hill. She is a kindred spirit and always seems to know exactly what I would do if I were there. She stands in my place so often in keeping our hospitality warm and gracious. She anticipates my needs and compensates for the frailties that seem to plague me in the aging process. She pampers and encourages me and always has a cup of tea at just the right moment.

In my life I have learned that I need three-dimensional mentoring. I need the women who have gone before. From the pages of Scripture come the testimonies of Esther who modeled submission—even to a pagan husband, of Hannah and Jochebed who took seriously their maternal responsibilities, of Mary the mother of our Lord who was obedient to the Lord whatever the cost, of Mary of Bethany who sat at the feet of Jesus to learn of Him, of Martha who was concerned with hospitality and the mundane needs of the Savior and of all who came to her home, of Priscilla who took seriously the admonition to be her husband's helper in ministry.

Throughout the pages of church history, other women appeared to inspire and encourage my heart. Katie Luther and Katherine Zell were not only women of great spiritual strength with some training in theological studies, but they were also active participants in the ministries of their husbands and able servants in the kingdom in their own right; yet they never wavered from honoring their husbands and giving priority to managing their households and caring for their families. Whatever they did beyond their homes was inspired by their desires to help their husbands.

Susanna Wesley is without peer in her maternal commitment, and Sarah Edwards was an extraordinary woman in managing her household, commanding the devotion of her husband, and rearing her children for service in the kingdom. Susannah Spurgeon was intimately involved in her husband's ministry. Although an invalid, she was his confidant, critic, public relations director, research assistant, editor, and loving helper.[2]

My mother and mother-in-love had a tremendous impact on my life in showing me the importance of intimacy with the Savior and the delight of serving others. Sarah Eddleman actually put me through a finishing school for First Ladies when I served on her personal staff at New Orleans Baptist Theological Seminary. She showed me first-hand how to prepare and preside over a gracious public home with a myriad of hospitality events. Ruth Hunt took up where Mrs. Eddleman left off during my years in Dallas when again and again I was included in hospitality at her Mount Vernon estate and learned the discipline of attention to every detail and offering your best "as unto the Lord." Edith Marie King introduced me to the beauty of interior design and the importance of letting each family member have his space and making it comfortable and uniquely his. Elisabeth Elliott and Jill Briscoe have modeled for me woman-to-woman biblical exposition and settled in my heart forever the importance of equipping women for kingdom ministries to other women.

You must not waste the experience and insights of those who have gone before just because they are considered to be part of a previous generation. You can sit at their feet and keep learning even when you feel quite secure in your own experience and wisdom.

In addition to women who are moving before me, I am blessed with peers who are mentoring friends. They are kindred spirits who share my commitment to family and ministry. Their husbands are colleagues of my husband. We attend meetings together, and we choose to spend some of our discretionary time together as well because we enjoy fellowship with one another. Jesus had His own peer group of friends upon whom He depended for fellowship and encouragement. We would do well to establish those bonds.

Then there are the young women in whom I am investing. They will come after me to serve the Lord and invest their time and energies and creativity in kingdom pursuits. I have the privilege of bearing testimony to them of the joys, challenges, and rewards in service to Christ. I also have the responsibility to affirm and encourage them as I seek to model a servant's heart before them. I believe fervently that I have an investment to make in these younger women. They will have more energy and creativity than I; they may well be smarter with sharper minds, but they will not have my years of experience, and they will not have seen the Lord's work in my generation. So I do have something to pass on.

What are the guidelines for establishing special friendships? First, remember that intimate friendships are not fashioned in a moment or a day or a week or a month or even a year. They are built over time, beginning with the foundation of shared commitments as well as common interests. Intimate friendships demand unselfish devotion, unconditional love, a heart set on service, time for listening as well as talking, sensitivity to the needs of another, discerning wisdom on how to help your friend be her best. Getting a friend is a task worthy of time and energy. You must invest yourself as well as your creativity and giftedness in the life of another.

How do you function as a friend? You study one another and learn strengths and observe weaknesses. You love someone so much that her problems become your own. You understand her because you can easily put yourself in her place. You are trustworthy enough that she can place her deepest secrets and confidences in your safekeeping. You are set apart unto the Lord in such a way that whatever comes from your mouth seems to come from God Himself. You are so immersed in His Word and wisdom that you can provide His answers. Your task is not to criticize but to construct. You are not as concerned with what you are getting as with what you can give. You are willing to be vulnerable, knowing that you may be hurt in the process since no friend but Jesus is perfect. You commit to spending time listening, talking, and deciding how you can invest wisely in the life of another. You determine to be there when you are needed.

Can You Have Friends in the Church?

Where should you look for friends? You need some friends who know your ministry demands—women you met during your preparation years, wives of other ministers whom you have met at conventions or other denominational gatherings, women whose husbands are pastors in other churches in your area.

Even from this pool of women, you want to choose carefully when it comes to intimate friends with whom you feel free to bare your soul and from whom you seek comfort in your deepest hurts. However, you will also find a fertile field from women within your congregation and perhaps even in your residential neighborhood. They will share your interest in hobbies or activities, or they may be women who are in the same season of life with children who are contemporaries with your children. These women are those to whom you naturally gravitate. Certainly, you should look for friends like these with whom you can shop or share gardening ideas or swap child care or enjoy lunch and a museum visit or take in garage sales. You can do fun things together; you can help one another in a pinch; you can share conversation.

Hobbies are important for ministers and their wives, and they provide a great opportunity for friendships within your congregation. For some years I really enjoyed needlepoint—until a piece into which I had put a great deal of time and energy literally blew out of a car in a remote region of Syria. Then I moved on to more intangible things—reading and research and collecting rare books, finding new places for afternoon tea and collecting tea accessories, listening to music, and traveling with my husband. You need to encourage your husband to develop hobbies as well. Some ministers have trouble retiring when they should because they have built their lives around church ministry, and they have no vision of serving the Lord or even living beyond the walls of the church. That is sad indeed—for the church as well as the pastor and his wife.

You would be wise to avoid sharing confidential information about your family and other church members with women in the church family. There are some adjustments to be made when you are a public figure. First Ladies must use restraint in what they share and with whom they share confidential information.

Even though it may appear to be unfair, a pastor is not allowed the failures of other men. He is on a pedestal in the eyes of his congregation and the community. A pastor's wife is not to build a façade of perfection around her husband, but neither is she to tear him down and in so doing lessen the respect he holds in the church and community. She can be his critic privately in constructive ways, but in public she needs to build him up and support his leadership and honor his position.

A preacher's wife should be open to the entire church membership. As with the preacher, you are given the privilege of serving all. The parsonage should be warm and hospitable.

While my husband and I served the First Baptist Church of Fayetteville, I planned my hospitality a year in advance. In September I had a Sunday morning breakfast at the parsonage for the college department with the University of Arkansas coaching staff and varsity football team as our special guests, followed by a Bible lesson and worship service at the church. Every Thursday at 9:00 in the evening, university students came for The Lion's Den, during which Paige taught a Bible lesson and fielded questions. At Thanksgiving, I invited the senior citizen group for a potluck lunch, and I provided the turkey and the beverage. At Christmas I had an open house for the deacons and a party for the staff. At Easter I had a party for the children's division and an event for the preschoolers. In May, I had a formal dinner for high school graduates and their dates. I invited various groups to come to the parsonage, but I also tried to be spontaneous in having smaller gatherings when appropriate. During this pastorate I did not have much household help, so I had to plan ahead and prepare food in advance. Hospitality was my main ministry because I could prepare for the events in my home as I supervised my children.

Vitalizing Volunteers

The church has suffered from its loss of women volunteers to undergird its various ministries. When women made the exodus from the home and into the workplace, they had no energy or time left to do much volunteering. However, I have noted in recent years that many women have been returning to homemaking and thus again are willing to invest their time in kingdom ministries. I have also noted that even women who are balancing home with marketplace careers seem to find a snitch of time here and there to give to the Lord.

One of the happy tasks of the First Lady is to set an example of volunteering, to present opportunities in the church and community for volunteers, and then to motivate women to give back their time and energy as well as their money. You are in a unique position for marshaling an army of volunteers. You can lose some excellent talent and labor by waiting for people to step up to the plate. Sometimes you need to put your finger on a woman whose gifts you have noticed and invite her to join you in a particular ministry.

Here are some ideas for mobilizing a volunteer ministry among the women who come under your influence.

1. Volunteers need to know precisely what you want them to do—a job description.
2. Volunteers need training. When the women volunteer to decorate Magnolia Hill at Christmas, they are primarily committing their time and energy. Our resident florist and decorator, Cindy Bush, offers a class in holiday decorating that culminates with decorating Magnolia Hill for Christmas. The women are taught valuable skills

and have a master craftswoman to guide them through preparing the decorations.

3. Volunteers need the authority and resources to do what you have assigned them to do.

4. Volunteers need flexibility. They will need more time to accomplish their assignments than would a paid staff member because they are weaving their volunteer duties into the warp and woof of their regular responsibilities. Sometimes they need time off, and they need to feel free to respond to their own family emergencies. They are able to volunteer because they are willing to sacrifice a second income in order to be available to their families.

5. Volunteers need to be treated with respect.

6. Volunteers need to know they are appreciated. We provide all the materials and select the Christmas theme for Magnolia Hill, but volunteers spend long hours and expend much energy and creativity to make it all happen. I select a gift to be given to each one of these faithful helpers as a token of our gratitude.

Winston Churchill said, "Success is moving from one failure to the next with enthusiasm." When you focus on your failures, it is like looking in a mirror—the focus is on you; but when you look beyond those failures, you are looking through a window, and there will be some joy out there on which you can fix your gaze. God wants your living to be in the "pleasant" tense. He also expects your life to be your deed rather than your creed. In other words, live what you say you believe.

When you go to a cutting garden to retrieve a bouquet, you choose flowers with roots firmly planted. The flowers are beautiful, fragrant, and thus they will be useful. But from the moment you snip that bloom, it is dying because it has been separated from its root. The same principle works in the spiritual arena. When you are rooted in the Lord, the beauty of Jesus can be seen in you, and His fragrance permeates your life and the world in which you live and move. Beware of cutting off your roots lest you become ineffective spiritually.

> "Life has not contained much trouble for thee, yet, darling son, but when it comes, remember that thy Mother has assured thee that there is comfort and ease in the grand fact that God Is."
>
> — Hannah Whithall Smith

CHAPTER 8

In the Eye of the Storm

Some have suggested that the Christian faith has been tried and found wanting, but G. K. Chesterton declared that Christianity had been "found difficult and left untried." Most believers, including ministers and their wives, have not begun to tap the resources the Lord makes available to them for dealing with the woes of life.

In a sense, believers can be happier after their trials because the greatest joy is realized when you contrast that joy with the greatest sorrow. No calm is any more evident than that which follows a storm. The sunshine that follows a dreary rainy day is all the brighter. Even so, the peace that follows crisis and tragedy is sweet, deep, and wonderful beyond description. You become rich through losses; you will be lifted up after your falls; you will fill your cup only after you have emptied it; you will find life abundant only after dying to yourself.

Virtues attributed to you prove to be genuine only after you have been tested. If you can sing in the dungeon of despair, as did the apostle Paul, can you imagine what melodious refrain you will waft in the heavenly portals? If you can praise the Lord in the midst of the fire, can you envision what glorious worship you will offer to Him when you reach the heavenly throne?

Ministers and their wives can be deceived into believing that to live and work in the midst of a congregation of believers should be "heaven" and thus bring perfect happiness. They see work for God as the path to heavenly reward. My friend Susie Hawkins says, "Preachers and their wives will work until Jesus comes or drop dead first." They see carrying the cross as merely the fastest way to the crown. They need to be reminded that this world is not home or heaven! They are not promised rest for today. They are not assured victory in earthly battles. Rather, full joy and rest and victory await those who serve the Lord on the other side—in the heavenlies. Trials are like an unpaved path toward the feet of the blessed Jesus (Heb. 12:11). To sit at His feet demands dying to self and with single-minded purpose to take up the task of obedience.

Every minister's wife will experience agony and ecstasy, the best and the worst, the good and the bad. Only when the Lord allows you to go through the experiences of pain and suffering do you reach for His strength and providence. He must be found faithful in meeting your needs in order for you to have a worthy testimony for someone else. Accompanying your tears must be a determination to trust the Lord and believe that He is able to deliver from any fiery furnace.

A *Humorous* Note

A pastor and his family were riding a roller coaster. The pastor remarked to the apprehensive couple behind him: "It's OK; I live on one of these!"

One of the greatest heartaches for the wives of preachers is the feeling of rootlessness that comes when you seemingly have no control over where you live, rear your children, and do your ministry. Missionaries struggle even more because they are uprooted from family and friends and all that is familiar and then planted in a strange land and sometimes with a hostile people. After years of making their field of service home, they return to the land of their birth for adjustments almost as challenging with only a few months or perhaps a year before the cycle continues.

Loneliness

Loneliness is not a problem for every minister's wife. However, by true definition it may apply to more than you would think. Being in the midst of people all the time does not ensure that you will not be lonely. Some of the loneliest people I know have no privacy. A lonely woman tends to have no close friend. Many ministers' wives refuse to make close friends and settle for acquaintances with whom they are friendly because of the dangers of close friendships for public figures. However, everyone ought to have at least one person who knows her well enough to recognize weaknesses as well as strengths and love her unconditionally.

In a strong marriage your husband is your best friend, but couples will have disagreements. If your husband is your only close friend, such disagreements seem to wipe out your entire support system. Also, men and women are different; they do not think and respond in the same way. Therefore, they never completely understand each other.

Loneliness is also exacerbated by the fact that ministry wives don't get to see their husbands enough. In a sense, ministers belong to the church, the community, the denomination, and in some cases the world. Early in our marriage, my husband committed to include me in every way he could. I committed to be satisfied with the ways he found to do so. I travel with him most of the time. That means some inconvenience for him and has often demanded a financial investment on his part. On the other hand, for me it means long hours of waiting (I've done everything from needlepoint, to reading magazines and books, to grading papers, to making to-do lists) and often a grueling schedule with 4:00 A.M. wake-up calls and midnight suppers. Only a husband and wife can decide how to deal with the monster of ministry demands.

Paige and I also deliberately plan time together away from our field of service—sometimes only an extra day on the road or a few days at the end of an overseas assignment. When our children were young, we scheduled uninterrupted family time to be away from home and the telephones.

Fatigue

Fatigue is another enemy that quenches enthusiasm and breeds dissatisfaction. When you exceed your physical limits and ignore your body signals for rest and renewal, you will eventually be forced to slow down. Didn't the psalmist say, "He makes me to lie down. . . ." That He will if you don't do it for yourself. When you wait until your body and mind rebel and refuse to go further, you may pay a fearful cost. Even Jesus took time for periodic rest and relaxation away from His ministries to the throngs of people who followed Him everywhere. You can avoid breakdowns physically, emotionally, and spiritually by simply following the divine mandate concerning rest and renewal. You cannot blame God for the abuse you heap on your body and mind with too much work. In fact, you make yourself vulnerable to Satan when you are worn out and too exhausted to be alert to his attack.

Closely related to fatigue is what the great preacher Charles Spurgeon used to call "fainting fits." You will have times when you feel that you have nowhere to turn. Your joy, optimism, strength, and courage are gone. You may be a child of light, but you are walking in pitch darkness with no end of the tunnel in sight. Spurgeon suggested several causes for such deep despair on the part of a preacher.

- With the frailties and infirmities associated with humanity, a man will experience tribulation and suffering as do all children of God. But preachers and their families seem to have more than their share!
- Some men have physical infirmities with which to deal.

- Ministers have the unique task of bearing up under the burdens of others. They see much more than the average man of what is wrong in the world, especially among believers.

- A leader stands apart from others in many ways. Often you can talk only with the Lord. You do not have a personal human counselor and comforter. The sedentary habits that seem to characterize your life can leave you more vulnerable to despondency.

- "The hour of great success" ought to lift the preacher to the height of ecstasy, but he may become more vulnerable. The unbelievable strength supplied by the Lord during the battle subsides once the goal is achieved because the preacher becomes confident of his own personal wisdom and ability.

- The time before great achievement can be just as devastating as the minister looks at the difficulties and obstacles that seem to block his path. He forgets that the darkest night comes before the dawning of the day.

- Another weakness for the preacher is the temptation to abandon the Sabbath of rest and move ahead. This test is especially challenging because the day of rest for a preacher is a day of greatest toil. He may try to rest another day, but the challenges of a burgeoning ministry and expectations of his congregation may make that difficult indeed. Yet Jesus took time to rest even when the people thronged to Him for help. A time of rest is absolutely essential. Can't you sometimes do more in the long run by doing less in the short term?

- The crushing blow, the climax of a series of difficulties, was experienced by Jesus, who had a traitor in His inner circle. My husband experienced that same kind of hurt in his ministry. There is nothing quite as devastating.[1]

How do you fight fainting fits? For the preacher and his wife, there is no way except in the presence of the blessed Jesus. Trite as it may seem, it works. I find great comfort in the Book of Psalms. I use the words of the psalmist to express my own prayers. I get alone with the Lord and cry out to Him. My tears flow, and I may sob uncontrollably for a time; but when I have poured out my heart before the Lord and emptied myself, His Spirit can then fill me with His presence and bring comfort.

For my husband the principle is also true. He does not have the same kind of emotional release, but he does have to get alone with the Lord and come to the end of himself and be willing to lose everything—his ministry, his reputation, his position, his friends—if that is what it takes to please the Lord. When he and I are willing, then we find that our God is able!

Financial Foes

Ministers are professionals; they are overworked public servants as well as underpaid spiritual leaders. Clergymen rank next to the bottom in salary and compensation; whereas they are at the top of the heap in educational preparation. In other words, they are often below the blue-collar level in what they earn while ranking with the top-earning physicians, dentists, lawyers, judges, university professors, and scientists in their education and training.

Southern Baptist ministers are fortunate that their denomination underwrites a large portion of their theological training. That is not true for most ministers. Therefore, they graduate from seminary with so much indebtedness that sometimes they must find secular employment in order to have enough compensation to repay their debts.

While being unable to provide for his family as he desires is demeaning to the minister, it is sometimes even more frustrating to the minister's wife as she seeks to stretch their small budget by doing without or by entering the job market herself. It is a pity that churches do not realize that to refuse to care for the minister and his family in an appropriate way cuts his effectiveness and may deny the congregation the service of a First Lady.

Ministers also have a lot of overhead that other professionals do not have. For example, they must continue to build their libraries, and they need to subscribe to a variety of periodicals if they are going to do the best sermon preparation. They need updating of skills in conferences, and they need the networking with other ministers found in conventions. They frequently have the expense of hospitality in their homes as well as entertaining church members and guests in restaurants. They are expected to give more gifts and to respond to emergency needs. All of these items can be addressed in expense accounts if a church is sensitive to needs of their pastor.

In addition, because pastors and their wives are public figures and leaders in the community, they are expected to dress accordingly. Frequently the minister's salary does not begin to stretch to include a category for clothing. A church should take pride in seeing to it that their minister and his family are able to represent them well.

There are two sides to this coin of financial accountability. Some pastors could never make enough money. Some pastors' wives—however much they have—spend what they do not have! With every increase in salary, they extend their expenses. Educational loans go unpaid; credit cards are maxed; purchases are made with every penny coming in; nothing is saved; sometimes no tithe is returned to the Lord. They are obsessed with having what everyone else has—vehicles, appliances, furniture, designer clothing, exotic vacations. This attitude will carry you down a dead-end street or put you on a merry-go-round that never stops.

If you are living beyond your means, if your outgo exceeds your income, if you have unsecured debt, let me encourage you to seek help immediately. One of the best financial authorities in this generation is Mary Hunt. She has published books and a monthly newsletter that give concrete suggestions on stewardship, enabling you to provide for your family and be faithful to the Lord.

The Big Break—Pulpit Committees

Dealing with pulpit committees is an art in itself. Your husband will usually have the first contact alone; but if the committee is a good one, they will want to meet you early in the process. The committee is interviewing your husband. Your main role is to listen carefully so that you can be a help to him in your private deliberations on the matter and can pray throughout the process that the Lord will reveal His will to your husband and even to you.

You can also help your husband by learning as much as you can about the committee. He will probably have a list of their names. If not, the two of you should try to compile such a list with notes to help you remember each person's name. If the committee sends your husband bulletins or newsletters, you should read the information carefully to become familiar with the church and its ministries as well as with the names of leaders and other staff members. As a bit of information surfaces, add it to your notes. Often with this kind of preparation during your visit to the field, you can make an individual feel special just by showing your familiarity with him and his work in the church.

After arriving on the field, get to know your congregation by visiting them in their homes or workplace. When we arrived in Arkansas, I carefully read through names on the church roll. Then I took my baby and preschooler to run errands and visit businesses on the town square. I often recognized the name of a church member and used that as an opening to get acquainted and sometimes to encourage someone who had dropped out of church to return to the fold.

Before and after worship services, I greeted people in the auditorium. I not only met visitors, but I also had conversations with our members. I volunteered with the welcome wagon to visit newcomers, sharing information about the community and letting them know that my husband was pastor of the First Baptist Church. Keeping notes helped me identify people and carry on meaningful conversations in the future.

Moving to a new location is never easy for the minister or his family. Some psychologists believe that the only trauma to outrank moving is the death of a spouse, a divorce, or a jail term. Saying good-bye to the people who have loved and encouraged you—even if they happen to be in the minority—is not easy, however happy you may be to get out of a difficult situation.

Settling into a new ministry also has its challenges, beginning with learning your way around the church facility as well as the community. You also have faces and names to connect, and you are expected to take the initiative in getting to know members of the congregation. That means lots of visits to church members when your heart may be longing to spend your time in evangelistic visitation and in getting new members for your congregation. People are slow to change. Give yourself time to live among your new church members and get to know them and the community. Learn why things are as they are before you suggest changes. You can help to expedite changes you want to make by communicating to your people the same teachable heart that you want them to have!

Again it seems that the minister's wife draws the short end of the stick in changing locations. While the minister may pack his books and office files (often a secretary or other staff member will assist), his wife must pack, or at least oversee the packing of, an entire household (and perhaps his books and files as well). She is also probably the one who must find housing in the new location, while at the same time getting their current residence ready for the market and then enduring all the interruptions and inconveniences associated with showing a house on the market.

Once the move begins, she must oversee preparation of the house at the new location (cleaning, repairs, etc.), engineer the move, and then settle the family into its new home (hopefully without transition housing, which would require two moves and an unsettled interim). While settling her new household, she is expected to learn names and faces and accept hospitality from new parishioners as well as immersing herself in the life of their new congregation.

All this upheaval is in addition to her efforts to help her children adjust to new schools, new friends, and a new neighborhood. When we moved from Arkansas to Texas, Armour was in the second grade. I thought his transition would be a breeze. Wrong conclusion! Not only did he have new textbooks (which essentially wiped out his limited vocabulary), but also his new teacher had a different way of forming letters so that he had to relearn his writing skills as well. Even the recess games were different as he was introduced to soccer for the first time. Add to that the fact that his new teacher didn't seem to like children, and you have an unusually traumatic situation!

Why do ministers move? For some it is a conviction that the Lord is directing to a new field of service. That decision may be made in the light of human wisdom that cries out against the change. When we left Arkansas and a church full of people whom we loved and who loved us, our church was one of the best in the state; our ministry had been productive in reaching the nearby university campus; we had a spacious home in a wonderful neighborhood; our children were well settled and loved their home and friends. God directed us to leave this security to go to a fledgling Bible college with only twelve full-time students under the umbrella of a large church—not without its own problems. We had to take on a double mortgage to buy a home since we had been in a parsonage. Our large personal library was not easy to settle. The financial remuneration stayed essentially the same. There were no human reasons for us to move, but it became quickly evident that God was calling us out. That move changed the entire direction of our lives. We remained in Dallas almost eighteen years, and now in North Carolina we are entering our third decade of doing theological education.

On the other hand, some ministers are quick to change ministries in order to go to a larger and more prestigious congregation or to secure a bigger salary and more benefits. They are not willing to accept the difficulties and challenges of building a work. This mind-set is tragic not only for the minister but also for his family. It takes time to build a great work.

When Johnny and Janet Hunt went to the First Baptist Church of Woodstock, the congregation was small and the facilities limited. The church was essentially "nowheresville." No one had heard of it, nor did anyone know Johnny Hunt. I first went to the church to speak to a women's group—small but enthusiastic. But as the years have rolled by and the Hunts have invested their time and energy and creativity with faithful commitment to the task, God has made that congregation one of the flagship churches of this generation. The church has a radio and television ministry; they have a premier program for women, which has served as a model throughout the country; they have put a host of volunteers overseas and are known far and wide for their international missionary outreach. Johnny Hunt has had the opportunity to go to pulpits with more prestige and better salaries, but he and Janet feel that God has planted them at Woodstock. With supreme faithfulness they are extending the outreach of that congregation literally around the world.

A comfort to my heart has always been the old gospel hymn, "This world is not my home; I'm just a' passing through." You as believers are merely pilgrims on this earth, and you will be home when you join the Lord for eternity in your heavenly abode. To surrender wholeheartedly to Him and establish a perfect trust in Him is all you need to feel His firm foundation. If you have a hunger for God's Word and a plan for spiritual growth in your own life, you will learn to respond to the Lord's leadership in your life. That means joy in serving Him and an overwhelming desire to share your faith and encourage the saints.

Resignations and Terminations

Moving because you have been called to another field is a challenge—physically, emotionally, and socially. Every call isn't marked by a burning bush or a thundering voice from heaven. In fact, accepting some calls doesn't even make good sense. Yet a wife must be supportive of her husband's decision to go out.

To move because your husband has been terminated or is being forced to resign by internal pressures is another matter. There are few hurts any greater than what you experience when you are attacked by a person whom you thought was your friend and a godly believer. Certainly you can add to the equation an overwhelming spiritual struggle on why God allowed you to get into such a situation and why He would not remove you in a way that would bring the least suffering possible to your family. You never stop to consider whether your husband may have missed God's will in the beginning or whether even the heartache of this experience is within the Father's plan for fashioning both you and your husband more into His image, thereby equipping you for even greater ministry. Suffering is a choice tool of the Lord to mold your character, but you must beware of the tendency to focus so much on yourself that you breed self-centeredness. In times like these, more than ever, you need a fresh word from God, and to hear it you must be quiet and wait.

You are tempted to indulge in martyrdom or self-pity, both of which are destructive and inappropriate for believers. You may try to compare your own pain to what you see as the pain of someone else. A sparkling smile and joyful spirit can mask your private pain and personal disappointments and keep your inner emotions in tow.

Remember not to abandon what you have learned in the light just because you are in darkness. The Lord is still on His throne, and He still cares for you! Never stop praying even when, because nothing is happening, you don't think He is listening. God delights in every communication from His children. Learn to live one day at a time. Go about your daily tasks with determination to do each "as unto the Lord." Don't think about what is coming; just take one step at a time, concentrating on the present moment and pleasing God.

Don't resist the tears; they are an effective cleansing and physical release. Find a private place and pour out your heart to the Lord. I prefer to pray aloud because I feel as if the Lord is having a conversation with me. No one can meet your needs as effectively as the Lord Himself: He has eyes that see your suffering; He has ears that hear your cries; He has arms that will carry you in your brokenness; He has hands that will lead you through the darkness; He has wisdom that will give you hope and direction; He has compassion that will never let you go!

My husband was fired by the trustees of Criswell College. Losing a job is considered one of the five most stressful life changes you can experience.

It ranks alongside the loss of a loved one. You not only lose your source of income, but you feel as if you have been robbed of your identity.

Paige's firing became a public matter splattered in newspapers across the nation. It is never easy to bear your private grief in the public arena; I prefer to do my crying in private places. Prayer chains and well-meaning friends, together with the media, ensure that the private is made public. The board rescinded their action under pressure, and my husband remained as president until he chose to resign. However, no one could erase the innuendos and accusations floating around. The fact that there was no evidence to support those accusations, which were never even clearly stated to us, much less to the public, did not matter. I am thinking, *Who, if not we the accused, has a better reason for knowing what the charges are against us?* To have your character and integrity questioned is the greatest blow, especially from fellow believers.

That current college board had a different vision from the board that hired my husband and those who served during several decades of its growth from a dozen full-time students to almost five hundred students and from a small Bible institute to a college with baccalaureate and master's degree programs. My husband believed the governing board had a right to make those changes. If he could not adapt to them for reasons of conscience and conviction, then he needed to leave. And that we did! However, the Lord did not release us for seven months, which must rank as some of the darkest days of our lives and ministry.

Facing the stress of knowing the board wanted us out, Paige and I carried the burden of realizing that the jobs of professors who shared our vision were also in jeopardy, and the students who were there because of my husband's vision were determined to walk out when he left—in the middle of the semester. We were stripped of support staff to force us out more quickly. Yet my husband did not feel the freedom to take the easy way and accept one of the exit offers coming to him almost immediately; he had to wait for God to release Him.

During those months of unbelievable agony, watching the hurt of elderly parents, the growing bitterness of our children, the tragedy of unwarranted dismissals of loyal staff members, and feeling my own personal pain from betrayal by people I thought were intimate friends, I had to go to church; I had to cross the paths of people who smiled and seemed solicitous of our family, yet who were constantly working to get rid of my husband at whatever cost.

The pain that comes from betrayal by friends or injustice when you have poured your life into ministry brings great suffering. Suffering has been described as the "splash zone" of someone else's sin. When my husband inadvertently leaves the shower on, I bend over to turn on the water for a leisurely bath and suffer a real splash zone, ruining my newly coiffured hair in the process! Oh, that the splash zones were limited to water!

Often I remind myself that when the going gets tough, the tough get going, and I want to go—anywhere just to get my family out of the line of fire. But God reminds me that the tough do indeed get going but not to another battle until they have given their best energies to winning the one they are already fighting and not until the Commander-in-Chief reassigns them. Meanwhile, there is healing "balm in Gilead."

Although the tendency is to withdraw from everyone when you are hurting, you should not shut yourself off from others. The presence of God will be your strength; His power will remind you of your inadequacy and His sufficiency. Jesus did not shut down His ministry during personal attack. He relied upon the Father's strength and the fellowship with His inner circle. Don't waste your energy worrying about things you cannot change, and don't dwell on glories of the past; keep your eyes focused on what the Lord has for you to do now. Yes, you can lay your soul bare before the Lord; you can ask why and wrestle with Him even as did the patriarch Jacob. However, you cannot presume to put a deadline on the timing of His answer nor can you demand a particular answer. His joy is an ever-flowing font, and you must draw from its waters for your personal joy.

The tears of grief can be a cleansing flood, cleaning out your heart and purging your life. That could be what enables you to have a happy spirit and optimistic outlook in the midst of the hard lessons of life. On the one hand, grief can reveal your sinfulness; on the other hand, it can be a measure for your character.

Yes, in His timing, He did reassign us. By waiting, all those students who were devoted to my husband and the principles for which he stood were able to complete their semester. Faculty and staff members who were in jeopardy because of loyalty to us were able to negotiate staying or find places to go. God in His mercy kept us in theological education so that we were able to take a group of those professors with us to continue the vision God had given all of us for equipping men and women for kingdom ministries.

One of my greatest struggles during this dark hour was what to say and how to worship with this dark cloud over my head. My husband was preaching in other churches on the weekends, but I was at the scene of the battle. My emotions ran the gamut from anger to despair to outright doubt that a loving God could allow something like this to happen to one of His faithful servants. In my better moments I was concerned about how this matter would affect the kingdom of Christ. A public attack of Christians/church leaders upon one of their own could not be a helpful testimony. How could a victim do damage control? I needed not only to survive but also to glorify the Lord in the process.

Here are some answers that worked for me. I found myself drawing closer to the Lord and clinging to Him. I began to focus on the blessings I was already enjoying. I even went back to journals and the record of past blessings. I called upon a network of supporters, most of whom were outside the church.

Our extended family joined us for Christmas. I tried to put aside my sorrow to avoid casting a shadow over the holiday celebration. On Christmas Eve my parents and siblings simultaneously determined to gather around and fervently pray for us. Throughout the months of struggle, they were always available, and their uplifting calls would come at the moments of deepest despair.

Ministry friends throughout the country and even overseas heard about our hurts and called and wrote letters of encouragement. Immediately after the firing of my husband became public, without our request or knowledge a group of pastors from the largest churches in our convention called for a meeting with the college board and, at their own expense, flew into Dallas for that meeting.

People within the congregation to whom the board was accountable stood with us and made their support known publicly. My husband was offered positions in ministry, and one evangelist friend sent us a check that covered a large portion of our legal fees. Generally legal services are not necessary among Christians, and we refused to file suit on fellow believers. However, because there were unsubstantiated accusations of impropriety and attempts to purchase my husband's departure as well as danger to loyal faculty and students, we did secure the services of a Christian attorney for consultation. We paid for his services out of our own limited resources. We were determined to remain people of integrity, obeying the mandates of Scripture as we understood them but doing everything we could to protect our own Christian testimony.

Over the months I found a way to give the burden of this overwhelming hurt to the Lord. I discovered that I could pour out my anger and hurt in His presence. He listened, and His presence seemed to put everything into perspective. My deep dependence on the hymnal of Israel—the Psalms—began during these difficult days. I found that I could use the words of the psalmist to express my own feelings.

You should never doubt the power of prayer, nor did I. However, I also found the need to do something. I discovered that I could make choices with the Lord's help to do what I could emotionally do. I continued my church attendance with regularity, but in my own church I often entered after the service began and left during the final prayer to avoid having to greet people; and since my husband was not the pastor, I could attend services in some area churches where we had students and friends. I determined in my heart to be governed by the same faith and values that had ordered my life over the years. That meant investing in the lives of others, focusing with my whole heart on pleasing God without concern for the choices of others.

The greatest tragedy for my husband and me was the effect of these events on our children who were young adults completing university training. There was no way to avoid their knowing what was happening. Our daughter was in her senior year at the college where my husband served. Both our son and daughter knew intimately the administrators and board members involved. They were at first disbelieving, then disillusioned, then angry, and finally bitter. When you are going through an experience of injustice, if you have young children or teens, tell them as little as possible, although it is far better for them to hear what they need to know from you than from rumors floating around throughout the church.

When the dust has settled, your entire family needs time for healing. That healing takes a long time—longer than the decade since our own experience. However, the healing comes, even in unexpected ways. Growing in the Lord seasons your own character and gives you a different perspective in the rearview mirror of life. Sometimes God works in the hearts of the perpetrators to bring conviction prompting them to seek forgiveness from you and your family.

God also restores what the locusts have eaten; and as often is the case, the subsequent opportunities for us did overshadow what had gone before. God never deserted us or cast our ministry aside; rather, He opened new doors for service. Despite our own personal mistakes and the mistakes of others, He continued working His plan for our lives.

Has time healed the wounds? Not completely. Recovery from such radical surgery is not so simple. However, the scar tissue has formed, and the most excruciating pain has subsided. The healing is still in process. It is easy to forget that God can use the mistakes of others to accomplish His purpose in your life.

For Paige and me, our ministry was rudely interrupted; seemingly an investment of our time had been wasted; the outpouring of our gifts and energies had been thwarted; but God did not leave us alone (Ps. 48:14). I began to look for opportunities of service. During our last few months in Dallas, I was distracted by preparations for the wedding of our only daughter. I determined to pour myself into building special memories for her. Making and executing these plans opened doors for sharing Christ with vendors and people with whom I was working.

Paige and I are now in the midst of the greatest ministry opportunities we have ever had—far beyond our dreams and goals; and we are loved by our colleagues, our board members, our personal staff. We are received lovingly and graciously in the churches of our denomination, and Paige has even served as president of its national convention.

Is the hurt gone? No. Do I remember the anguish of those tragic events? Yes. Does our family have some scars? Yes. My greatest remaining heartache is for my children. Their faith was shaken to the core, and they didn't have our years of maturing faith on which to lean. Sometimes I wonder if they will ever completely heal, and that is important to me because my own wounds cannot heal until I know my children have survived.

How do I deal with those wounds after a decade of rebuilding?

- I keep my focus on the present and how I can please God in what He has given me to do today in the here and now.
- I can be faithful to spend my time with Him, reading His Word and praying for my own needs as well as for the needs of those whom I love.
- I must forgive even when there is no request for forgiveness. I have to trust the providences of God, knowing that He could have stopped the attack on my husband. But He chose to allow Paige and me to go through a crushing experience, to drink of the cup of His sufferings. He does not waste pain and suffering; He works it for our good. I can choose to forgive just as He chose to forgive.

• Finally, I can work out ways to communicate not only my feelings but also the lessons learned and even more important the faithfulness of God. These events are forever a part of my "living letter" of testimony. I have written private words in my personal journals and shared public testimony as God has prompted me to do so. In my correspondence with a special friend, I shared these words:

> We are still moving up the mountain—the peak has an extraordinary glow and keeps my focus in the heavens where it hides beyond the clouds. When I reach its pinnacle, you'll hear a victorious shout, but meantime I have recovered the songs of praise, and my perspective gets better each day. Please do continue to pray for my children. . . . I'll be in the showcase . . . at the Monday evening banquet, which we tried so hard to decline but finally agreed to attend. Hopefully the Lord's grace will shine through my own frailties.

Dated 1994, this note speaks of a journey that is still not over, but my Guide is ever faithful, and I am moving through the fire and the deep water (Isa. 43:2).

How do you settle into a new work? An attitude of joyful optimism will build an expectancy in your own heart as well as in the hearts of your children. Of course, there is curiosity over a new place and new people, but you can add to that an attitude of gratitude for new opportunity.

The only way to move forward in putting down roots and settling into a new place is to put your former ministry behind you. There will be memories and missed traditions. Our family misses the Tex-Mex cuisine of Texas, and the distinctive vinegar-based shredded pork barbecue of North Carolina does not agree with our palates. But we have come to love the climate that allows us to use our deck almost year-round, and we like being within a couple of hours of the mountains or the beach.

When you unpack your household belongings, you must also pack up the past and store it for a rainy day. Begin to look around and put down your roots in your new location. I had only seen the house in which I was to live one time, and my walk-through was quick and limited. When I arrived in North Carolina, the house was bare and had some definite challenges—so much so that our new board had offered to help us find housing off campus. But from my arrival, ascending the gentle hill and viewing the most magnificent magnolia tree I had ever seen, I was inspired to name the president's official residence Magnolia Hill. The name was embraced by all, and through our decade here I have spent much time and energy giving the residence warmth and personality and a tradition for hospitality. The progress has seemed painstakingly slow, and there is still much to be done, but my heart has a vision, and my energies and creativity have been attuned to the task before me. I have missed people, favorite foods, and some special cultural events; but from the time I entered the portals of Magnolia Hill as the First Lady of Southeastern Baptist Theological Seminary, I have never looked back to mourn over ministries in the past; rather, I have focused my dreams and energies and creativity on what I can do in this wonderful home in North Carolina.

The Advantages of Adversities

Jesus Himself cried out to the Father from the cross, "Why have You forsaken Me?" Have you ever felt abandoned by God? I have had those moments of hopelessness when I felt utterly alone and rejected—even by God. Joni Tada has been associated with the phrase "severe mercy." Through a tragic accident she was saddled with a severe handicap, leaving her completely paralyzed. But Joni would be the first to bear testimony that God did not leave her alone. In His mercy He used that tragedy in her life to draw her to Himself so that she testified, "I instinctively knew I was where God wanted me."

The great Christian apologist C. S. Lewis is often quoted as predicting that if you keep ignoring God, "He will whisper to you in your pleasures and shout to you in your pain." Sometimes for a minister's wife the expectation for shared gains in ministry becomes the reality of shared pain.

Hannah Whithall Smith (1832–1911), the wife of a famous nineteenth-century evangelist, walked in faith despite overwhelming tragedy in her own life. Shortly after she reluctantly allowed the columns she had written for her husband's newsletter to be published, her husband destroyed his ministry through personal scandal. Instead of repentance he chose bitterness and depression. One of Smith's daughters abandoned her husband, and another chose to marry the atheist Bertrand Russell. Her teenage son died from scarlet fever. Nevertheless, Hannah Smith refused to give in to her circumstances. Rather, she believed that God loved her; she walked in faith; and she passed on to others the joy of knowing Jesus regardless of circumstances. This Quaker homemaker's "secret" for living a happy life is still being shared around the world through the book she penned—a devotional classic on personal holiness and one of the most remarkable books circulating since its release in 1875, more than a century ago.

Hannah Smith was one preacher's wife who refused to allow her husband's downfall or her children's wrong choices to destroy her capacity for happiness and joy. She refused to question God's innate goodness, faithfulness, and love. She would not covet what seemed to be the good fortune of others but remained content with the circumstances God allowed in her own life. Discontent and ingratitude were simply not compatible with the indwelling joy of her Christian faith.[2]

Smith realized that joy was her birthright as a child of God. She experienced joy as a foretaste of God. Her spiritual longings were satisfied with this heavenly taste of God. She possessed it as a sign of the Spirit of God dwelling in her heart. Although the emotions of happiness could ebb and flow with the events of the day, the reality of God's glory and goodness could not be diminished by circumstances. As darkness can always be pushed back by the light, so tragedy and disappointment are covered with the presence of the Lord Jesus. Smith simply did "what she could" as did Mary of Bethany (Mark 14:8). She reared two grandchildren and spent her last years confined to a wheelchair, from which she penned these words:

> I am very happy and content in my narrow life, and
> with my lessening capabilities, and can say, 'Thy will be
> done' to my Divine Master from the very bottom of my
> heart. . . . I feel the lines have indeed fallen to me in a
> pleasant place.[3]

She realized that the grass under her feet was greener than what she could see under the feet of her neighbor on the other side of the street.

You, as I, have the choice of grasping His promises and building your own reservoir of the love of the Heavenly Father, who said, "I am sufficient. I am enough," and He is! His promises are not powerful until they become personal. You are not adequate in yourself. Ducking into a phone booth or prayer closet will not enable you to solve your problems. You will not go in one way and come out another so that you are faster than the wiles of the devil and able to leap over all trials and difficulties. You are not a superwoman, but you do have a God who is beyond super.

The Lord is there all the time as He was for the disciples caught in a storm on the lake. They asked Jesus if He cared if they perished. Jesus calmed the winds and then asked the disciples why they were afraid. In fact, He questioned their faith in Him to handle the situation (see Mark 4:35–41). If you let Him, the Lord will go beyond your dreams; He will overcome your fears; He will put together your broken pieces; He will even paint a rainbow out of your tears!

Your Stress Busters

You must build into your spiritual arsenal some stress busters—things you can do when stress, and even depression, invades your life to quench your joy and sabotage your ministry. The center of your relief will come from God's Word, which will prepare you for living life according to His principles. These principles are not merely pious platitudes to make you holy, but they include real-life directives to keep your body and mind whole!

You have to inventory your own life regularly. Are you getting enough rest? Are you eating and exercising appropriately? Are you taking care of the temple of God in which you live? I am personally amazed at how much more I can cope with problems and difficulties when I retreat from the pressures of my world long enough to get

> "The greatest honor you can give to Almighty God is to live gladfully, joyfully because of the knowledge of His love."
>
> —JULIAN OF NORWICH

needed physical rest. Even a long and brisk walk will clear my mind and provide a time for some uninterrupted conversation with the Lord. Have you forgotten the relaxation and play God intended in your life? Heavily committed and overscheduled people must intentionally set times for relaxation.

Why do churches expect too much from the pastor's wife? The primary reason is that the pastor's wife lets people prod and push her into overextending herself. Anyone who is capable and willing will find herself overburdened if she does not have the courage to say no. Learn your abilities and strengths by trial and error so that you can make the best choice of how to use your time and energy and creativity. It's simply a matter of stewardship.

Healing the Hurts

The Old Testament has a wonderful renewal plan that prepares the way for restoration, revival, and recommitment. The wives of preachers would do well to examine the jubilee in the Old Testament. There are many possibilities—perhaps a sabbatical. Seminary professors are freed from teaching and administrative assignments every seven years. They read and do research, think and meditate, rest and relax with full salary for a year away from campus. They are expected to be productive, but they can choose how to accomplish that productivity and refresh themselves in the process.

Missionaries have furloughs every two to four years during which they return to their birth country with full salary and benefits. They are to have reunion with family members, rebonding with home church, opportunity for special medical or dental procedures, time to take care of family business—meet needs of senior parents and visit with adult children.

Wives and mothers can come up with their own plans. Some may opt for a weekend alone once a year; others may take a week away every five years. Some may even choose one day a month. Whatever the time frame or venue in which the jubilee is taken, the purpose is to put aside mundane responsibilities to the family for a brief time to give yourself to rest and renewal. Every woman needs a time to be alone with God for an extended time without interruption. Begin by just sitting at the Savior's feet, drinking in His presence, filling yourself with His power. Then you will be ready to work on whatever projects are before you—a Bible study or devotional message, homeschooling lesson plans, personal and family goals, or family celebrations for the coming year. However, in the jubilee concept, productivity is not the most important goal; it should be no more than an optional by-product. Instead of being obsessed with quantity—more projects completed—why not look for the quality life changes that may evolve from giving God a quantity of time.

Difficult People

The minister's wife is constantly in the public eye. She sits at the head table at a banquet; she stands in the receiving line at a reception; she occupies her regular pew in the worship service; everyone knows who she is from the moment she appears on the scene. Her clothing is scrutinized, the behavior of her children is analyzed, her speech and manner are evaluated. Often she is held to a standard of perfection beyond what is expected of the pastor himself.

No church is without problem people who seem to sow discord and discontentment. They whine and complain; they accuse and backbite; they threaten and intimidate. A questioning shadow can arise around the minister and his family without any substantiating facts. Mere rumors can devastate the ministry of a godly man. Those who seek to defame the minister criticize him and his wife for what they do and what they have not done. They even know what the pastoral couple could have done. The minister's wife is criticized for helping her husband too much or not coming to his assistance enough.

What can the minister's wife do to deal with these troublesome people in a redemptive way?

- Pray for that individual's salvation. A genuine believer tries to emulate Christ in his behavior. To be converted is to be changed into the likeness of Jesus Christ. You cannot judge an individual's heart; all you can do is inspect the fruit. But if the fruit suggests an unbelieving heart, your first responsibility is to pray for that person's salvation.

- If you are convinced that the individual is a believer, you should pray that he would be convicted to move to a mature faith and that he would turn to Scripture and immerse himself in the Word to enable the Holy Spirit to guide him.

How do you deal with criticism? To be intimidated by your critics is to live in defeat and timidity. You may in fact miss the most exciting opportunities for service and spiritual growth. You can lose your individuality and destroy your faith. In fact, the only way to avoid criticism is to do nothing, say nothing, and be nothing.

The best antidote for fear of criticism is to move forward with energy and creativity despite your detractors. Your personal walk with God will make you stronger and more confident because your chief desire will be to please God rather than other people. God will give grace to handle criticism in the right way. He is righteous in His judgments, and His vindication is far better than any you can achieve by your own retaliation.

While most criticisms that come your way may be unjustified, some criticism is valid and offers constructive discernment. Coping with criticism and handling stress require the presence of the Spirit of God in your life. Satan has no greater victory than to pull believers into the pit of ungodly and worldly responses. You would do well to lay all before the Lord and there sift out criticism from wise counsel. Try to be objective and impartial in considering the matter. If the criticism is justified, you may need to make some changes.

Jesus was betrayed by one of His twelve most intimate friends and deserted by another who denied knowing Him. Consider His method of dealing with undeserved criticism: Pray for those who hurt you and love those who are against you. You will find an inner peace and healing. Expect criticism; learn from it; don't be devastated by it.

- Pray that God will speak to this individual in a way he cannot misunderstand and help him to find God's purpose for him. Sometimes personal attacks come as a result of an individual's frustration when he himself is out of the will of God.

- Pray for that individual's contentment. Ask God's blessing on him. Determine to follow the biblical admonition to love your enemies and to pray for those who despitefully use you. When you are obedient to the divine mandate, you remain under the umbrella of God's protection. Years ago my husband began a practice that has enabled him to deal with the difficult people in his life. When someone attacks him unjustly, he becomes proactive in expressing his interest and concern for that person—a necktie, a floral bouquet, or a fruit basket. When you seek to please God with your response, God cleanses your heart from bitterness.

- Finally, a strong pulpit ministry over the years will address the matter of personal holiness and a Christian lifestyle in which all responses of a Christian should be based on the question: What would Jesus do? Nothing convicts and convinces like the Word of God.

If your husband is the difficult person in your life, focus on the things he does right and refuse to fall into the trap of criticizing him for all he leaves undone. If you hear constructive suggestions that would help him and augment his ministry, find a way to pass those along in a loving way.

As hard as it is to imagine, the difficult people who bring grief and sorrow to your life have a role to play in your spiritual maturing process. They will draw you, with your hurting heart and frustrated spirit, closer to the Lord. You have the opportunity to obey certain mandates in Scripture that you otherwise would have to ignore. For example, you are to "love your enemies" and to "pray for them who despitefully use you." Without an antagonist in your life, you would never have the opportunity to exercise these disciplines.

You will find that biblical principles really do work. As you begin to do the acts of love toward the one who has made herself your enemy and as you pray for her on a regular basis, you will find that God will change your heart. Instead of anger and frustration, you will begin to have loving compassion for the difficult person in your life.

You will find your own emotional and physical health improving. Many illnesses and sieges of depression come because you allow anger and bitterness and all-consuming hurt to take control of your life. During a stressful year in my life, I was hit from all sides in particularly sensitive areas. Then like being rolled over by an eighteen-wheeler, my arthritis and asthma—both of which had been minor irritations—attacked me with a vengeance. I found myself sinking into deeper depression and hopelessness. But in the midst of this night season in my life, I chose to release my hurt and grief to the Lord and allow Him to work. I found a verse in Psalm 42, which became my treasure: "Yet I will praise Him." I realized that I could be grateful in the midst of my storm; I could choose to do the right thing myself; I could claim the promise that somewhere down the line I would praise the Lord for restoring what the locusts had eaten as He had done before in my life. Of course, the fresh wounds are there; the tears flow. I am still on my knees; I continue to cry out to the Lord; but now I am committed to giving Him time, and I am waiting not in anguish but in anticipation of what He will do!

Finally, I am going to be proactive and expectant. I will practice doing what I know pleases God, however futile it may seem. I will forgive and in

Dottie's Dictum for Dealing with a Difficult Person

- See this person through the eyes of Christ. Stand in her shoes.
- Be positive, kind, encouraging; keep a cheerful countenance.
- Guard your tongue—not just what you say but how you say it!
- Treat others as you would like to be treated.
- Show your interest in the person by asking about her and her family.
- Overlook criticism and unkind comments.
- Be yourself; let your actions speak for you; don't tear down others to make yourself look good; don't toot your own horn.
- Exercise integrity in commitments, whatever anyone else may do.

so doing release my hurts and open myself to divine forgiveness since Jesus promised to forgive me by the same measure I forgive others (Luke 11:2–4).

The Advantages of Adversities

One of the chief complaints of ministry wives is the feeling that you are always on display and that your family must endure fishbowl living. Unfortunately, that is First Lady living, but perhaps it could be worse. Mrs. Thomas Cranmer, wife of the first Anglican archbishop of Canterbury, was to be neither seen nor heard! She was forced to seclude herself from the public. In fact, when she traveled with her husband, she had to ride in a box with ventilating holes in the lid. Why? Married clergy were not widely accepted in England until the 1600s.

In America the wife of pastor Jonathan Edwards followed the custom of wearing her wedding dress to church on her first Sunday as a bride. She had the privilege of choosing the text for that Sunday's sermon. Sarah Edwards selected Romans 8:35, "Who shall separate us from the love of Christ?" She was assigned seating on a high bench facing the congregation, which put her in a position where everyone in the congregation could watch her every expression or movement.[4]

Things have indeed changed for the wives of ministers. Public scrutiny of the minister's wife seems to be relished by congregation and community. Everyone wants to know what the minister's wife is wearing, how she does her hair and makeup, and what she does with her time.

Challenges, Trials, Testings

A delightful vacation we Pattersons enjoyed together as a family included several nights in Yellowstone National Park. The excitement I felt in anticipating the beauties of nature I had seen as a teenager and now would have the opportunity to show my own teens was considerably dampened as we entered the park.

Lightning-sparked forest fires, which had been allowed to burn without interference, had ravaged huge chunks of the beautiful forest. Only the man-made structures were carefully preserved. Where there had once been lush vegetation—beautiful and stately trees, green mountainsides, and flower-filled meadows, now this great park was marred with black earth, burned trees, and more devastation than I could have ever imagined. The nation's most famous wilderness lay in smoldering ruin. However, God had not forsaken His vast creation. The ashes are nutrient rich and thus eventually provide perfect fertilizer for new forestation. In fact, some burning and fire are necessary for continued growth and healthiness in the great wilderness. Within a year after the unrelenting fires, the heavy winter snowfall, the rain-blessed spring, and a generous outpouring of the creative handiwork of God would yield patches of greenery and wild flowers even in the midst of the great devastation.

You will have sorrows and disappointments and failures, and they will appear as worthless ashes and refuse; but God will use the ashes as fertilizer for your spiritual growth (Isa. 61:1–3). At times a pastor's wife must bear without resentment the failures of others. Whether these failures come through misunderstanding or through the downright moral deficiency of another, the pastor's wife must accept the injustice and resulting hurt. The burning fire becomes a beautiful blessing in leading you in spiritual pilgrimage to the growth God wants to give. In the rearview mirror of life, it is not the days and weeks and years of suffering that stand out; rather, it is the moments of joy that punctuate every season of sorrow that burn themselves into your memory. Coaches who train athletes say that there is no gain without pain (Heb. 12:5–8, 11). That is true in all of life.

My husband and I have made visits to Berlin. We were there during the darkest days when the Iron Curtain kept out all the light of hope; we visited again shortly after the wall came down as hope began to filter through the darkness; and we were there recently when the wall was gone and the curtain torn away. The difference was as between night and day. During our first visit the guide told us that officials from Communist East Berlin used to dump garbage over on the Western/American side of the line. The West responded with pouring over the wall fresh vegetables, good cuts of meat, luscious fruits. The guide concluded, "Each gives what he has to give!" How true is that analogy in life.

No one goes through life unscathed. You may not have heard the dreaded diagnosis of cancer; you may not have had a child or relative break your heart; your husband or father may not have lost his job; you may not have been treated unjustly. Just wait—the time will come when you will experience some suffering (1 Pet. 4:12–16). When you receive the rubbish of criticism, the refuse of injustice, and the trash of bitterness, you can return what you have—namely, love, joy, peace, longsuffering, kindness, goodness, faithfulness, gentleness, self-control, what believers know as the "fruit of the Spirit" (Gal. 5:22–23).

As you deal with the storms of life, remember that the Lord can indeed calm the storm, and sometimes He does just that. But at other times He lets the storm rage and simply calms you, His child.

In the midst of the storms of life, you must learn to appreciate the quiet moments. Virginia Baucom, an elderly Raleigh woman, has owned a night-blooming cereus plant for more than a decade. This half-dead looking cactus with octopus arms strapped with twine to an old oak tree as if on life support only blooms from midnight to dawn and now in its old age blooms once a year. Virginia can predict that special night with precision!

When the cereus blooms, a strong and alluring perfume wafts through the night air. Its cluster of long and slender translucent white petals are as big as a man's hand, and, according to Virginia, they unfurl with the slow elegance of a minuet. Tiny tendrils inside the bloom look like angels dancing. This matchless plant is a reminder than nothing lasts, for it will disappear by morning light. Nevertheless, just as Virginia faithfully watches for the blooming cereus and cherishes its beauty and fragrance while it lasts, you are reminded that life is but a vapor. Only what's done for Christ will last; so you must exude a fragrance and beauty of life that permeates your world with Christ and His fruit.

> "Gratitude unlocks the fullness of life. It turns what we have into enough, and more. It turns denial into acceptance, chaos to order, confusion to clarity. It can turn a meal into a feast, a house into a home, a stranger into a friend. Gratitude makes sense of our past, brings peace for today, and creates a vision for tomorrow."
>
> — Melody Beattie

Conclusion

The definition of *success* for every preacher's wife is the same as it is for her husband and all believers—obedience! In reality, you are supposed to do as any other wife and mother in the church. You are to serve "as unto the Lord." The question is not how much you can serve the Lord or even how you might go about glorifying Him with your ministries. Rather, your first task is to obtain food for your own soul, consistently nourishing your spirit and heart from His Word and through your communication with Him so that you are comforted, encouraged, instructed, and corrected according to His Word.

First Ladies are unsung heroines. They are often great women—not only for their spiritual sensitivities but also for their contributions to the community and nation. They love their families; they love the Lord Jesus and His church. They are marked by genuine commitment, sincere faith, and humble service. A heroine is willing to put everything on the line in a selfless and successful effort to save the life of another. The New Testament speaks of this discipline as "losing" your life or "dying" to self, which opens the way for you to offer noteworthy and exemplary service to the Lord and to others. Perhaps a mother who is willing to lay down her life for her own husband or child is merely doing her duty and responding naturally to protect those whom she loves. On the other hand, a woman who would lay down her life for someone she doesn't know or one to whom she is not related is extraordinary in that she puts her life on the line in a way that is beyond human reason.

The wives of ministers have a unique opportunity to serve not only their families but also their congregations, neighborhoods, and communities unselfishly and wholeheartedly. Such spontaneous, voluntary service may bring to them the respect and honor due a genuine heroine!

An Attitude of Gratitude

Seldom is a pastor's wife a stranger in a new city, for the congregation will usually welcome her and assist the family in getting settled. She is often invited to be a part of various clubs and organizations. The pastor and his wife usually have a respected position in the community from the moment they arrive and the opportunity for a warm association with the finest people in their community.

Nothing can equal the privilege of walking alongside a God-called and God-anointed minister, praying for him, encouraging him, sharing both joys and sorrows, protecting his time and energy, extending his ministries by your strength and help. A preacher's wife also has the joy of rearing her children in a home committed to Christ and in a setting where love and faith unite in a common purpose of serving Christ. Special guests in the home and visitors to the church offer her children a new view of the world and its people.

The wife of a preacher can extend loving concern and gracious service to the congregation. She can comfort those who grieve, counsel those who are confused, and encourage those who are disheartened. Of course, some people are always waiting to offer criticism, but others will love her despite her mistakes and admire her for her contributions.

God doesn't call any minister's wife to do anything He doesn't enable her to do. He doesn't enable you to do anything He doesn't equip you to do. He doesn't equip you to do anything He doesn't empower you to do. Quitters are never winners, and winners are never quitters.

Gratitude is more than a trite thank-you; it doesn't find ultimate expression in even the most gracious handwritten note. Gratitude speaks of satisfaction and contentment and joy. It reframes all of life. When your heart is grateful, your attitude is one of thanksgiving. However little you may have is enough to give you contentment. Though many problems pursue you, you are not discouraged.

Gratitude appreciates what has gone before—your family heritage and your own experiences of life. It brings contentment with your present situation however bleak it may appear. It gives you an excitement for what is to come. Your house is home; your job is ministry; your enemies are loved; your friends are honored; your suffering is the path to victory.

Counsel for the Congregation

The pastor's wife may be made or broken by the people in her husband's congregation. She will make mistakes, especially in the early years of ministry. However, in most cases, her decisions are based on what she feels the Lord would have her do—choosing what is best for her family and for the church. Her lack of experience may precipitate some clumsy efforts, and she should be allowed to fail and learn from her mistakes.

The congregation can help their minister and his family by allowing them privacy. Give the pastor at least one day off each week. If the pastor sets aside a day for his wife, honor it. If the pastor plans a weekly evening at home with his family, help him guard it. Limit your telephone calls to genuine emergencies. Learn to contact other staff members with emergencies when the pastor is taking a day away from the church field.

Treat the pastor as you would like to be treated. Place nonemergency calls to his office during office hours rather than waiting until evenings or weekends. Be sure the pastor's workload allows him adequate time with his wife and family. Give him an extended weekend occasionally without counting those days as vacation and allow him to have a holiday with his extended family. Someone in the church needs to take the initiative to discuss with the pastor how he can honor his family commitments within the context of broader ministries.

Don't expect too much of the minister's wife. Let her give her primary energies to being a wife and mother and keeping her home. Let her find her own place for service within the church. Honor her seasons of life. When she has toddlers and preschoolers, she'll miss more services because of sick babies. When she has teens, she'll have more supervision and chauffeuring to do. Honor her priorities. Don't look at her as an appendage of her husband; recognize her gifts; express appreciation to her directly for her contributions; introduce her with pride as the First Lady of your congregation!

Affirm the children of the pastor. Recognize their strengths and accomplishments. Be patient with their failures; replace your criticism with gentle and loving correction when that is needed. Respect and honor their parents, and you will win their hearts.

The minister should receive an adequate salary. In many cases he has prepared himself with graduate and post-graduate education. All that education and maintaining a supportive library have costs, and these should be considered when setting the minister's salary. Apart from salary, he should also have budget allotments for the extra expenses he incurs in doing his job—a housing allowance, car expense, library purchases, travel costs, and hospitality. The minister is in the public eye, which in itself has costs. Many churches do not offer their pastors salaries that are commensurate with the median income of their professional membership. Churches should consult with tax experts and perhaps denominational consultants in order to structure the pastor's compensation so that they do the most for a pastor with the resources available.

Postscript for Preachers

A preacher can make his wife shine and glow in the awesome task she has assumed upon becoming his helper. He needs to remember who held the ladder while he climbed to success!

The preacher should be proud of his wife, and that should be evident in what he says and does. He should give her credit for her wise counsel and good ideas. When praise comes to him for their joint ministry, he ought to share it generously with her. She needs constant assurances of her husband's love and appreciation. The preacher's complete devotion can be appropriated through common courtesies, romantic affection, worthy recognition, and gracious praise. A preacher dare not let his physical weariness keep him from pouring out tender affection upon his wife and showering her with acts of kindness.

Stephen Olford, while serving as pastor of the Calvary Baptist Church in New York City, instituted the weekly practice of celebrating Heather's Day (named in honor of his wife). This day was to be an uninterrupted time for him and his wife to enjoy each other. His church knew about the day and respected his choice to "cheer up his wife" on a regular basis (Deut. 24:5 KJV). The preacher and his wife need to retreat away from the routines of life for time to give attention to one another.

The preacher needs to guard his wife's health. Not only should she have regular physical exams, but he should watch for any danger signals lest she have a medical problem in the making. He should also encourage and make possible regular sleep patterns for her as well as retreats away for physical, emotional, and spiritual renewal. He should be sure that their recreation is sometimes geared to what she enjoys.

Second, the preacher's wife yearns to be included in her husband's ministry:

- By the discussion of dreams and goals for family and church.

- In visiting and counseling where her feminine insights and sensitivities might be helpful and might perhaps protect her husband from an unseemly situation.
- In sermon preparation by enlisting her help to locate scintillating illustrative material.
- By encouraging her constructive evaluation of his pulpit ministry.
- Through asking his wife to accompany him to conventions, conferences, and revivals so that she might also enjoy fellowship, inspiration, and edification.

The preacher's wife ought to be her husband's chief confidante, dearest friend, and closest colleague.

The pastor needs to share the load in parenting. By assuming his responsibility as leader of the household, he is available to make the tough decisions. Taking the initiative in family worship means assuming genuine spiritual leadership, not in title only. He can encourage by word and deed the respect his children should accord the First Lady of his household. Spending time with each child personally and with them collectively provides for him an accurate pulse on what is going on with the children. The pastor's wife ought to have some time for herself regularly—time for spiritual nurture, for planning, and even for relaxation and renewal. However, the pastor's involvement in the household does not mean doing housework and baby-sitting to compensate for his wife's employment.

If a minister is receiving full-time compensation from his church, he cannot with integrity adjust his hours in order to cover for his wife while she is out working elsewhere. Because a minister does not punch time clocks and works according to his own schedule—often without a specific job description—he may be tempted to become the flexible one in the home. The decision as to whether a wife is employed is one the clergy couple must make themselves, but the pastor dare not shirk his responsibilities in order to become the keeper of the home and nurturer of the children while his wife climbs the professional ladder of her own pursuits.

Congregations should be attentive to the needs of their pastoral families. Being a First Lady in the church is a time-consuming task added to the responsibilities of wife and mother. A pastor will find it easier to be as effective as possible if his wife is available to manage the household and help him in ministry.

As the preacher "dwell[s] with [his wife] according to knowledge" (1 Pet. 3:7 KJV), he can encourage his wife's educational preparations by providing open doors for her continuing edification through attendance at seminars and conferences. Perhaps a portion of the book budget could be allotted for purchasing volumes that would be helpful in equipping her.

Time must be spent to identify her gifts and to help open doors for her to use those gifts. Paige commits for me to write and speak much more often than I would ever have the courage to do on my own, and he lives with the inevitable inconvenience by deadlines imposed on the family, and especially on him.

The minister's wife may need protection from a host of well-meaning people and even herself. Overcommitment is always a danger for the capable and willing worker. A pastor is the key to protecting his wife. Sometimes he must do this in a public way—from the pulpit or in his weekly news column—in order to keep her from being overloaded, to give her time to recover from illness, or to allow her to pour extra energies into some important family project. A husband can be most effective in channeling his wife's energies so that she does not exhaust herself in doing things that are not in line with her primary gifts. Sometimes a person or group in the church will not take "no" for an answer from the preacher's wife; but when the preacher as a protector, graciously but firmly intervenes, the matter is solved.

Every minister's wife will not be a shining star to guide wise men or women, but each has the capacity to concentrate her energies as an angel of the home, singing peace and good will and bringing heaven to earth. As she seeks to make her preacher happy and contented and as free as possible to do the work to which he has been called, she needs the prayers of her husband, his loving counsel and concern, his unfailing respect, and his willingness to share her burdens even as she shares his. Every preacher should start by treating his wife at least as courteously as he would treat other women in the church!

Favour is deceitful, and beauty is vain: but a woman
that feareth the LORD, she shall be praised.
Give her of the fruit of her hands; and let her own
Works praise her in the gates (Prov. 31:30–31 KJV).

Addendum for Ministers' Wives

Be yourself—genuine and sincere without pretense. Keep in mind that you are always and forever a work in progress. God is never finished! Nurture the personality and gifts God has uniquely bestowed upon you. Don't pretend to be someone you are not, but be all you can be with the equipping and opportunities God has given specifically to you. Develop your talents and giftedness; use your skills and creativity appropriately.

Don't waste time comparing yourself and what you have with others and what they have. Determine to look your best with the resources available to you. Do what you can to make your home attractive and inviting within your budget. Use your time wisely.

Learn to say "no" just as graciously as you say "yes." Don't fall into the negative voice and "kickative" mood. Take a positive approach to doing the most with your time and energies.

Invest heavily in your family, and the interest accrued will pay wonderful dividends in the church. Stay out of authoritative positions in the church. Participate enthusiastically and consistently in the programs of the church, but let your husband and the official staff cast the vision and execute the overall plans. You will have unofficial input and plenty of opportunity to share ideas and dreams.

Treat all your congregation graciously. Don't get caught in the rat race of licking the boots of those who seem important because of their status or resources, while lording it over those who are lower on the totem pole.

Someone has suggested that every minister's wife needs the hide of a rhinoceros, and that is good advice. You should not be swayed by what others say about you.

The key for every preacher's wife is that there are choices to be made. I believe wholeheartedly that God blesses choices that are based on the mandates of Scripture. I also have discovered that the seasons of life affect those choices. When my children were living at home, I was unable to do many of the things I do now. When we were in a fledgling Bible institute, we did not have the breadth of ministry we now have. In our first full-time pastorate, we did not have the salary and benefits we have now after four decades of ministry. As the old adage goes, you can indeed have it all—just not all at once!

My own life has been governed by ironclad priorities, which I believe come from Scripture. Regardless of professional skills, academic preparation, opportunities based on gifts or training or luck of the draw, I have made choices. I am first and foremost a wife and mother and grandmother. I often remind myself that along with my honorable profession of being a wife and mother and homemaker, I am also leading an interesting life in my own right as the First Lady of Southeastern Seminary.

Whatever I do as a theologian is always going to come after my commitments to home and family. I functioned with the same priorities as a seminary student in early church assignments, or as the First Lady of a Bible institute with a handful of students, as I do now in a large seminary with greater responsibilities. The rest is yet to come, and I fully believe that it will be the BEST as well (Eccles. 7:8).

Endnotes

Introduction

1. Marilyn Brown Oden, *The Minister's Wife: Person or Position?* (Nashville: Abingdon, 1966), 27.
2. Jim Lowry, "Expectations Pressure Baptists' First Ladies," *Florida Baptist Witness*, 15 January 1987, 3.

Chapter 1

1. If you would like to read more about the prayer basket, see an article by one of my former students, Cynthia Neighbors, "Prayer Baskets," *The Minister's Family*, Spring 2000, 40–41.
2. Charles E. Hambrick-Stowe, "Ordering Their Private World," *Christian Heritage*, 41:18.

Chapter 2

1. Every minister's wife should do a careful personal study of the pastoral Epistles—1 and 2 Timothy and Titus—in order to learn what the Bible

says about church order. As their popular designation suggests, these letters were written by the apostle Paul especially for pastors and church leaders. George Knight's *The Commentary on the Pastoral Epistles* (Grand Rapids: Wm. Eerdmans Publishing Company, 1992) will be especially helpful in such a study.

2. Lori Joseph and Adrienne Lewis, *USA Today* Snapshot, 4 June 2001.
3. Ruth Hayden, *Mrs. Delany: Her Life and Flowers* (London: British Museum Press, 1980), 12, 62–65.
4. James F. Findlay, Jr., *Dwight L. Moody: American Evangelist, 1837–1899*, Chicago: University, 1969), 333–34.
5. Jennifer White, "Personal" in *Bottom Line*, 1 November 2000.

Chapter 3

1. For an extended treatment of adultery by a church leader, see Jan Winebrenner and Debra Frazier, *When a Leader Falls* (Minneapolis: Bethany House Publishers, 1993).
2. Mary LaGrand Bouma, "Ministers' Wives: The Walking Wounded," *Leadership*, Winter 1980, 63.
3. *Parade* Magazine, 9 September 2001, 16.

Chapter 4

1. Elisabeth D. Dodds, *Marriage to a Difficult Man* (Philadelphia: Westminster Press, 1976), 37–39.
2. For additional help in parenting, see Tedd Tripp, *Shepherding a Child's Heart* (Wapwallopen, Pa.: Shepherd Press, 1995), and in my own volume *The Family: Unchanging Principles for Changing Times* (Nashville: Broadman & Holman, 2002).
3. Elisabeth D. Dodds, *Marriage to a Difficult Man* (Philadelphia: The Westminster Press, 1976), 46–53.
4. Ibid., 53–54.

Chapter 5

1. Although there are many more modern editions, I still rely on Emily Post, *Etiquette: The Blue Book of Social Usage* (New York: Funk & Wagnalls Company), which has continued to be updated over the years.
2. Information on tea preparation and enjoyment from the Dutchess of York comes from listening to and reading accounts of her media interviews.
3. Look for inexpensive creative accessories for your hospitality at the Dollar Store, Pier One, Tuesday Morning, Salvation Army, yard sales, and flea markets. Look for ideas in department and specialty stores and magazines.
4. There are a number of household experts with excellent suggestions for maintaining an efficient and sufficient household: Don Aslett, Sandra Felton, Amy Young, and Peggy Jones. Look for their individual volumes.
5. My favorite financial guru is Mary Hunt. I avidly read her *Cheapskate Monthly* and her books and recommend them to my students.
6. For Southern Baptist clergy, contact the Annuity Board, P. O. Box 2190, Dallas, TX 75221, 800-262-0511, and request "For Ministers' Wives" by Frank Schwall, Jr., or ask your questions of one of their efficient consultants. For other clergy, consult your denominational headquarters.

Chapter 6

1. Every minister's wife should have a copy of *Robert's Rules of Order* or some other resource on parliamentary procedure.
2. For a study of the biblical guidelines concerning a woman's role in the church, I suggest James R. Beck and Craig L. Blomberg, eds., *Two Views on Women in Ministry* (Grand Rapids: Zondervan Press, 2001).

3. I can recommend the class seminar taught by Florence and Marita Littauer in locations throughout the country as well as Carol Kent, *Speak Up with Confidence* (Colorado Springs: Navpress, 1996), which is used in our communication classes for women at Southeastern Baptist Theological Seminary.

Chapter 7

1. Roland Bainton, *Women of the Reformation in Germany and Italy* (Minneapolis: Augsburg Press, 1971), 66–67.
2. Nothing will enrich your life any more than reading biographies of great First Ladies of the church. For example, Elisabeth D. Dodds, *Marriage to a Difficult Man: The "Uncommon Union" of Jonathan and Sarah Edwards* (Philadelphia: The Westminster Press, 1976); Arnold A. Dallimore, *Susanna Wesley* (Grand Rapids: Baker Book House, 1993); Sandy Dengler, *Susanna Wesley* (Chicago: Moody Press, 1987).

Chapter 8

1. C. H. Spurgeon, *Lectures to My Students* (Grand Rapids: Zondervan, 1954), 154–65.
2. For more from the pen of Hannah Whithall Smith, see David Hazard, *A Christian's Secret of a Happy Life or Taken from Safe Within Your Love: A 40-Day Journey in the Company of Hannah W. Smith* (Minneapolis: Bethany House Publishers, 1992).
3. Jodi Searls, "Hannah Whithall Smith" in *Just Between Us* (Brookfield, WI: Telling the Truth Media Ministries, Winter 1999), 27.
4. Elisabeth D. Dodds, *Marriage to a Difficult Man* (Philadelphia: Westminster Press, 1976), 28–29.

Index